# Intermediate Range

# Intermediate Range

The Forensic Evidence in the Killing of Trayvon Martin

## Michael A. Knox

Crime Science Books

A Division of Knox & Associates, LLC

ISBN-13: 978-0-61568-781-0
ISBN-10: 0615687814

Published in the United States of America by:

Crime Science Books
A Division of Knox & Associates, LLC
P. O. Box 8081
Jacksonville, FL 32239

www.crimesciencebooks.com

About the Cover: The image on the front cover is a creative representation of the key elements of this case: an armed man walks away from an encounter with a teen dressed in a hooded sweatshirt carrying a bag of candy and a can of tea. The image is not intended to accurately depict any of the actual events that took place. The image is also not intended to either promote or disparage the products represented, only to include them as they have been included prominently in the public discourse associated with the killing of Trayvon Martin.

*To A. and A., my greatest accomplishments;*
*M., L., and E., my junior forensic team;*
*and R., for getting me there.*

*"Things are not always what they seem; the first appearance deceives many; the intelligence of a few perceives what has been carefully hidden."*

—PLATO IN *THE PHAEDRUS*

SIR ARTHUR CONAN DOYLE, author and creator of the intellectual detective character, Sherlock Holmes, recounted an exchange between Holmes and Inspector MacDonald in *The Valley of Fear*. MacDonald, reading from a report, deduced that a man named John Douglas had been the victim of a heinous homicide.

"[H]ow did you get at Mr. Douglas and the fact that he had been horribly murdered?" Holmes inquired.

It was in the report, MacDonald replied. "It didn't say 'horrible': that's not a recognized official term," the inspector told Holmes before explaining the information that led him to his deduction. "It added that the case was undoubtedly one of murder, but that no arrest had been made, and that the case was one which presented some very perplexing and extraordinary features."

Holmes wished not to presume what happened. "The temptation to form premature theories upon insufficient data," Holmes explained, "is the bane of our profession."

The evening of February 26, 2012, police in Sanford, Florida, discovered just what Holmes meant, only it wasn't the police that were forming "premature theories upon insufficient data," but the news media and the public who quickly took an unprecedented interest in what would ordinarily have been a brief story on the eleven o'clock local news.

But this case was different. George Zimmerman, a resident

of the Retreat at Twin Lakes, a gated townhouse community in the Central Florida city, was on his way to do some Sunday grocery shopping when he spotted a young black teenager named Trayvon Martin, dressed in a hooded sweatshirt, walking between houses in the rain. The guy looked suspicious, Zimmerman, the captain of the Twin Lakes neighborhood watch, thought, so he called police. Minutes later, Trayvon Martin lay dead in the grass between two rows of back-to-back buildings.

Because you are reading this book, chances are you have already heard about this case. You're probably familiar with the fact that Sanford police did not charge Zimmerman with the killing and a special prosecutor was appointed who quickly charged the neighborhood watch leader with second-degree murder, bypassing a grand jury by foregoing the charge of murder with premeditation—first degree murder as it is called in Florida. You probably also know that the case was propelled into the national spotlight and that racial overtones dominated much of the public discourse on the killing.

But chances also are that there's much about this case that you don't know. Even if you have closely followed media coverage of the case, you will read in this book about evidence that hasn't been mentioned anywhere in mainstream media, evidence that not even the bloggers have uncovered or understood. You will read about analysis of the physical evidence that has as yet gone untold. You will learn, as Plato wrote in *The Phaedrus*, that things are not always what they seem.

What sets this book apart from other accounts of the killing of Trayvon Martin is that it is written not by a journalist or a blogger or a family friend of either Zimmerman or Martin, but by a forensic consultant: someone who specializes in the reconstruction of crime scenes; someone who spent over fifteen years as a police officer in Jacksonville, Florida, about two hours north of Sanford; someone who personally knows and has worked with Angela Corey, the special prosecutor in the case, and her two main assistants, Bernie de la Rionda and John Guy; someone who has traveled the world teaching police officials how to investigate crime scenes; someone who has testified numerous times in state and federal courts around the nation as an expert in the reconstruction of crime scene events.

This isn't a book about the social implications of Trayvon Martin's murder. It isn't about race or about profiling. It isn't about whether or not Trayvon Martin's hooded sweatshirt played a role in his death. It isn't about gun control or Stand Your Ground laws or whether Zimmerman should or shouldn't have been carrying a pistol. And it isn't about whether prosecutors should or should not have charged George Zimmerman with second-degree murder.

This is a book about the actual forensic evidence in the case against the neighborhood watch leader. It is based on the publicly-released evidence in the killing: documents, reports, recordings of witness interviews, and photographs taken by Sanford police. There is no special inside information in this account. But unless you have read every page, listened to every recording, and viewed every photograph that has been made public in the prosecution's case against Zimmerman, you haven't heard about much of what you'll read in this book. Even if you have read and listened to everything about this case, unless you have nearly two decades experience in forensic investigations and all the accompanying training and education, you probably haven't gained the appreciation for the evidence that you will get from reading this book.

I have made every effort to include any piece of information that has any forensic relevance to this case. Commentary has been limited as much as possible to that which explains my professional view of what the evidence means. Quotations have been carefully edited so as not to alter the apparent meaning, and the actual words of those involved have been used as much as possible in lieu of paraphrasing so as not to impose my interpretation on the reader.

While researching this book, I found a number of examples of journalists either altering the meaning of certain statements through paraphrasing or outright misquoting what was said. While many of these examples were benign, some were not. One New York Times article, for example, described Zimmerman's call to Sanford police about the "real suspicious guy" he saw walking through his complex.

"This guy seemed to be up to no good; like he was on drugs or something; in a gray hoodie," the reporters wrote. "Asked to describe him further, he said, 'He looks black.'"

But Zimmerman wasn't asked to "describe him further"; he was asked about the person's race.

"Okay, and this guy is he white, black, or Hispanic?" the dispatcher asked.

Zimmerman replied, "He looks black."

Disingenuously at best, the New York Times reporters altered the meaning of the exchange making it appear that Martin's race was foremost on Zimmerman's mind. But there is a significant difference between an open-ended inquiry to "describe him further" and a three-option, multiple choice question aimed specifically at determining the person's race.

As a forensic consultant and crime scene reconstructionist, I am not an advocate for either side but an advocate only for the truthful facts of what happened that February evening. It is this advocacy for the facts—the truth, the whole truth, and nothing but the truth—that has prompted the writing of this book to give those many, many people in this country who have become intrigued by this case a chance to learn what really happened when George Zimmerman killed Trayvon Martin.

In this book, I will not argue the issue of whether Zimmerman should have been arrested on February 26, or in the weeks that followed, or, as was finally the case, on April 11, forty-five days after the shooting took place. I will not argue whether he should be found guilty or not guilty of second-degree murder or manslaughter or any other crime. I will leave that for the attorneys who so craftily and artfully argue their cases as advocates for their clients, whether they be someone charged with a crime or the citizens of the State of Florida. And I will leave it to you, the reader, to form your own opinion of Zimmerman's guilt or innocence.

What I present in this book is a complete account of the forensic evidence of this case. Using the same techniques, methods, and scientific background I use in every case I reconstruct for clients around the country, I reconstruct this case and explain what the forensic evidence undoubtedly proves about what happened when Trayvon Martin was killed.

I have remained as objective and unbiased as possible, and have carefully chosen the words that I have written so as not to imply bias. I have, for example, avoided calling the shooting a "murder" but have opted instead to say "killing"; murder is a criminal charge, one over which I have no interest and no control. I have, in journalistic fashion, used last names only throughout much of the text to avoid an apparent bias that has crept into many accounts of this case: referring to the victim, warmly, as "Trayvon" but to the killer, coldly, as "Zimmerman". I have never met either one of them and have no stake in the outcome of the case.[†]

Despite my best efforts to seek the truth, there will be those who believe what they want to believe about what happened that evening. Speculation and conspiracy theories about the killing run deep. Some have claimed that two shots were fired, not one. Others have claimed that they can hear Zimmerman cocking or even loading his pistol while talking with police about the "real suspicious guy" he was about to follow. Some claim that the lead Sanford police detective, Chris Serino, a man who wanted to arrest Zimmerman for manslaughter, actually led witnesses to say things that help the neighborhood watchman's case. Others have claimed more broadly that the Sanford Police Department went out of their way to protect Zimmerman. Some have claimed that Witness 6, the man who spoke to Zimmerman and Martin as they struggled and told them he was calling 911, was actually an accomplice to the killing. Some bloggers have even speculated that another person in a white t-shirt was involved in the killing in a murder conspiracy that has been swept under the rug by police, and, the bloggers believe, Zimmerman's friend, Frank Taaffe, was the elusive man in white.

On one side come arguments that Trayvon Martin was

---

†    Some have argued that common journalistic practice has one refer to an adult by last name and a child by first name. At 17-years-old, standing 5'11" tall, and weighing 158 pounds, Trayvon Martin was, at least physically, not a child. Referring to him by first name while referring to Zimmerman by last name communicates an unfair bias that doesn't belong in any factual recounting of the evidence in this case.

nothing but a trouble-making thug; on the other side come arguments that George Zimmerman was a cold-blooded, racist, psychopathic killer who stalked Trayvon Martin and then concocted elaborate lies that twisted the truth in his favor.

But there are also those who will always believe that President Kennedy was shot by a sniper on the grassy knoll, that men never landed on the moon but faked it in a secret studio somewhere, and that the Twin Towers were brought down by explosives placed by agents of the United States government.

For those people—whether supporters of Martin or Zimmerman—who are willing to manipulate evidence to fit their notion of what happened, who will ignore facts that don't support their beliefs, and who will believe something even in the absence of any compelling evidence, this book will probably not be well appreciated. But for those readers who truly want to know what happened at the Retreat at Twin Lakes the evening of February 26, 2012, keep reading because this book is for you. There are at least three sides to every story, including this one: Zimmerman's side, Martin's side, and the truth, which lies somewhere in between.

# Skittles

*"If I had a son, he'd look like Trayvon."*

—President Barack Obama

THE UNMISTAKABLE RED BAG has a rainbow on it and pictures of the little green, orange, yellow, red, and purple candies that are inside. There are no blue candies, though, at least not in the red bag. Then there's the Arizona Iced Tea, a tall aluminum can of the beverage that, despite its name, is made by a New York-based company. The two products made a cameo appearance in what was to become a nationwide media event that captivated Americans and forced them to face their fears and prejudices in ways few events have.

But this isn't a case about Skittles or Arizona Iced Tea. It isn't a case about hoodies or about race or about guns. It's a case about physical evidence. It's a case about putting aside preconceptions and prejudices and taking the time to evaluate evidence before coming to a conclusion about what really happened on a rainy February evening in Sanford, Florida. It's a case about 911 calls, about injuries to a man's head and face, about gunshot residue from a pistol that was in contact with a sweatshirt but not in contact with the skin on the other side. It is a case about who was heard screaming for help, who was on top of the two-person fracas, about who was the first person to push, shove, or throw a punch. It is a case that should teach us how not to jump to conclusions, how not to let our notion of the events shape the facts as we perceive them. It is a case about the difference between truth and perception.

Nobody really knows what happened between two rows of buildings inside the gated Twin Lakes community, a neighborhood that had seen its fair share of crime in recent months. Residents of the 263 homes in the complex were motivated to organize a neighborhood watch group, and a twenty-eight-year-old insurance underwriter named George Zimmerman

tackled the task of leading the newly-formed group; a neighborhood newsletter published in February 2012 listed Zimmerman as the watch captain. Zimmerman's zeal in that role is evi-
dent in the many emails he sent to Sanford police volunteer
services coordinator Wendy Dorival as early as August 31,
2011. He coordinated a meeting in which police presented
neighborhood watch plans to residents of the gated community,
and he even corrected an error on a flyer that mistakenly listed
his name as "Greg". In the coming months, he and Dorival corresponded about an array of topics ranging from the printing of
contact cards to the status of a home invasion investigation.

Zimmerman wasn't shy about calling Sanford police to report who he believed was a suspicious person. Records showed
that he placed calls on August 3, August 4, and October 6,
2011, and again on February 2, 2012, just 24 days before he
shot and killed Trayvon Martin. In all four of those calls, Zimmerman identified the suspicious person as a black male. But
Zimmerman also made other calls to police that did not involve
suspicious black males.

While Zimmerman's penchant for proactively phoning police to report people he suspected of criminal activity may seem
overzealous, crime statistics for the Twin Lakes community suggest otherwise. Over a two-year period from March 15, 2010,
through March 14, 2012, there were thirty reported crimes inside the gated subdivision including seven burglaries, seven
thefts, six assaults, three drug offenses, six other crimes, and,
of course, one negligent manslaughter—the killing of Trayvon
Martin.

On July 29, 2011, a woman residing on Retreat View Circle
awoke to find her rear sliding glass door open. Her car keys
were missing from the dining room table, and when she went
out the front door, she found that her 2011 Ford Fusion was
missing as well. The car was found abandoned at another location. On August 23, another female Twin Lakes resident reported that someone had broken a window to burglarize her
home and had stolen a Sony Playstation and eleven games. The
crimes were never solved.

The shooting death of seventeen-year-old Trayvon Martin

sparked outrage across the nation by supporters who saw the killing as the result of racially-motivated profiling. Martin, who was black, was walking back to the home of his father's fiancée who lived in the gated community. He had gone to a nearby convenience store where he bought the now-infamous Skittles and Arizona Iced Tea. Zimmerman, the son of a white father and Peruvian mother, was leaving home enroute to a nearby Target store to do his weekly grocery shopping when he spotted Martin, clothed in a hooded sweatshirt, walking near a previously-burglarized building in the rain. Zimmerman phoned Sanford police and relayed his suspicion. But before police arrived, Martin lay dead from a single gunshot wound to the chest.

The son of a retired Virginia magistrate, Zimmerman was in his final semester at Seminole State College seeking an Associate's degree in criminal justice. He told police that he wanted to be a judge one day. Perhaps it was his interest in justice that motivated his desire to rid the neighborhood of the crime that had been plaguing it. But Zimmerman clearly was not the only resident concerned about crime in the complex. One of Zimmerman's neighbors told Reuters journalist Chris Francescani that she believed Zimmerman was concerned about crime, not race.

"Let's talk about the elephant in the room. I'm black, OK?" the woman told Francescani. "There were black boys robbing houses in this neighborhood. . . . That's why George was suspicious of Trayvon Martin."

Originally constructed starting in 2004, Twin Lakes had suffered as a result of the plunge in Florida's housing market, and the 1,400-square-foot units that had once sold for $250,000 had plunged as low as $80,000. As had happened throughout the state, foreclosures led to homes that had once been occupied by first-time homeowners being taken over by transient renters, and, in turn, the complex experienced an upsurge in burglaries, vandalism, and drug activity. According to a March 25 Tampa Bay Times article, on the day of the shooting, forty of the homes were vacant "and more than half of the residents were renters." Fear of crime had been increasing among the residents of Twin Lakes, and witnesses attributed a number of these crimes to young black males.

On August 3, 2011, Twin Lakes resident Olivia Bertalan was at home with her infant son while her husband, Michael, was away at work. Two black men rang her doorbell several times before entering her home through a rear sliding glass door. Bertalan hid in her baby's bedroom and called police. Francescani wrote that Bertalan "tried to coo her crying child into silence and armed herself with a pair of rusty scissors." This was the crime about which Zimmerman corresponded with Dorival in emails. Zimmerman's wife, Shellie, was at home when the crime occurred, and she saw a black male run behind their residence. She reported what she saw to police.

On October 2, Zimmerman emailed Dorival to ask about an arrest in the case. "I understand a suspect was arrested in the home invasion case in my neighborhood," wrote Zimmerman. "Is that information correct?"

After returning from vacation on October 10, Dorival wrote back. "I made a query in the system and I found out that we received a fingerprint match on the burglary and identified a suspect," wrote Dorival. "The system does not indicate an arrest." She explained that she would have to contact the investigator and would get back with Zimmerman. The next day Dorival emailed Zimmerman to tell him that she had heard from the investigator. "She says they have identified a suspect," Dorival told Zimmerman, "but have not been able to locate him." The five-foot-ten-inch, one-hundred-seventy-five-pound suspect described by Bertalan was identified as Emmanuel Burgess. Bertalan picked him out of a photo spread. The other black male suspect was not identified.

◈

Trayvon Benjamin Martin was a junior at Dr. Michael M. Krop Senior High School and lived with his mother and older brother in Miami Gardens, a South Florida suburb about four hours drive south from Sanford along Florida's Turnpike. Martin's parents, Sybrina Fulton and Tracy Martin, were divorced in 1999. On the day of the shooting, Martin and his father were visiting the elder Martin's fiancée, Brandy Green, and her 14-year-old son, Chad, at their home in Twin Lakes. Martin had been to Twin Lakes before, and he was staying with Green while his father handled some business in Orlando.

According to website postings by his family, at age nine Martin saved his father's life by pulling him from a burning kitchen. Martin "loved sports and horseback riding" and "had a bright future ahead of him with dreams of attending college and becoming an aviation mechanic." His family described him as kindhearted, even-tempered, and thoughtful—a peaceful person. Martin's mother told columnist Charles Blow that her son had not been involved in a violent confrontation since preschool. Martin helped feed his quadriplegic uncle, babysat his young cousins, and baked cookies. Before Martin left his soon-to-be stepmother's home to go to the store, he asked Chad if he wanted anything from the store. Chad asked for Skittles. The little round candies that Martin was carrying when he was killed weren't even for himself.

Often going by the nickname "Slimm", Martin died just twenty-one days after his seventeenth birthday. According to a March 22 article in the Miami Herald, Martin spent his birthday with his family and "ate a home-cooked meal followed by cake, opened presents that included Levis jeans, Adidas sneakers and a bottle of Issey Miyake cologne." According to the Herald, Martin "wanted to fly or fix planes, struggled in chemistry, loved sports video games and went to New York for the first time two summers ago, seeing the Empire State Building, the Statue of Liberty and a Broadway musical, The Addams Family." He had hoped to go to college at the Univesity of Miami or Florida A&M University.

"[H]e had a girlfriend and spent endless hours talking or texting on his cell phone," the Miami Herald reported. "Other times he was quiet, listening to the soundtrack of R&B, reggae, rap and gospel music flowing through his ear buds or watching half-hour re-runs of Martin, his favorite show."

"Tray was a beautiful child. He was raised to have manners and be respectful. He was a teenager who still had a lot of kid in him," Martin's father told the Herald. "He still loved to go to

Chuck E. Cheese with his cousins and would bake them choco-
late chip cookies when he was babysitting them."

"He loved flying and working with his hands," Martin's
mother explained. "He wanted to be a pilot or work as a mechanic in aviation. He was mechanically inclined and could fix
just about anything."

Martin's English teacher, Michelle Kypriss, described the
teen as "extremely creative". "He just loved building things,"
Kypriss said. "He really was intrigued by how things worked."
According to a March 17 article in the Orlando Sentinel,
Kypriss described the high school junior as "an A and B student
who majored in cheerfulness."

"He had been so looking forward to going to his junior
prom, and he had already started talking about all the senior
activities in high school," Martin's mother said. "He will never
do any of those things."

"He wasn't threatening," sixteen-year-old Brian Paz, Martin's childhood friend, told the Miami Herald. "There was no
reason for George Zimmerman to pull out a gun and kill him.
He was too peaceful for that."

Despite his virtues, Martin had his vices. His Twitter handle
was "@no_limit_nigga", and he had been suspended three
times from his Miami-Dade county high school for being tardy,
tagging graffiti, and possessing a small amount of marijuana.
On March 26, journalist Francis Robles with the Miami Herald,
Martin's hometown newspaper, reported that "a more complicated portrait" of Martin had emerged showing "a teenager
whose problems at school ranged from getting spotted defacing
lockers to getting caught with a marijuana baggie and women's
jewelry."

According to Robles, in October 2011, a school police investigator, while watching surveillance monitors, spotted Martin in
an unauthorized area of the campus. The investigator reported
that Martin was "hiding and being suspicious." The policeman
watched as Martin wrote "WTF" on a door, the common text-
messaging abbreviation for "what the fuck." The following day,
the policeman found Martin and searched his book bag. The officer reportedly found twelve pieces of women's jewelry and a

screwdriver, which he described as a "burglary tool". Among the items of jewelry were a watch and "silver wedding bands and earrings with diamonds."

"Martin replied it's not mine," Robles quoted the policeman's report. "A friend gave it to me." Martin refused to name the friend. Though not arrested or disciplined for possessing the jewelry, Martin was suspended for the graffiti.

His family acknowledged the suspension but claimed to have no knowledge of the jewelry or the "burglary tool". "It's completely irrelevant to what happened Feb. 26," Robles quoted Martin family attorney Benjamin Crump. "They never heard this, and don't believe it's true. If it were true, why wouldn't they call the parents? Why wasn't he arrested?"

"No evidence ever surfaced that the jewelry was stolen," the Herald reported.

Martin's supporters dismissed the reports as nothing more than an attempt to defame the dead teen. "They killed my son, and now they are trying to kill his reputation," Martin's mother said. Exactly who "they" are was never explained.

Martin's third suspension from school came four months later when school police found him in possession of a bag containing marijuana residue and a pipe used to smoke the drug. Toxicology testing showed that Martin had both active and metabolized marijuana in his system when he was killed.

After his son's third suspension from school, Tracy Martin brought his son to stay with him in Sanford for a change in social scenery. The elder Martin wanted his son to go to college and did not want his son to fail. As the New York Times reported, he brought his son to Sanford "to keep him from hanging around Miami, doing nothing, and to talk some sense into him."

Natalie Jackson, another Martin family attorney, was quoted by the Herald as saying, "This is someone in a school writing a report, rumor as far as I'm concerned." But Jackson's statement belies the fact that the report was an official police report written by a policeman who, at the time, could not have known that Martin would later be shot and killed by a man in another county four hours away.

The Reverend Al Sharpton claimed that the school records were meaningless because Zimmerman knew nothing about them when he killed Martin. "[H]e didn't interview him before he shot him," Sharpton said.

"The only thing that's relevant is what Zimmerman knew," Sharpton explained. "Let's not play this double standard of trying to damage who is dead and sanitize who is the cause of the death." But while Zimmerman didn't know about Martin's high school suspensions, he did tell the police dispatcher that he thought Martin was "on drugs or something" and his suspicion of Martin was raised in much the same way as the school policeman's suspicion was raised when he saw Martin in an unauthorized area of the school.

But Martin's troubles in school were not due to violence. "Trayvon was not a violent or dangerous child," Kypriss said. "He was not known for misbehaving. He was suspended because he was late too many times."

◈

The lives of Trayvon Martin and George Zimmerman collided on February 26, 2012. It was a rainy Sunday evening. Martin had gone to a nearby 7-11 store where he purchased a tall can of Arizona Iced Tea and a bag of Skittles. Walking back to the home of his father's fiancée, Martin was spotted by Zimmerman, walking between two buildings near a home that Zimmerman had previously called Sanford police about after it had been burglarized. Zimmerman thought that Martin, dressed in a dark-colored hooded sweatshirt and walking in the rain, appeared suspicious. Zimmerman would later explain that he had never seen the teenager in the complex, and the high-school athlete did not appear to be a resident caught in the rain or an avid athlete who would work out in the rain.

Zimmerman called police. After explaining to the dispatcher that there had been some break-ins in the neighborhood, Zimmerman expresses his suspicion. "This guy looks like he's up to no good, or he's on drugs or something," the neighborhood watch captain explained. "It's raining and he's just walking around, looking about." The call lasted just over four minutes. The next time Zimmerman spoke to police, Martin, an unarmed black teenager, was dead.

In the weeks following the tragic shooting, Sanford police and prosecutors declined to arrest Zimmerman citing Florida's Stand Your Ground law, a recently-enacted piece of legislation that removed the long-standing requirement for a person to retreat from a confrontation before using deadly force. Stand Your Ground gave citizens in Florida the legal right to use deadly force when faced with the fear of imminent death or great bodily harm so long as the person was in a place where he or she was legally allowed to be and was not in the process of committing a crime when the confrontation took place. Prosecutors and police administrators felt that Zimmerman's claims of self defense could not be refuted and, therefore, decided that he could not be prosecuted for Martin's death. Little did they know that news media attention and public perception would make that decision one of the worst of their careers.

◈

While Trayvon Martin had no reported history of violence, George Zimmerman did. In 2005, Zimmerman was arrested after he shoved an undercover alcohol enforcement agent who was arresting Zimmerman's underage friend at a popular college bar. While agents were processing the arrested friend, Zimmerman approach to ask what was going on. Paul Fleischman, a special agent with Florida's Division of Alcoholic Beverages and Tobacco, identified himself to Zimmerman and told him to "wait off to the side" where he would explain the situation after the agents finished processing the prisoners. Fleischman later told FBI agents that Zimmerman "had an angry demeanor" and told the beverage agent "that he did not care who he was." Zimmerman shoved Fleischman before being subdued by Fleischman and the other four beverage agents. Zimmerman was initially charged with several felonies but was able to get the charges dismissed by complying with the conditions of a pre-trial intervention program.

After the shooting, Zimmerman explained to the lead investigator, Chris Serino, that he was at a bar with several friends and had gone to the restroom. When he came out, a female told Zimmerman that his "buddy just got drug out of here by the neck by some big dude." Zimmerman thought his friend, who was known to dance with other men's girlfriend's, had caused a fight. "When I got out there, this guy—a big guy—had him by the neck up against the wall," Zimmerman told Serino. Zimmerman said that when he yelled at the big guy, the big guy yelled back—something like "step the fuck back." Zimmerman stepped toward the big guy. The big guy threw Zimmerman back. Then Zimmerman grabbed the big guy and pushed him into a wall. Only problem was, the big guy was a cop.

That same year, Zimmerman and his ex-fiancée—whose name has not been released by officials—filed for injunctions for protection against each other after trading allegations of domestic violence. The two met in 2001 while she was working as a hairdresser at a local Supercuts. Zimmerman came in to get his hair cut, and the two struck up a conversation. He told her that he had recently moved to Florida from Virginia and was living with his family in Oviedo. He was working as an agent for Allstate. Zimmerman returned to Supercuts later that day and asked the woman out on a date. They continued dating, and by 2002 or 2003 they were engaged to be married.

But after the engagement, Zimmerman "began to exhibit overly protective and territorial behavior", according to an FBI report dated March 30, 2012. Zimmerman would tell his fiancée that she needed to "dress more conservatively", and the couple increasingly argued. Zimmerman went to weekly counseling sessions at a church in Oviedo over a year-long period. His fiancée accompanied him to the sessions "about a quarter of the time."

But the relationship continued to deteriorate. According to the FBI report, Zimmerman allegedly struck his fiancée "in the mouth with an open hand because she was chewing gum." The woman told agents that she had "previously, but playfully, hit Zimmerman in his mouth while he was chewing gum but Zimmerman didn't like it and this was his way of retaliating."

Zimmerman began having contact with other woman that his fiancée considered inappropriate. She learned that he had been telling people he was no longer engaged, and she eventually discovered that he was advertising himself as single on a dating website. When she confronted him about it, a heated argument ensued, and the two began to "push one another aggressively." Zimmerman kicked the woman's dog in the stomach. She ended the relationship the next morning after Zimmerman left for work.

After she moved out, Zimmerman often called her to apologize and told her that he wanted to get back together. The two went out on several dates, but, according to the FBI, the woman "soon realized that although Zimmerman was a good talker and could be very persuasive, he hadn't really changed and she was no longer interested in reconciliation."

The woman told the FBI that Zimmerman "had a bad temper" and she thought it "had something to do with the side effects of Accutane," an acne medication Zimmerman used.

"The worst behavior he exhibited," the FBI report says, "was when he talked about killing himself." Zimmerman's ex-fiancée "explained that following some of their more intense arguments he would get depressed and talk about driving his car into a lake or taking a bunch of pills." But the woman apparently did not take the threats seriously; she told the FBI that she "believed that behavior was designed to get her attention or to garner her sympathy."

Zimmerman's former fiancée told FBI agents about an incident that occurred sometime after their relationship had fallen apart. One evening while she was returning home, she saw Zimmerman drive away from her townhouse complex. The woman phoned her ex-fiancée who initially claimed to be at another location. She confronted him with the fact that she had just seen him leaving the complex, and he confessed that he had come there to see her because he was upset about his grandmother's declining health. She allowed Zimmerman to visit her for awhile, but when he wanted to stay the night, she demurred. Zimmerman grabbed the woman's cell phone, put it in his pocket, and "said he wasn't going to leave." The woman "attempted to remove the phone from his pocket but Zimmerman pushed her away." The woman's dog then bit Zimmerman, and she was "able to retrieve her cellphone and call police." But when police arrived, Zimmerman was gone.

At the urging of officers, Zimmerman's ex-fiancée filed for an injunction. The day after police served Zimmerman with the injunction, he filed one against her in which he alleged that the woman had "accused him of being a womanizer and had scratched his face after he refused to stay with her at her apartment." The former couple "went to court and a mutual one-year injunction order was filed." The two went on with their separate lives.

In 2010, Zimmerman contacted his former fiancée, and the two met on several occasions in 2010 and 2011. The woman had been married in 2007, but that relationship fell apart in February 2011. Zimmerman, also married by that time, complained that his wife did not want to have children, but he did.

The woman told FBI agents that Zimmerman "often talked about wanting to be a police officer", and she "described him as being passionate about the prospect." She described Zimmerman as "very driven as was his whole family." The woman felt that Zimmerman's Peruvian mother married a white American to improve her "status", and she believed that her ex-fiancée's mother did not like her because her mother was Puerto Rican and her father was Argentinian. She believed that Zimmerman's mother wanted her son to marry a white woman.

Zimmerman's ex-fiancée told FBI agents that Zimmerman's "mother and grandmother exercised a lot of control over [him] and he always seemed to want to please them." In a television interview with Sean Hannity, Zimmerman explained that he was raised by his mother and grandmother because his father was in the military and was often gone. In fact, Zimmerman explained, English is his second language because he spoke Spanish most of the time at home.

Zimmerman's former fiancée told FBI agents that she never saw the man get into any physical confrontations with anyone other than her. In fact, she doubted that he would ever be a police officer because she "did not consider him to be the type of person to put himself in harm's way." She "never heard Zimmerman talk about weapons and never saw any weapons during their relationship." When asked about the shooting of Trayvon Martin, the woman told the FBI that "Zimmerman was the last person she would expect to be involved in anything like that."

While Zimmerman had some reported history of violence, he did not have a history of racial prejudice. In middle school, a young black student named Anthony Woodson befriended Zimmerman despite a seemingly-racist remark about Woodson tripping over his lip. Woodson, however, knew that Zimmerman wasn't a racist because he was in the company of two black students, an Asian, and a Hispanic. Zimmerman's father described their family as "multi-racial"; not only was Zimmerman's mother Hispanic, he had an Afro-Peruvian grandfather. Nobody in Zimmerman's inner circle describes him as a racist.

Even Zimmerman's ex-fiancée told the FBI that she did not believe he was a racist. During their relationship, the woman "observed Zimmerman as he socialized and played basketball with white, black and Hispanic men." She also explained that he "never exhibited any biases or prejudices against anyone and did not use racial epithets of any kind". The woman even told agents that Zimmerman "has never shown anything but support for his brother" who is gay.

Zimmerman's relationship with Sanford police had not always been amicable. In 2011, public outcry over alleged misconduct by Sanford police grabbed Zimmerman's attention. In December 2010, Justin Collison, the 21-year-old son of a Sanford police lieutenant, was accused of beating a homeless black man named Sherman Ware who was hospitalized as a result of the attack. Despite the statements of numerous witnesses, Sanford police refused to arrest Collison. Public outrage over the incident resulted in the resignation of Sanford's police chief, Brian Tooley. Zimmerman, angered by the event, spoke at a public hearing. "I would just like to state that the law is written in black and white," Zimmerman said. "It should not and cannot be enforced in the gray for those that are in the thin blue line."

Despite Zimmerman's multi-racial background, the shooting death of Trayvon Martin became a polarizing force that brought racial tensions in the United States to the surface. Many were convinced that Zimmerman profiled Martin because of his race. Early media accounts presented Zimmerman as white, presumably because of his last name. When Zimmerman's father pointed out that he was half Peruvian, some in the media began referring to the neighborhood watch volunteer as a "white Hispanic". Critics saw that play on words as a feeble attempt to keep Martin's race a central issue in the case pointing out that Barack Obama, the President of the United States, was himself born to an African father and a white mother, though most people, including the president himself, identified him as a black man, and nobody in mainstream media ever referred to the president as a "white African-American".

President Obama spoke about the case when a reporter inquired at a press conference in late March. "I think all of us have to do some soul searching to figure out how does something like this happen," the President said. "And that means we examine the laws and the context for what happened, as well as the specifics of the incident."

"I think every parent in America," President Obama said, "should be able to understand why it is absolutely imperative to investigate every aspect of this and that everybody pulls together—federal, state, and local—to figure out exactly how this tragedy happened."

"But my main message," the president added, "is to the parents of Trayvon Martin. You know, if I had a son, he'd look like Trayvon. And, you know, I think they are right to expect that all of us as Americans are going to take this with the seriousness it deserves and that we're going to get to the bottom of exactly what happened."

In response to the shooting, civil rights leader Jesse Jackson said: "Blacks are under attack." "We're surprised that everyone else is surprised," Jackson said, referring to the perception among black people in America that racism is alive and well. Jackson, speaking in the weeks between the shooting and the eventual murder charges, said Zimmerman's "lack of appearance in the court system is a source of embarrassment and humiliation" to the nation. The Reverend Al Sharpton went further comparing the death of Trayvon Martin and the ensuing battle to have his killer arrested to the trial and crucifixion of Jesus Christ.

NBC fired a reporter and a producer in an audio doctoring scandal that also brought down a local news reporter for a Miami NBC station. The three were involved in airing an edited clip of Zimmerman's call to police in which he was heard to say, referring to Martin, that "this guy looks like he's up to no good. He looks black." In fact, after Zimmerman stated that Martin appeared to be "up to no good", the dispatcher asked if Martin was "black, white, or Hispanic". Zimmerman responded: "He looks black."

In Sanford, police Sergeant Arthur Barns told the FBI in April that "the African American Community would be in an 'uproar' if Zimmerman is not charged." "The community will be satisfied," the FBI report explains, "if an arrest takes place." Barns, a black man born and raised in Sanford, told the Bureau that about half of Sanford's nearly sixty-thousand residents believed the shooting was a hate crime.

The racial overtones of this case contributed to the nation's collective rush to judgment. How could an over-zealous neighborhood watch volunteer shoot and kill a black teenager carrying nothing but a cell phone, a bag of Skittles, and an Arizona Iced Tea just for walking through a neighborhood he had every right to be in? A strong sense that he was profiled for being a young black male dressed in a hoodie gripped the nation.

The case catapulted to the top of the nation's attention as the days and weeks passed without charges against Martin's killer. Calls for Zimmerman's arrest were met with the realization that Sanford officials were not planning to charge Zimmerman with a crime. Outrage, protests, and calls for justice were heard from coast to coast before any substantive information about this case was made public. Speculation became fact. Fact became myth. Sanford police chief Bill Lee stepped down and was eventually fired. A special prosecutor was appointed by Governor Rick Scott, and within weeks, Zimmerman was charged with second-degree murder. But little in the news media made Americans aware of the truth of what really happened at Twin Lakes the evening of February 26, 2012.

The nation's ignorance of the facts is slowly waning. Discovery documents have been released: the autopsy report, details of the police investigation, 911 call recordings, George Zimmerman's statements to police, photographs of Zimmerman's injuries. Release of this information has led to a shift in public perception about what really took place that night.

What still has not taken place in the media or the public discourse about this case is any genuine analysis of the forensic evidence, taken in context to reconstruct the events of the shooting with any real appreciation of the forensic science that has become so commonplace in the investigation of fatal shootings and other criminal matters. Some evidence has been misinterpreted, other evidence ignored altogether.

Until the evidence is collected in context, until the puzzle pieces are put together, we will not truly understand what took place in that gated community in Sanford, Florida, on a rainy night that, until Trayvon Martin died, was just another night in any neighborhood in any city in the United States. But when we take a critical, in-depth, objective look at this case from the standpoint of the most reliable evidence available—the physical evidence—we will begin to understand what has happened in this country since a neighborhood watch volunteer and a teenage boy collided in a tragic sequence of events that has forever changed the way Americans perceive race relations, guns, violence, and justice in this country. What follows on these pages is just such an analysis.

# Puzzle Pieces

*"It has always been only George Zimmerman's word and his version that Trayvon Martin attacked him."*

—BENJAMIN CRUMP, MARTIN FAMILY ATTORNEY

EIGHTEENTH-CENTURY LONDON ENGRAVER and mapmaker John Spilsbury put one of his maps on a piece of wood and used a marquetry saw to cut around the borders of the countries. Spilsbury's simple but intriguing invention came to be known as "dissections", and the cutouts were used mostly as educational tools to teach students about geography. In the late 1800s cardboard "jigsaw puzzles" appeared as a children's toy. As the twentieth century emerged, jigsaw puzzles became as popular with adults as with children. Puzzle patterns were made more intricate, the images more pleasing. With the onset of the Great Depression, jigsaw puzzles grew popular as an inexpensive form of entertainment for a cash-strapped society.

The mention of a modern-day jigsaw puzzle conjures up images of a sophisticated photograph cut into hundreds of tiny pieces that only fit together one way. Puzzlers often rely on the box top to guide them through the assembly process by comparing the pieces to the picture, determining along the way where each tiny cardboard component fits.

A jigsaw puzzle analogy can be used to describe much of what takes place in forensic science. But the forensic scientist has no box top for guidance, and the likelihood is that a number of the pieces will be missing. Still, the process of determining what happened during an event such as a shooting can be accurately accomplished. If enough pieces of a puzzle are in place, the picture becomes apparent even if significant details are missing. How clear the picture becomes is, of course, dependent on the number and quality of available pieces. If the right pieces are present, the right conclusions can be drawn.

Dr. Max Houck defines forensic science as "the science of spatial and temporal relationships between people, places, and things involved in crimes." Forensic science, much like geology, astronomy, archeology, and paleontology, is a historical science that deals with proxy data. "The events under study have already occurred and are in the past," Houck explains. "A forensic scientist does not view the crime as it occurs [but] must assist the investigation through the analysis of the physical remains of the criminal activity."

The forensic scientist deals in time periods that are much shorter than most other scientists relying on proxy data, but he or she must also deal in details that are significantly finer. The archeologist, for example, may deal in time spans of hundreds or even thousands of years, but will likely be dealing in much grosser detail than the forensic scientist. The archeologist will view the collective actions of a group whereas the forensic scientist will view the minute actions of individuals. "Because of this abstraction," Houck explains, "we can only test hypotheses about what could have produced the proxy data we see. We cannot test the actual events that did produce that data." We are limited, as Houck explains, by the asymmetry of time: the past cannot be undone.

A forensic scientist's view of a crime is guided by the Locard Exchange Principle: every contact leaves a trace. Developed by 19th-century French criminologist Edmond Locard, the principle tells us that connections in the events are implied by connections in the evidence. What one thing gives, the other receives. Whenever someone enters a crime scene, he leaves something that wasn't there before, and he takes with him something that was.

While Locard's Exchange Principle is foundational to forensic science, it must not be so construed as to mean that, if no evidence of an event was found, the event never happened. The oft-used phrase, "the absence of evidence is not evidence of absence," while hotly debated as a matter of science and philosophy, sums up conceptually how one should carefully approach the reconstruction of criminal events. Clearly, there is a difference between a lack of evidence after careful searching, study, and research and a lack of evidence due to a deficiency of research, insufficient study, or a poorly executed crime scene search. We must recognize that our ability to interpret evidence is necessarily limited by our ability to find it. "When two items come into contact," Dr. Houck explains, "information may be exchanged; this exchange of information occurs, even if the results are not identifiable or are too small to be found." We work with the evidence we have, but not every crime is intrinsically soluble. In some cases, there simply are not enough pieces to see what the puzzle is supposed to look like.

But as the protests began in the weeks following the killing of Trayvon Martin, the puzzle pieces had yet to be seen. Martin's and Zimmerman's supporters alike knew almost nothing about the case for which they so vehemently argued their respective positions. Nobody was listening. Truth be damned, the media pundits and protest leaders felt that they knew what took place at Twin Lakes the evening that Trayvon Martin was killed.

Even as documents about the case became public, much of what was written on those pages was completely ignored, and what wasn't ignored was twisted and distorted by both sides to weave arguments for or against charging Zimmerman with the killing. And what was happening was a textbook example of exactly what a forensic scientist trains *not* to do: make the evidence fit one's notion of what took place. But few people making decisions about this case were forensic scientists, and almost nobody in the media or court of public opinion was interested in making their notion of the case fit the evidence. "People will generally accept facts as truth," Andy Rooney once explained, "only if the facts agree with what they already believe."

The forensic scientist cannot afford to follow this line of thinking. To do so results in letting the guilty go free and incarcerating the innocent—or worse. In science, there is a term for the human tendency to shape facts to fit one's hypothesis: it's called confirmation bias, and it most often happens without the biased viewer of the evidence even realizing what's happening.

In forensic investigations, confirmation bias leads to ignored or misinterpreted evidence because the investigator or scientist seeks to prove what he or she believes has taken place. But the problem with this approach is that there is no bar against which one can determine just when a case has been proven. How much evidence is needed to know for sure what really happened? When is the investigation done? There's no way to really answer these questions because the evidence that is considered has not been weighed against the evidence that is ignored.

◈

In the field of forensic science, there is a discipline dealing exclusively with putting together the puzzle pieces in context, a discipline known as crime scene reconstruction. The Association for Crime Scene Reconstruction defines it: "To gain explicit knowledge of the series of events that surround the commission of a crime using deductive and inductive reasoning, physical evidence, scientific methods, and their interrelationships." The crime scene reconstructionist is a generalist in forensic science, a person who assembles the evidence together in context to determine what happened. What was the sequence of events? Where were victims and suspects and how were they positioned? What's the nature and extent of the gunshot wounds? What type of weapon was used to commit the crime? What is the relationship between bloodstain pattern evidence and the events that took place? What are the connections between people, places, and things involved in the crime? How did human factors such as perception and visibility affect what took place? Who fired the fatal bullet? Who shot first? Who fell last?

The crime scene provides a snapshot of what took place, frozen in time, the culmination of a series of events that occurred over the course of seconds, minutes, hours, and even days. The asymmetry of time tells us that what we have found at the crime scene was collected in sequence from first to last, and we must unravel that sequence, generally working backward from last to first. But our snapshot does not begin when the criminal first enters the scene and end when he leaves. Instead, our snapshot includes data that were there perhaps long before the arrival of the offender, and it likewise includes changes to the scene and evidence that have occurred during the interval of time from when the criminal fled the scene to when the crime is investigated. Even if the scene has been undisturbed by people or animals, during that time changes occur. Much like a faded old photograph found in a box in one's closet, evidence that once was clear can become muddled—especially on a rainy evening.

Unlike practitioners of many other forensic science disciplines, crime scene reconstructionists are a relatively rare breed. There are just over a dozen certified by the International Association for Identification, the sole certifying body nationwide. To achieve such status, applicants must meet minimum training and experience requirements and must be active in their field of practice. They take a 300-question exam and complete a packet of practical scenario questions.

The crime scene reconstructionist is not a sociologist. He is not a philosopher. He is not a policy maker. He is not an advocate for a cause, a criminal, or a criminal's victim. He is—at least as much as any human being can be—an objective, unbiased observer of facts and evidence, a person whose duty to the criminal justice system is to analyze the evidence, explain the facts, and educate the jury.

But up until now, the killing of Trayvon Martin has not been about analyzing anything. It has not been about facts or explanations. And it certainly has not been about educating anyone. So much of the news and social media coverage of this case has focused on biased, slanted opinions about what took place that night. Few Americans have really appreciated the depth and breadth of the event because few have appreciated the facts, and even fewer have understood them.

◈

Long considered the father of modern criminalistics, Dr. Paul Kirk explains the relationship between evidence in a crime and the people involved. "All criminal investigation is concerned with people and with things," Kirk wrote. "Only people commit crimes, but they invariably do so through the medium of things." The process of crime scene reconstruction is often viewed as a physical evidence problem, and in many ways it is, which means that we tend to be less interested in "why" than we are in "who" and "what". However, crime is ultimately a human act, and no reconstruction of a human act can be wholly separated from the underlying human behavior. It is human behavior that drives the events that take place at a crime scene. It is human behavior that we are reconstructing.

The killing of Trayvon Martin is no different. Unlike many forensic science cases, the question of "who" has never been disputed. The question of "what", however, is the focus of dispute, but to understand "what", one must understand "why". To answer either of those questions, one must put aside any preconceptions of what took place and begin with a critical analysis of the physical evidence that exists, viewed in context to determine just what really took place at the Retreat at Twin Lakes that February evening.

The question of "why" in any criminal case is necessarily interwoven with the question of "what". An offender's *modus operandi* or method of operation—explained in the "what"—tells the forensic investigator a great deal about the crime, about how it took place and about why the offender chose to perform certain acts. *Modus operandi* is about expediency. It is about executing the crime and then getting away with it as efficiently and effectively as possible. Criminals often adjust their method of operation to accommodate factors that they encounter while committing a crime: a rapist known to find victims only on the first floor of a building may suddenly rape a woman living on the second floor because he couldn't find a suitable victim on the first floor; a robber may switch vehicles after learning that the description of his original getaway vehicle has been compromised, or he may change his method of escape altogether; a killer may change his preferred weapon finding another weapon to be easier to use, more effective at killing, or less likely to attract attention.

Then there is the criminal's signature, the actions that represent his psychological motivation for the crimes he commits. Signature elements are those crime scene behaviors that must be present for the criminal to live out his fantasy or to otherwise achieve pleasure from the crime. Signature behaviors typically have nothing to do with expediency or with evading capture; in fact, they often   slow the process of committing the crime and add to the risk of capture. A burglar may defecate on the floor of his victims' residences. A robber may force female victims to strip. A rapist may penetrate his victims with a particular object. A killer may carry away a trophy from his prey.

Signature and *modus operandi* elements of a crime represent planning and preparation. While they may not always be dictated by organized planning, they do require some level of aforethought, even if only in the twinkling of an eye.

But, despite the seemingly overwhelming rate of homicidal violence in the United States, killing other people is not an inherently human trait. Killing is, in fact, a learned behavior, one that carries with it many differing and often-conflicting motivations. People kill for money, power, control, anger, lust, and, among other reasons, survival.

Renowned expert and author on the topic of human aggression and the psychology of combat Dave Grossman, a professor of psychology and former military man, explains that during World War II, only about fifteen to twenty percent of combat infantry troops were willing to fire their rifles at enemy soldiers. He explains how physical and mechanical distance affects a soldier's ability to kill: hand-to-hand killing is more difficult than firing from a distance with a gun, and killing with a gun is more difficult than killing with artillery or bombs, weapons with which the killers rarely see their victims. But more importantly, Grossman explains how emotional distance tears down one's inherent barriers to killing: it's easier to kill someone you don't see as human, or who you see as less than you, as worthy of killing, or as a beast.

While the World War II infantryman was unlikely to kill, Grossman explains that the Korean War infantryman was much more motivated: one in two were willing to fire their rifles at enemy soldiers. And by Vietnam, almost every single soldier on the battlefield was a trained, willing killer—over ninety percent. But why the dramatic change in the infantryman's willingness to kill? Grossman explains that the military learned what society still has not: that killing is learned. During World War II, the infantryman received rifle training in which he fired at round bulls-eye targets; when he hit them, nothing happened. But by Vietnam, the military learned to use human silhouette targets that fell when the soldier-in-training hit it. Today, the military has gone ever further using video game-like simulators that provide full feedback—sound, blood, and death.

But George Zimmerman had none of this training. He had never been in the military. He had no real police training, only criminal justice classes he had taken at a local college. He even had apparently-limited firearms training; his only documented firearms training came on November 7, 2009, when he attended a six-hour firearms safety training course in order to obtain his Florida permit to carry a concealed firearm.

Real-life shooting incidents occur much differently than they are commonly portrayed on television and in movies. Shooting incidents are quick, dynamic events, often taking only a few seconds from the first shot to the last. There is a vast body of research on the use of deadly force. An understanding of the dynamics of shootings, including an understanding of the human factors, physiology, and biomechanical aspects of shooting incidents is necessary to properly comprehend the events and interpret the evidence.

One cannot understand the human factors of shooting incidents without understanding fear. Police psychologist Alexis Artwohl and law enforcement expert Loren Christensen provide a working definition of fear: "Fear is an automatic physical reaction to a perceived threat that will result in predictable physical, emotional, perceptual, and cognitive changes because of high physical arousal states." Fear is the body's way of telling someone that his or her life is in danger and that immediate action is required; "profound chemical changes" occur to make one "instinctively, and without hesitation, do one of three things to save [one's] life: fight, flight, or freeze." Police instructor Stephen Bunting describes the nature of those changes: "As the blood flow is enhanced to the large muscles, it is diverted away from other areas of the body. The brain receives less blood; the organism is seeking only to survive and therefore has a reduced need and ability to think or reason." Author Charles Silberman explains the concept of fight or flight:

> From a physiological standpoint, what we call fear is a series of complex changes in the endocrine system that alerts us to danger and makes it possible for us to respond effectively, whether we choose to attack or flee. The first stage—the one we associate most closely with fear or tension—prepares the entire body for fight or flight: the heart rate and systolic blood pressure go up; blood flow through the brain and the skeletal muscles increases by as much as 100 percent; digestion is impaired; and so on.

In a shooting situation, people revert to what they have been trained to do. Law enforcement tactical experts Ronald Adams, Thomas McTernan, and Charles Remsberg describe this phenomon: "[W]hen you are under sudden stress and fear, your pupils dilating, your heart thumping, your lungs heaving, your adrenalin surging, your stomach and bowels in turmoil, your ability to distinguish time, colors and distance diminished, you revert without thinking to the habits you have learned in training." Actions become automatic, and the shooter may act without conscious thought. Without proper training, however, physical skills will probably not occur correctly under stress. Bunting explains that a "physical skill must be performed 3,000 to 5,000 times before it can occur without conscious thought in a crisis."

Artwohl and Christensen describe a number of perceptual changes that can occur as a result of fear: (1) tunnel vision may occur resulting in a loss of peripheral vision and depth perception, as well as inhibiting one's ability to see beyond a threat; (2) heightened visual clarity may—despite tunnel vision —cause one to see certain details in vivid, almost surrealistic detail; (3) time may seem distorted resulting in events seeming to have taken much longer, or to have occurred much more rapidly, than they actually did; (4) dissociation may occur in which a person feels strangely separated from the event as if it is a dream; and, (5) temporary paralysis may cause one to be momentarily unable to move despite desperately trying to do so.

Grossman and Christensen explain that these sensory distortions rarely occur in normal life; aside from deadly force encounters, such distortions occur frequently only among hunters who often experience auditory exclusion and slow-motion time. Bunting explains that "the increased auditory and visual focus and acuities are directed toward the threat." As a consequence, the shooter may clearly see the person he is shooting at but may not see his surroundings, and those surroundings are what provide a visual context for understanding what is happening, such as when a person falls to the ground.

Grossman explains that, in addition to the various perceptual distortions commonly experienced by those involved in deadly force encounters, fear and panic can lead to what he terms the "endless do-loop." In such a state, a fear-stressed person may fall into a loop in which an act is endlessly repeated despite its futility. This type of stress response leads to seemingly unimaginable behavior; people trapped in a burning building, for example, may repeatedly try to exit through a locked door rather than going to another exit. A shooter may also fire repeatedly and even continue to try to fire an empty weapon; such a phenomenon can be associated with the shooter's perceptually-distorted belief that the firearm is not working because he does not hear his shots.

◈

In the aftermath of the killing, Martin family attorney Benjamin Crump quipped: "It has always been only George Zimmerman's word and his version that Trayvon Martin attacked him." But Crump is wrong. There exists something much more compelling, much more reliable, and much less ambiguous than Zimmerman's word: the physical evidence. And until that evidence is fully analyzed in context, nobody will know clearly what happened at Twin Lakes—at least nobody other than George Zimmerman.

On May 27, Zimmerman's attorney, Mark O'Mara, appeared on CNN's *Piers Morgan Tonight*. "It's several pieces of the puzzle that we now have to put together," O'Mara said. "I would only ask that everyone wait until we have the whole pieces—all of them together—to look and see what the whole picture is."

# Fucking Coons

*"These assholes—they always get away."*

—GEORGE ZIMMERMAN TO THE POLICE DISPATCHER

"HEY, WE'VE HAD SOME break-ins in my neighborhood, and there's this real suspicious guy," George Zimmerman told the Sanford police dispatcher. "This guy looks like he's up to no good, or he's on drugs or something. It's raining and he's just walking around, looking about." Zimmerman, reportedly on his way to the grocery store, called the Sanford police non-emergency number to report seeing who he thought was a suspicious person walking in the rain in the Twin Lakes complex.

This was not Zimmerman's first call to Sanford police to report someone suspicious in his neighborhood. Just as he had done at least four times since the previous August, Zimmerman decided to share his suspicion that a young black male was "up to no good" with the police agency that he had, by February, developed at least somewhat of a working relationship with. If nothing else, the neighborhood watch volunteer had proven that he wasn't shy about sharing his suspicions of neighborhood wanderers with Sanford's boys in blue, and on February 26, a recording captured the now-infamous four-minute-thirteen-second call. Later it was learned that Zimmerman placed forty-six 911 and non-emergency calls to Sanford police over the eight year period leading up to the shooting. Although every call to police is recorded, the audio of only six of those calls survived to become part of the case because routine call recordings to Sanford police are destroyed after six months.

According to records, Zimmerman called the non-emergency line in November 2006 to report a Toyota pickup that had been "driving around the neighborhood" for several minutes. In June 2009, he reported a disturbance near the gated community's shared pool. In October 2010, he called to report a woman in a blue Jeep who appeared to be yelling at elderly passengers in the vehicle.

In April 2011, Zimmerman called police to report an incident involving a black boy between seven and nine years old. Then Zimmerman called twice in August 2011, once in October 2011, and once in early February 2012 to report seeing suspicious black males in the gated community.

But Zimmerman wasn't the only person calling Sanford police to the Twin Lakes subdivision. Police received 402 calls from Twin Lakes' residents from January 1, 2011 until the February 26, 2012 shooting. But this call would prove to be arguably the most significant call ever placed to Sanford police.

"This guy—is he white, black, or Hispanic?" the dispatcher asked Zimmerman.

"He looks black," Zimmerman responds, twenty-nine seconds into the call.

"Did you see what he was wearing?"

"Yeah, a dark hoodie, like a gray hoodie, and either jeans or sweatpants and white tennis shoes." Martin was dressed in a dark gray Fruit of the Loom hooded sweatshirt.

Zimmerman told the dispatcher that Martin "was just staring" and that he was "looking at all the houses."

"Now he's just staring at me," Zimmerman said forty-eight seconds after placing the call. As he explained to the dispatcher that he was near the clubhouse, Zimmerman said, "Yeah, now he's coming toward me." There was some background noise, but Zimmerman was still in his truck one minute into the call.

"OK," the dispatcher replied.

"He's got his hand in his waistband," Zimmerman said, followed by more background sound. Several seconds later, Zimmerman continued, "And he's a black male." Immediately afterward, Zimmerman moved his truck's gear shift, placing the truck in gear to follow Martin past the clubhouse onto Twin Trees Lane. It was one minute and nine seconds after Zimmerman called police.

"How old would you say he looks?" the dispatcher inquired.

"[L]ate teens."

"Late teens. OK."

"Something's wrong with him," Zimmerman said. "Yeah,

he's coming to check me out." Zimmerman was still in his vehicle.

"He's got something in his hands," Zimmerman explained. "I don't know what his deal is."

"Just let me know if he does anything, OK?" the dispatcher asked.

"How long until you get an officer over here?" Zimmerman inquired.

"[W]e've got someone on the way," the dispatcher explained. "Just let me know if this guy does anything else."

"OK," Zimmerman replied. "These assholes—they always get away." Zimmerman's comment, one minute and thirty-seven seconds after he phoned Sanford police, would come to be part of the allegations against him. Six seconds later, the sound of the truck's gear selector is heard as Zimmerman puts the truck in park. The distance from the front of the clubhouse to where Zimmerman parked his truck is about three hundred fifty feet; he drove that distance in thirty-three seconds, a speed of about seven miles per hour, a jogging pace.

Over the next several seconds, Zimmerman tried to tell the dispatcher how to find him after coming through the front entrance of the complex. "When you come to the clubhouse you come straight in and make a left," Zimmerman explained. "Actually, you would go past the clubhouse."

"So, it's on the left-hand side from the clubhouse?" the dispatcher clarified.

"No, you go straight through the entrance, and then you make a left." The audio background was contained; Zimmerman was still in his vehicle. "[G]o straight in, don't turn, and make a left.

"Shit," Zimmerman exclaimed. "He's running." It was two minutes and seven seconds after Zimmerman called police.

"He's running?" the dispatcher replied. "Which way is he running?" Zimmerman opens the door to his truck.

"Down towards the other entrance to the neighborhood," Zimmerman replied, his voice strained. The door chime dinged politely in the background, and the car door closed just as Zimmerman completed his sentence, two minutes and fourteen seconds after the call began.

"Which entrance is that that he's heading toward?" the dispatcher inquired.

"The back entrance," Zimmerman replied. He sounded winded as though he was running or, at least, moving briskly. The back entrance is near Brandy Green's home, the residence where Martin was staying.

Then, two minutes and twenty-one seconds into the call, Zimmerman muttered something under his breath, three words that would become one of the most hotly-debated issues of the case and that would drive much of the public's belief that George Zimmerman, the son of a white father and a Peruvian mother, was a racist.

◈

What Zimmerman muttered under his breath is not clearly discernible on the police recording of the telephone call. In fact, it would be quite easy to listen to the recording and not even realize that he said it.

Sanford police, clearly suspecting that his comment had an impact on what took place that night, sent the recording to the FBI's Forensic Audio, Video, and Image Analysis Unit, known in Bureau jargon as FAVIAU. While it is not clear from the redacted Sanford police investigation report just what investigators thought Zimmerman muttered, FAVIAU reported being asked to determine the word Zimmerman said "following the word 'fucking' at approximately 2 minutes and 20 seconds" into the call. But FAVIAU wasn't able to determine anything. The FBI report stated simply that the request "could not be done due to weak signal level and poor recording quality." Whatever it was that Zimmerman said, the nation's top law enforcement agency had no clue.

While the FAVIAU's report stood on safe forensic ground, it did nothing to clear up the issue. So just what did Zimmerman say? Using audio enhancement software, the one-second clip can be cleaned up to make the words more apparent. Clean out the background noise. Equalize the sound to improve quality of the vocal range. Slow the clip down. Listen to the cadence.

Many have suggested that Zimmerman muttered, "fucking coons", an obsolete racial slur that is rarely heard in modern mainstream diction. Nowhere in the publicly-released investigative evidence did the Sanford police, special prosecutor Angela Corey's office, the Florida Department of Law Enforcement, or the FBI uncover credible evidence that George Zimmerman is a racist or that he ever used the word "coon" at any time before placing the now-infamous call to Sanford police. Even Zimmerman's ex-fiancée, a woman who at one time had a restraining order against the neighborhood watch volunteer, told the FBI that Zimmerman was no racist.

So if Zimmerman didn't say "coon", what did he say? Fifty-three-year-old former news anchor Joe Oliver, claiming to be Zimmerman's "close friend", appeared on ABC's Good Morning America and gave an explanation: Zimmerman said "goon", not "coon".

"Goon is apparently a term of endearment in the high schools these days," Oliver, who is black, explained. "I don't know of anyone younger than 40 who uses coon as a racial epithet."

While many in the public and the media were, at best, skeptical of Oliver's claim that Zimmerman used a "term of endearment", almost nobody in the nation was aware that Sanford's lead investigator in the Martin shooting case, Detective Chris Serino, used the word "goon" twice while interviewing Zimmerman on February 29, just three days after the killing.

During the audio-recorded interview, Serino asked Zimmerman if he had ever heard of "Murphy's Law".

"Yes," Zimmerman answered.

"Well, that's what happened," Serino replied. "This person wasn't doing anything bad." Serino asked Zimmerman if he knew the name of the person that died.

Zimmerman replied, "Trayvon Martin."

"Trayvon Benjamin Martin," Serino added. "He was born in 1995, February the fifth. He was seventeen years old, an athlete, probably somewhere someone who was going to be in aeronautics, a kid with a future, a kid with folks that care. In his possession we found a can of iced tea and a bag of Skittles, and about forty-two dollars in cash. Not the goon."

Later in the interview, responding to Zimmerman's claim that Martin attacked him, Serino asked, "What do you think set him off?"

"I don't know," Zimmerman replied.

"Had he been a goon, a bad kid," Serino added, "two thumbs-up, you know, but he does not fit the profile of what occurred, which is another unfortunate thing that we got going on here."

It's clear from the cadence of the recording clip that Zimmerman muttered four syllables. It is equally clear that the second and third of those syllables formed the profane word "fucking". But there have been many suggestions as to what the full phrase really was including "these fucking coons", "these fucking goons", "these fucking cones", "these fucking punks"—even "it's fucking cold".

As part of their investigation into the shooting, the FBI interviewed Josh Memminger, a gang intelligence investigator with the Sanford Police Department. During their March 4 interview, the Bureau spoke specifically with Memminger about gangs in the Sanford area that refer to themselves as "goons". The report states that there are "currently three different groups of Goons" operating in Sanford and going by the names "14th Street Goons", "Washington Oaks Goons", and "Midway Goons". The membership of all three groups is exclusively African-American. Memminger was not aware of any documented members of the three groups who lived in Twin Lakes. According to Memminger, during times of cold weather, members of the groups were "known to wear hoodies and dress in layers."

CNN aired stories in which two different audio experts with the cable network enhanced the recording. The first time it sounded like Zimmerman said "coons"; the second time it sounded much more like he said "cold". But the temperature that rainy night was sixty-three degrees, and Zimmerman was wearing a jacket.

Zimmerman himself said that the words he uttered were "these fucking punks." Sanford police questioned him about it.

In July, nearly five months after the shooting, Zimmerman and his attorney, Mark O'Mara, were interviewed in Sanford by Fox News personality Sean Hannity, the first television interview granted by the embattled neighborhood watchman. Hannity asked Zimmerman what he said on that recording. Zimmerman replied, simply, "Punks."

Whatever Zimmerman said, one fact remains: without a high-quality enhancement of the audio, the prosecutors will not be able to prove that what Zimmerman said in that brief second was a racial epithet directed toward Trayvon Martin, and, in fact, they have not alleged anything of the sort. The prosecution, despite FAVIAU's inability to discern what was said, alleges in the probable cause affidavit that Zimmerman said, "these fucking punks." What Zimmerman told Sanford police about the muttered comment is apparently what prosecutors plan to tell a jury.

◈

Two minutes and twenty-two seconds into the call, after Zimmerman muttered those three controversial words under his breath, the dispatcher, realizing that Zimmerman was running, asked, "Are you following him?"

After a two-second pause, Zimmerman, still sounding winded, responded, "Yeah."

"OK, we don't need you to do that," the dispatcher chided.

After a brief pause, Zimmerman acknowledged the dispatcher saying, simply, "OK."

"Alright, sir. What is your name?"

"George," Zimmerman replied. "He ran." It was two minutes and thirty-seven seconds after Zimmerman called police, ten seconds after the dispatcher's chiding. Moments later—two minutes and forty-two seconds into the call—background noise that sounded like wind passing over the microphone of Zimmerman's phone subsided. The noise started when Zimmerman got out of his car and began following Martin. It lasted a total of twenty-three seconds.

◈

"All right, George, what's you last name?" the dispatcher asked.

"Zimmerman."

"And George, what's the phone number you're calling from?"

Zimmerman recited the number.

"All right, George, we do have them on the way," the dispatcher reassured him. "Do you want to meet the officer when they get out there?"

"Yeah," Zimmerman affirmed.

"Alright, where are you going to meet with them at?"

Zimmerman began explaining. "If they come in through the gate, tell them to go straight past the clubhouse . . . and make a left," Zimmerman said, "and then they go past the mailboxes —that's my truck. . . ."

"What address are you parked in front of?"

"I don't know. It's a cut-through so I don't know the address."

"OK. Do you live in the area?" the dispatcher inquired.

Zimmerman affirmed.

"What's your apartment number?" the dispatcher asked.

"It's a home. It's 1950—oh, crap. I don't want to give it all out. I don't know where this kid is," Zimmerman said reservedly. Martin was gone, at least from Zimmerman's view. It was three minutes and thirty-seven seconds after Zimmerman phoned Sanford police.

"OK," the dispatcher acknowledged. "Do you want to just meet with them right near the mailboxes then?" The mailboxes are in the opposite direction of where Trayvon Martin ran and where George Zimmerman followed.

"Yeah," Zimmerman said, "that's fine." Then Zimmerman asked if the officer could just call him instead.

"OK, yeah. That's no problem," the dispatcher affirmed.

Zimmerman confirmed that the dispatcher had his phone number.

"OK. No problem," the dispatcher said. "I'll let them know to call you when they're in the area."

"Thanks."

"You're welcome."

Four minutes and thirteen seconds after it began, Zimmerman's call to police ended. The next time George Zimmerman spoke to Sanford police, Trayvon Martin was dead.

# Get Off, Get Off

*"He said this man was watching him, so he put his hoodie on."*

— DEEDEE, TRAYVON MARTIN'S GIRLFRIEND

"THIS YOUNG LADY CONNECTS the dots," Martin family attorney Benjamin Crump told an audience at a March 20 press conference. "Arrest George Zimmerman for the killing of Trayvon Martin in cold blood, today."

Crump was referring to statements of the 16-year-old girlfriend of Trayvon Martin, a girl known only by her first name of DeeDee. "We don't understand how he's not arrested," Crump said. "The family worries that the more time passes it will be swept under the rug."

But the case wasn't swept under the rug. Just three days later, Florida Governor Rick Scott appointed a special prosecutor, Jacksonville State Attorney Angela Corey, to take over the case. Within weeks, Corey announced that Zimmerman had been charged with second-degree murder.

Twenty-three days after the shooting, Crump revealed that DeeDee had been talking with Martin in the moments leading up to the shooting, a fact that was not even known to police or prosecutors. Crump allowed portions of a recorded interview of the girl to be aired during an ABC News exclusive report. The interview was conducted by Crump himself.

"He said this man was watching him, so he put his hoodie on. He said he lost the man," DeeDee told Crump. "I asked Trayvon to run, and he said he was going to walk fast. I told him to run, but he said he was not going to run."

DeeDee described what happened right before Martin was killed. "Trayvon said, 'What are you following me for?' and the man said, 'What are you doing here?' Next thing I hear is somebody pushing, and somebody pushed Trayvon because the headset just fell. I called him again, and he didn't answer the phone."

Martin's father, Tracy Martin, reacted to hearing the girl's account of her conversation with his son. "He knew he was being followed and tried to get away from the guy, and the guy still caught up with him," the elder Martin said. "And that's the most disturbing part. He thought he had got away from the guy, and the guy backtracked for him."

DeeDee's statements were interpreted as proving that Zimmerman attacked Martin. Many in the news media were still reporting that screams for help heard in the background of a 911 call from a witness were those of Trayvon Martin, a claim that would later prove unlikely. The news media, unaware of the substance of the police investigation into the shooting, would learn that the elder Martin told an investigator that the screaming person was not his son.[†]

The Martin family had grown leery of the Sanford police investigation and decided not to share the girl's account of the phone call with the local police agency. "We're going to turn this over to the Justice Department," Crump said, "because the family does not trust the Sanford Police Department to have anything to do with the investigation." Phone records proved that the call had, in fact, taken place.

On April 2, Bernie de la Rionda, assistant to special prosecutor Angela Corey, recorded a twenty-two minute question-and-answer session with DeeDee who had traveled to Jacksonville where the assistant state attorney was based. A tall, bald-headed attorney with a rim of brown hair wrapped around his head and a thick mustache, de la Rionda speaks in a fast-paced, projected manner with just a slight hint of a Spanish accent. Flanked by investigator T. C. O'Steen and several unnamed agents with the Florida Department of Law Enforcement, the prosecutor inquired about DeeDee's involvement with Trayvon Martin.

She had known Martin since kindergarten, the girl explained. When de la Rionda inquired about the seriousness of their relationship, DeeDee replied, "We were getting there."

---

†    Tracy Martin would later claim that he never made such a statement.

DeeDee told the prosecutor that she had been talking with Martin off and on since that morning, and that she had been on the phone with him while he walked to a nearby store to get candy and a drink "for his little brother." She said that the conversation did not take place during one continuous call but rather multiple calls because her "phone was acting up."

On his way back from the store, Martin told DeeDee that it had begun to rain, so he took shelter in a "mail area".

"This man is watching me," Martin told his girlfriend. He described the man as white and said that the man was in a car and was talking on the phone. According to DeeDee, Martin started walking because the man was following him.

DeeDee would tell de la Rionda that Martin said, "The man looking crazy." Martin also used the word "creepy" to describe the following stranger.

"He put his hoodie on," DeeDee told de la Rionda. The girl said Martin was "about to run from the back." She told him to "go to his [dad's] house."

"So the next thing I hear," the girl explained, "he [was] just running, and I could hear that the wind [was] blowing." Eventually, Martin told his girlfriend that he had "lost" the following stranger. "He was breathing hard," the girl said.

DeeDee told de la Rionda that Martin's voice changed. "I know he was scared," she said.

"He started walking back again," the girl told de la Rionda, "and I told him, 'Keep running.'" But Martin told her that he wasn't going to run.

"He said he ain't gonna run," DeeDee explained, "'cause he said he [was] right by his [father's] house."

"[I]n a couple minutes, he said the man [was] following him again," the girl said. "I say, 'Run!'" But Martin told his girlfriend that he was not going to run; he was still out of breath.[†]

---

† DeeDee's reference to a "a couple minutes" coincides with Zimmerman's call to police and his later statement in his television interview with Sean Hannity that Martin attacked him about thirty seconds after the call to police ended. That call lasted approximately one-and-a-half minutes from the time that Zimmerman stopped running and told the dispatcher, "He ran."

◈

"He said the guy was getting close to him," DeeDee said. "He told me the guy was getting real close to him. Next I hear, 'Why you following me for?'"

The girl heard another voice. "I hear this man—sounded like an old man—say, 'What are you doing around here?'" DeeDee explained.

The girl called out to Martin. "Trayvon, Trayvon," she inquired. "What's going on?"

"You could hear that somebody bumped Trayvon," she explained, "'cause I could hear the grass."

She called out to her boyfriend again with no response. Before the call ended, DeeDee heard Martin yell, "Get off! Get off!"

"And the next thing," the girl said, "the phone just shut off."

DeeDee told de la Rionda that she didn't hear any screams, and she did not hear the gunshot. The girl tried to call Martin again, but nobody answered.

# Screaming for Help

*"He just looked so messed up."*

—Witness #11 in a Statement to Sanford Police

"9-1-1. Do you need police, fire, or medical?" the Sanford emergency dispatcher answered.

"Maybe both. I'm not sure," the caller said. Known only as Witness 11, the female caller dialed 911 after hearing a person yelling outside her home. The screaming male voice was recorded in the background. "Maybe both. There's just someone screaming outside," she told the dispatcher.

Part of the North American Numbering Plan, 911 are the three digits used throughout the United States and Canada for quickly dialing police during an emergency. In 1968, at the urging of the Federal Communications Commission, AT&T, then the sole telecommunications provider in the United States, agreed to implement the three-digit number for emergency use. The number became part of the N11 system of numbers such as 411 for "information" and 611, which was dialed for repair service. The digits were also designed based on the area code rules and numbering plan that were in place so that switching equipment could recognize the digits and route the call appropriately. Today, the 911 system not only directs calls quickly to emergency services, but it also provides the caller's phone number and address (if the call is placed from a land line) so that, even if no conversation takes place, the police can respond to find out what's wrong.

"Is it a male or a female?" the dispatcher asked.

"It sounds like a male."

"And you don't know why?"

"I don't know why," the woman answered. "I think they're yelling help, but I don't know. Send someone quick, please." The concern in her voice was waxing.

"Does he look hurt to you?" the dispatcher asked.

"I can't see. I don't want to go out there. I don't know what's going on."

"So you think he's yelling help?" the dispatcher asked again.

"Yes," the woman responded abruptly.

"Alright what is your name—?" The dispatcher's question was interrupted by the loud sound of a gunshot forty seconds into the call.

"There's gunshots!" the woman exclaimed.

"You just heard gunshots?"

"Yes."

"How many?"

"Just one." The woman yells at her boyfriend in the background, telling him to "get down."

"Is he no longer yelling?" the dispatcher inquired.

"No one's—I don't know," the woman responded.

"Is he right outside?" the dispatcher asked.

"Yeah, pretty much," the woman responded with tension apparent in her voice, "out the back, yeah."

The male in the background says, "There's gunshots."

"Is he in front of it or behind that address?" the dispatcher asked.

"He's behind my house," the woman replied.

"I don't hear him yelling anymore," the dispatcher said. "Do you hear anything?"

"No, I don't," the woman replied, "because I'm hiding upstairs. There was a gunshot right outside our house."

After a moment, the woman said, "You've obviously sent someone already, right?"

"Yes, it's in dispatch. What's your name and phone number?"

The woman's response has been redacted from the recording.

"Do you hear any vehicles leaving or anyone else?" the dispatcher asked. "Do you hear anything right now?"

"There's people yelling out there," the woman replied, "but I don't want to go down there."

"OK, multiple people are yelling now?"

"Yeah."

"OK." The dispatcher is typing in the background. "Alright, well we do have officers on the way. Just call us back if you do hear or see anything else suspicious like any vehicles leaving or anything like that, OK?"

"OK."

"Alright, thank you." The call ended two minutes and eighteen seconds after it began.

◈

There is a male voice screaming in the background, an impassioned and desperate cry for help. At least sixteen distinct screams are heard, including one that occurs after the shot is fired. Although difficult to tell for certain, it sounds like only one voice. Whose voice it was is a critical question for this case.

Sanford police turned to the FBI for answers. The Forensic Audio, Video, and Image Analysis Unit, better known as FAVIAU, examined the recording. But, once again, the Bureau couldn't help. Examiners Kenneth Marr and Dr. Hirotaka Nakasone tried to "conduct a voice comparison examination of the designated area" of the recording of Witness 11's call to police.

"During the 45 second segment," the FAVIAU examiners wrote, "the designated screaming voice is audible for approximately 18.82 seconds in the background while a neighbor talks to the 911 dispatcher." The examiners explained that only during a fraction of that duration was the voice heard by itself, without interference from the talking caller and 911 dispatcher. "Of the 18.82 seconds, the screaming voice is superimposed for approximately 16.29 seconds by a simultaneous exchange between the calling female neighbor and the 911 female dispatcher." According to the FBI examiners, the "total duration of the screaming voice without another voice overlapping is approximately 2.53 seconds long."

But those 2.53 seconds of screaming weren't enough for the Bureau to work with. "Voice comparison is not possible for the designated voices," the FAVIAU examiners reported, "due to extreme stress and unsuitable audio quality." The FBI examiners explained:

Critical listening and digital signal analyses further revealed that the screaming voice of the 911 call is of insufficient voice quality and duration to conduct a meaningful voice comparison with any other voice samples primarily due to the screaming voice being: (1) produced under an extreme emotional state, (2) limited in the number of words and phrases uttered, (3) superimposed by other voices most of the time, and (4) distant, reverberant and very low signal level.

The Sanford Police Department would have to rely on someone other than the FBI to tell them who was screaming for help.

◈

On the day of the shooting, Witness 11 provided Sanford police with a one-paragraph written statement about what she saw and heard. Writing in a staccato, broken style, she recorded her experience in just five sentences:

> Heard some scuffling and loud talking outside our back door. Muted tv because it got louder and wanted to hear what was going on. Heard a man yelling but couldn't make out what he was saying then same man started yelling help. We called 911 and while on phone heard gun shot. Ran upstairs so couldn't hear anymore until police where [sic] here!

On Friday, March 2, five days after the shooting, Sanford police investigator Chris Serino recorded an interview of Witness 11. Serino, a dark-haired, stocky-built, fast-talking man with a solid, raspy voice, was the lead detective on the case.

The part-Puerto Rican, part-Italian investigator asked the woman to describe what she saw. "We didn't see anything," the woman replied. "We only heard everything. We had our back door open, so we could hear everything going on, but we didn't see anything. It was too dark."

"OK, what did you hear?" Serino asked.

"[I]t sounded just like two or more men talking kind of loud," the woman replied, "and so I muted the TV to see what was going on, and at that point it kind of just sounded like scuffling around so that's when I . . . went to go get the phone. . . ."

"We've been having issues in the neighborhood already," the woman said."

"What kind of issues?" Serino asked.

"Break-ins and burglaries and stuff," the woman explained. "They've been telling us the minute you see anything [or] hear anything suspicious, just call 911." Seven reported burglaries and twenty-two other crimes over a two-year period had put Twin Lakes residents on edge.

Witness 11 told Serino that, while she was calling 911, one man was yelling, "Ah! Ah!" "Not a help yell," the woman explained, "but just yelling. . . . Then those yells kind of turned to, 'Help! Help! Help!'"[†]

"He yelled help many times," the woman said. "I heard the next door neighbor open his door and kind of say, you know, 'What are you guys doing?' and the guy said, 'Help! Help!' to him, too. And he was like, 'Well, I'm calling 911.'"[‡]

"We heard the gunshot, and it got quiet," the woman explained, "and that was about it."

"The conversations that you heard before you muted the TV," Serino inquired, "could you make out *anything* that was being said?"

"I really couldn't," the woman replied. "It was just kind of loud yelling."

"Was it an exchange?" Serino asked. "Would you call it an exchange of words?"

"Yes," she said. "Yes."

"How many did you hear back and forth as far as the yelling?" Serino asked. "Could you approximate?"

"I would say maybe three," the woman responded, "and I

---

†   Zimmerman told police that, while he was struggling with Martin, the teenager covered his mouth and was suffocating him. Witness 11's reference to a "Ah! Ah!" that turned into "Help! Help!" seems to corroborate Zimmerman's account.

‡   During his videotaped walk-through with Sanford police investigators, Zimmerman said that a man stepped out his back door. He said that he asked the man to help, but the man said he was calling 911. That man was apparently Witness 6.

would be kind of just guessing." The woman explained that the television was still on, unmuted, when that exchange took place.

"At first we just thought it was like a couple of drunk guys or something yelling," she explained. "That's just how it sounded like loud, belligerent kind of."

Witness 11 explained that she never saw the altercation, and she believed that her next door neighbor was the only person who did see anything.

"He didn't know George or the other guy at all," the woman said, "but he did describe both of them, and we know George was on the bottom getting pummeled and we saw George's face after. . . . He was the one yelling help the whole time."

"How did his face look when you first saw him?" Serino asked.

Witness 11 explained that she didn't want to go over to see Zimmerman, so a police officer brought a picture he snapped with his cell phone to her. "[A]t first we couldn't even recognize him because it looked like his nose was broken in a few spots," the woman explained. "His lip was all bloody, and he just looked completely out of it."

Witness 11, who knew Zimmerman from the homeowners' association meetings, didn't recognize the neighborhood watch leader until another woman said, "Oh, that's my neighbor!"

"And I kind of put two and two together," Witness 11 told Serino. "[H]e just looked so messed up."

"Have you ever spoken to him before?" Serino inquired.

"Just during meetings and stuff," the woman explained. "I'm on the board. . . . We'll talk, but not much. . . ."

"What's your impression of him . . . in general?" Serino asked. "A good person?"

"Yeah, he seems just really laid back," she said. "Calm, cool, collected. That's why, I mean, I couldn't really picture him doing anything crazy, like, or malicious. . . . I can't picture him loosing his cool, you know, unless he really felt like he needed to do something."

Serino asked if Zimmerman was confrontational. The woman explained that Zimmerman was passionate about the neighborhood watch program. "I think if he saw something going on, he would confront the person," she said, "but not confrontational in the sense like he's trying to have, you know, an altercation or something like that."

"So he's not like a little Nazi running around trying to, you know—?" Serino asked.

"No," the woman replied. "Absolutely not."

"He just wants the neighborhood to be safe," the woman told Serino.

Investigator Doris Singleton joined the conversation. "You would recognize his voice possibly?" she asked.

"I would," Witness 11 answered hesitantly, "but not—no, not in that situation, I wouldn't." She explained that "it just sounded like two men yelling."

Serino asked if the woman heard a "chase" outside.

"No, I didn't," she replied. "It sounded like it all started right on the sidewalk by our house there and then maybe like it bent the corner, and right there is where the scuffle started [and] kind of scooted down because it definitely went past the back of our house."

Serino and the other investigator verified with Witness 11 that she thought the altercation started "at the T", which is the spot where the cut-through sidewalk near where Zimmerman parked his truck meets the perpendicular sidewalk that passes behind the woman's house. This is the same spot where Zimmerman told investigators the altercation began.

◈

On March 19, Special Agent John Batchelor with the Florida Department of Law Enforcement, along with Investigator Jim Post with the State Attorney's Office in Seminole County, interviewed Witness 11 again. Batchelor, assigned to the case to conduct an independent review in the wake of public protests about the Sanford Police Department's handling of the case, recites a prepared statement at the inception of each recorded interview. Batchelor speaks in a slow, deliberate, monotonic dialogue that projects a certain dispassionate lack of interest in the case. He's there to do his job, and that's exactly what he's doing.

"The purpose and scope of inquiry today," Batchelor announced for the recording, "is to conduct an independent follow-up with regards to the shooting investigation that has been conducted by the Sanford Police Department in your community."

Batchelor handed the woman a copy of her written statement and had her authenticate that she, in fact, wrote it the day of the shooting.

"If you would, would you go through the events that occurred on February 26, 2012?" the agent asked.

The woman relayed her recollection of the events telling the investigators about hearing the scuffle, muting the television, and calling 911. She also mentioned the break-ins the community had been suffering.

"About how many 'helps' do you think you heard?" Batchelor asked.

"Maybe fifteen," the woman replied. "It was within a span of forty seconds, I'd say—the yelling started to the gunshot."

Batchelor asked if the woman at any time looked outside to see what was happening.

"No, because we couldn't see outside here even if we wanted to. We would've literally had to go out onto the porch and lift up the blinds to see."

Batchelor asked the witness if she was familiar with the sound of gunfire. "No, and that was a weird sound," she explained. "I mean, I knew what it was. There's no doubt about it, but . . . it wasn't what I expected it would sound like. It was more of a pop than what you hear in the movies."

◈

Witness 11 told police that her neighbor likely had a better view of what was happening. The neighbor, a man, came to be identified as Witness 6. On the day of the shooting, he wrote a statement for Sanford police in which he explained that he "heard yelling out back in [the] grass area" behind his home. "I opened [the] blinds," he wrote, "and saw clothing but everything [was] dark outside." Witness 6 opened his door and saw one man dressed in gray straddling another man wearing red; Martin was dressed in a gray hooded sweatshirt, Zimmerman in a red jacket. Witness 6 wrote that the man on top was "hitting" the man on the bottom, who was "yelling help". Witness 6 wrote in his statement twice that the "guy on the bottom" was the one calling for help. But instead of helping, Witness 6 "ran upstairs" and called 911.

"I just heard a shot right behind my house," Witness 6 told the 911 dispatcher. "They're wrestling right in the back of my porch."

"You just heard one shot go off?" the dispatcher asked.

"It was either that or a rock at the window or something. I don't know. The guy's yelling help and I'm not going outside."

Serino recorded an interview of Witness 6 the day of the shooting. The witness told Serino that he heard yelling and looked out his blinds and saw "kind of like a person out there." "I didn't know if it was a dog attack or something," the man explained, "so I opened my door. There was a black man with a black hoodie on top of either a white guy or, now that I've found out, I think it was a Hispanic guy with a red sweatshirt on on the ground yelling out 'Help!'"

Serino clarified if it was the person on the bottom that was calling for help.

"Yes," the witness answered affirmatively. There was no hesitation in his voice. "That was the one getting beat up, and he was the one with the red sweater on."

Witness 6, known only by the first name, John, was interviewed the day after the shooting by Orlando's Fox 35 News. "The guy on the bottom, who I believe had a red sweater on," Witness 6 said, "was yelling to me, 'Help! Help!' I told him to stop and I was calling 911."

On March 20, Special Agent Batchelor interviewed Witness 6. "[H]e could see a person facing away from him who appeared to be looking down toward the ground, while in some sort of vertical position," Batchelor reported. "It was only when he heard a males [sic] voice yelling 'help, help, help', that he observed a second guy pushing up or trying to get out from underneath this person." Again, Witness 6 described the person

on the bottom as the one wearing red. In the recorded interview, Witness 6 told Batchelor that he thought it was the guy
on the bottom who was yelling 'help' because the person on top
had his back to the witness, but the yelling sounded clear, not
like it was echoing off the buildings.

While Witness 6 was, the day of the shooting, unequivocal
in his belief that the person on the bottom of the fracas—the
one dressed in red—was the person yelling for help, nearly a
month later after the case had garnered much publicity, he was
far less certain. Batchelor reported that Witness 6 "indicated
that at no point could he see who was calling for help." When
Batchelor asked the witness about his earlier statement, Witness 6 said that he didn't know who was yelling. "[He] said of
his earlier statement," Batchelor reported, "that he never observed which individual was yelling help, he only made an assumption that the person on the bottom would be the one
yelling help."[†]

◈

Mary Cutcher and her roommate, Selma Mora Lamilla, were in
their kitchen when Cutcher heard "a little boy" crying behind
her home. Cutcher was officially identified as Witness 5, Mora
as Witness 16. Their names became publicly known when the
two women went on television with Martin family attorney,
Benjamin Crump, to tell their stories.

"We were in the kitchen. I heard the crying. It was a little
boy," Cutcher told reporters at a press conference with Martin's
parents and their attorney, Benjamin Crump. "As soon as the
gun went off, the crying stopped."

Cutcher claimed that her calls to police went unanswered
as she reached out to investigators to tell her story. But Cutcher
and Mora were interviewed by Detective Serino on March 2 at

---

[†]     On May 22, the Orlando Sentinel reported that four witnesses in the case
        had changed their stories, three of them "in ways that may damage Zim-
        merman." A fourth witness "abandoned her initial story, that she saw one
        person chasing another. Now, she says, she saw a single figure running."
        Witness 6 was one of the four story-changing witnesses the Sentinel re-
        ported on.

the Sanford Police Department. According to Serino's report, Mora told police she was "inside of her kitchen" when "she heard someone crying, just prior to hearing a gunshot ring out." Mora looked outside and "observed one individual standing over another individual who was lying on the ground."

The woman called out, "What's going on out there?" Nobody responded. She called out again. The standing person then said, "[J]ust call the police."

Cutcher told Serino that she heard a "whining" sound but couldn't hear "any words". "It just sounded like somebody was struggling, in trouble or hurting or something," Cutcher said. Cutcher said that she and Mora "didn't think much of it", but she started "walking around toward the sliding glass door" when she heard the gunshot.

"That's when I opened the sliding glass door," Cutcher said. "I see the kid laying on the ground." Cutcher explained that Martin's head was away from her, so she couldn't tell if he has "face up or face down at that time."

"The guy was standing with his feet," Cutcher continued, "one on each side of the kid, and he was leaning over him." Cutcher didn't know if Zimmerman was the shooter or just a passerby. Mora called out to Zimmerman several times, but he didn't respond. "He looked back and he acknowledged us," Cutcher said. "He knew we were there. He just—I think he didn't know what to say, didn't know what to do."

Zimmerman told the women to call police. Cutcher dialed 911. "I think someone's been shot," the woman told the 911 dispatcher.

"Why do you think someone's been shot?" the dispatcher asked.

"The kids are laying out in the backyard, and a gun just went off, and they said call 911," the woman frantically explained.

Cutcher's call is frantic and disjointed. She is talking as much with her children and Mora in the background as she is with the dispatcher. At one point in the call, she says that it's "the black guy" that is standing, but she had to ask Mora before saying so.

Cutcher told Serino that she eventually saw that "the kid was face down in the grass and not moving."

Cutcher told Serino that she didn't understand why she never heard any sounds of a fight. "I can't say [because] I didn't see it," Cutcher said, "but if there's a fight, you hear something, you hear movement, you hear hits or verbal or— you hear something, but I heard nothing but a little kid scared to death or like crying."

"Could you possibly associate that sound with somebody being smothered?" Serino asked. The woman took a deep breath and let out a long sigh.

Serino then asked if she ever heard any screaming. Cutcher didn't know how to answer the question, and Serino didn't push her to. "I don't know. I mean, it's so hard to remember," Cutcher said. "Everything happened so fast."

"But I feel in my heart . . . that he intended for this kid to die," Cutcher told Serino, "because there was no struggling going on at that point. You're self-defense? Shoot him in the leg. He's a seventeen-year-old, scrawny little kid."

It is clear from the 911 call that Cutcher saw very little, and Serino concluded as much during his interview with her. "She stated she does not know why the incident occurred," Serino reported, "and could not provide any other information pertaining to the occurrences prior to her hearing the 'whining' sounds she heard."

"I firmly believe this was not self-defense," Cutcher said at the press conference, "because I heard the crying, and if it was Zimmerman that was crying, Zimmerman would have continued crying after the shot went off."

Slate's David Weigel reported on April 6 about a meeting he had with Cutcher and Mora in which the two women showed him their view from inside their home. "When they heard the noise," writes Weigel, "—desperate, like '*aaaaaah, aaaaaah*'— they looked through the window blinds.

"No visibility. Two more whines. The sound of a gun going off," Weigel continues. "The two women raced over to their patio and went outside."

"Zimmerman is standing over Trayvon's body," Cutcher told

Weigel. "He's straddling him. He had his hands pressed on Trayvon's back. I called out, 'What's going on over there?' But he's facing away from us, and even when he turns it's not like we can see his facial features."[†]

Rebuffed by police, Cutcher became a public figure in a brewing battle to have Zimmerman arrested. On March 7, Cutcher was interviewed by WFTV reporter Daralene Jones. The Orlando television station reported that "police only took a two or three sentence statement from this woman." In response, Jones told viewers that she spent thirty minutes with Cutcher "on camera".

Exactly what led reporters to believe that Cutcher had not been interviewed by police is unclear, but Serino interviewed Cutcher for almost fifteen minutes five days before being interviewed by Jones. In that recorded interview, Cutcher had every opportunity to tell Serino about anything she saw that night, and she told him, in essence, everything she told Jones. In her interview with Jones, Cutcher refered to the five foot eleven inch, one hundred fifty-eight pound Martin as "the little boy".

"Cutcher believes even if Martin got the best of Zimmerman," Jones reported, "it's no excuse to kill an unarmed teenager half his size." A medical report from the day after the altercation lists Zimmerman as five feet seven-and-a-half inches tall and weighing two hundred four pounds—not "twice" Martin's size.

"I assumed he was going to be arrested," Cutcher told the reporter. "Common sense will tell you, and he wasn't."

During the interview, Jones asked Cutcher if she was certain that it was Martin who was crying. "I am a hundred percent—OK, ninety-nine point nine percent sure," Cutcher replied. "It was the little boy."

Cutcher described what she had learned from neighbors about the physical altercation that had taken place before Zimmerman and Martin ended up behind her house. "I think that

---

†    Weigel pointed out the odd, yet common, practice of many talking about this case to refer to the victim by his first name, Trayvon, but the shooter by his last name, Zimmerman. From a crime scene reconstruction standpoint, such name usage indicates the witness's bias. The use of the first name is warm and personal; the use of the last name is cold and distant.

the shooter probably got beat up and was very angry," Cutcher said, "but I really do believe the little kid was trying to get home."

Jones asked Cutcher what she thought happened that evening. While Cutcher was quick to say that she didn't know if her "opinion counts for much", but she speculated that Zimmerman was motivated by Martin's race. Cutcher said that Zimmerman was known "through the neighborhood" as not "being able to control" his temper "very well."[†]

"In the reports that I have seen and heard, he called in that there was a black boy . . . in a white neighborhood and it's suspicious," Cutcher surmised. But much like the whisper-around-the-circle game played by so many schoolchildren, the woman's more-than-second-hand knowledge of the call was false, and her retelling of the story betrayed her bias. "I think he was probably harassing the seventeen-year-old boy," Cutcher told the reporter. "I just think that people need to know the truth. I don't think he should be set free. I don't think he should get off this easy."

Cutcher admitted in the press conference with Crump that the crying and the account she gave about what took place afterward was, in her words, "the only thing I saw that night". Cutcher's belief that Zimmerman was not acting in self-defense is based on her assumption that, had he been, he would have "continued crying after the shot went off." But Cutcher's opinion is, at best, speculative, especially since she doesn't even know why someone was crying in the first place. If Zimmerman was "crying" in response to something that Martin was doing to him, he would quite likely have ended that crying when Martin, stopped by the shot, no longer had the upper hand.

What Cutcher, a woman who by her own admission saw none of the events that led up to the shooting, did by turning

---

[†] Later when Jones asked Cutcher if she could provide "specific examples" of Zimmerman losing his temper, Cutcher replied, "I have no specific examples. That's all hearsay and all rumor. I've only lived in this neighborhood for maybe three months." But of all the people interviewed by the Sanford police, the Florida Department of Law Enforcement, the FBI, and the special prosecutor, only Zimmerman's ex-fiancée said he had a bad temper. Cutcher admitted that she had never met Zimmerman.

to the news media was to take herself out of the realm of being an unbiased fact witness and injected herself into the realm of being an advocate for "the little boy", Trayvon, who was "ha-rassed" by that temper-ridden neighborhood watchman, Zim-merman. Crump seized upon Cutcher's statements as evidence that Zimmerman should have been arrested, but what Crump didn't know about this case, Sanford police did. What they knew about Mary Cutcher is that she saw almost nothing, yet still believed that Zimmerman should be charged with killing Martin. They also knew that what she did see was consistent with what Zimmerman himself told them about the shooting and about what he did afterward.

◈

The question of who was screaming for help was not answered by Witness 11 or by the FBI. Serino turned to the parents of both Martin and Zimmerman. Martin's mother was adamant that it was her son screaming for help on the recording.

On March 19, Zimmerman's father, Robert Zimmerman, Sr., told investigators that he was certain it was his son yelling for help. "That is absolutely, positively George Zimmerman," he said. "Myself, my wife, family members and friends know that that is George Zimmerman. There's no doubt who's yelling for help."

In his report, Serino wrote that, while listening to the recording of Witness 11's 911 call, he "could clearly hear a male's voice yelling either 'Help' or 'Help Me', fourteen . . . times in an approximately 38 second time span." "This voice was determined to be that of George Zimmerman," Serino wrote, "who was apparently yelling for help as he was being battered by Trayvon Martin."

It was Serino's interview with Martin's father that broke the tie. On February 28, Serino played the 911 recording for Tracy Martin. "I asked Mr. Martin if the voice calling for help was that of his son," Serino reported. "Mr. Martin, clearly emotionally impacted by the recording, quietly responded, 'no'." Serino did not record this exchange and no other investigators were present at the time, at least not close enough to hear what Martin said.

On April 2, CNN aired a story in which audio expert Tom Owen claimed to have determined that the voice screaming for help was not Zimmerman's. "It's done in a manner in which there's a comparison made between a known and an unknown voice," Owen explained. "In this instance, George Zimmerman is the known voice. He identified himself on the 911 call. We know who that is. We have the voice of the person screaming. We consider that the unknown because we don't know who that is at this point."

Owen explained that the current audio analysis software doesn't require verbatim speech. Instead, the biometric software looks at certain characteristics of the speech and attempts to make a match, much like a fingerprint. "We have the tape of Zimmerman, the tape of the screams. And we can start the comparison. And basically it's going to do this comparison," Owen said. "It will give me false rejection rates, some false acceptance rates and a likelihood ratio. This gray dot designates the lower end of the scale, which in essence translated as it's not him." But Owen admitted that his analysis is not an exact science.

While Owen's analysis was admittedly not exact, another audio expert interviewed by CNN provided an analysis that came across as mere guesswork. Ed Primeau told the news network that he did not believe it was Zimmerman who was screaming for help. "There's a huge chance this is not Zimmerman's voice. As a matter of fact, after 28 years of doing this, I would put my reputation on the line and say this is not George Zimmerman screaming."

"Can you put a percentage on that?" a woman asked.

"Boy, that's a tough question," Primeau replied. "I'm going to say about 95." There's something about guessing at a "tough question" that just isn't terribly scientific.

On April 2, Assistant State Attorney Bernie de la Rionda and Investigator O'Steen with the State Attorney's Office in Jacksonville met with Tracy Martin, Trayvon Martin's father, in Miami. According to O'Steen, the elder Martin explained that, when Serino played the 911 call recording for him, he "was emotionally upset and didn't give his full attention to the recording." Martin claimed that he told Serino "that he couldn't tell whose voice it was." The elder Martin denied telling Serino that the voice yelling for help was not his son's. "He has since listened to the 911 calls many times," O'Steen reported, "and is sure it was his son's voice calling for help."

# Who's on Top?

*"Like the blind men of the proverb, each
individual feels a piece of the elephant, and the
enormity of what he has found is
overwhelming enough to convince each blindly
groping observer that he had found the essence
of the beast."*

—PSYCHOLOGIST DAVE GROSSMAN IN *ON KILLING*

AS THE INVESTIGATION PROGRESSED, it became increasingly clear
that Zimmerman's claim of self-defense would rest largely on
whether he or Martin was the aggressor that February evening.
Many in the news media and the public would argue that the
over-zealous neighborhood watch leader was the aggressor by
following the unarmed, innocent Martin in the first place and
by ignoring what many perceived as an "order" from the police
dispatcher not to follow the teenager. But police and prosecutors were more keenly aware of the insipid details. Zimmerman
was already following Martin before the dispatcher told him
that Sanford police didn't need him to do that. Zimmerman
twice stated that he had lost sight of the "suspicious" teen. At
some point, Zimmerman again encountered Martin, and the
question to be answered centered on that encounter. The police
needed to know who was the first person to turn the encounter
physical.

The testimony of witnesses is critical to a successful and
proper crime scene reconstruction. Witnesses are often able to
provide key contextual information that allows the crime scene
analyst to piece together physical evidence in a meaningful way
and to make appropriate connections between items of physical
evidence that might not by themselves provide a complete pic-

ture of what took place. When employing information elicited from witness testimony, it is important to consider both the credibility and reliability of the witness. A credible witness is one who is apparently trustworthy and free from unmitigated bias; a reliable witness is one whose testimony comports with the physical evidence.

Forensic scientist and shooting reconstruction expert Bruce Moran describes the necessity of evaluating witness statements against the physical evidence. "Statements made by victims, suspects, and witnesses . . . can provide information as the basis for the development and testing of scenarios and theories," writes Moran. "[O]bservations by these participants can direct significance to certain items of physical evidence that might not otherwise be apparent to investigators . . . ." Moran writes that witness statements "should not be relied on as fact" and explains that "physical evidence and observations made at the shooting scene should be consciously correlated with participant statements to either support or refute them."

Psychologist Alexis Artwohl and police expert Loren Christensen explain that "human memory is fallible" and that fact is "one of the most important things to remember about investigating a shooting". "Few people have a photographic memory that is a totally accurate representation of reality," they write. "Human memory is subject to distortions and omissions even under nonstressful circumstances, and the stress of a traumatic incident only makes it worse." Inaccurate statements are not necessarily deceptive ones. Participants in a shooting incident will recount what they recall, but their recollection may be distorted. Fast-paced events such as shooting incidents leave great room for witnesses to confuse time-lines and event sequencing.

Psychologist Dave Grossman likens the information obtained from participants in a critical incident to blind men feeling an elephant. "Like the blind men of the proverb," Grossman explains, "each individual feels a piece of the elephant, and the enormity of what he has found is overwhelming enough to convince each blindly groping observer that he had found the essence of the beast." Grossman explains that it is important to put the testimony of each witness into context to gain insight into the complete picture. Grossman and Christensen explain that one of the blind men "says that he felt a tree, another reports a wall, and the third says he felt a big snake. In the end, each person comes away with different impressions of the experience, and only by gathering them all together can we hope to get a complete impression."

Virtually every experienced investigator is familiar with the diversity of witness testimony. In most cases, there will be as many differing accounts of what took place as there are witnesses interviewed, and their descriptions of the events and people involved can be so drastically different that one is left wondering if these people were really witnesses to the same crime. Descriptions of an offender's height can vary by more than a foot, weight by dozens of pounds. Hair and eye color will vary. Facial hair, no facial hair. Deep voice, raspy voice, high voice, soft voice. Statements made by participants will be recounted in surprisingly different ways, and even the locations where things took place can be so far off from what the physical evidence shows that the variances seem inexplicable.

The fact that something in a witness's statement is wrong doesn't imply that the witness is lying; it only means that his or her recollection of the events is flawed. Human memory is fallible. Anyone who has forgotten the name of a person he just met or who has walked from one end of her house to the other only to forget why she was going there in the first place should understand that our minds just aren't as reliable as we'd like them to be. Witnesses often create details in their minds because our human tendency is to fill in the blanks. We are creatures that don't like *not knowing* something, so our minds trick us into believing our imagination.

And by our very nature we are prejudiced creatures, and not just with respect to race. We all have our perspective, our vantage point, the personal platform from which we view the world. We see things in terms of what we understand, what we relate to, what we know. We're affected by culture, by the movies we watch, the television we enjoy, the books we read, the company we keep, the ideals we learned as a child, the lessons we learned as an adult. And all of this influences how we view the world.

The truth, however, lies not in the grand scheme of what any one witness says, but in the culmination of little snippets from each witness's testimony. Witnesses may be adamant that their recollection is correct, and thus they will appear to be truthful. In fact, they are telling the truth as they know it. *60 Minutes* host, Lesley Stahl, explained the problems with witness memory in a story about a man falsely convicted of rape. "We now know memory is not like a video tape recorder," Stahl explained. "You don't just record an event and play it back. Instead memory is malleable, full of holes, easily contaminated, and susceptible to suggestion."

In that story, Stahl interviewed psychology professor Gary Wells, an expert in eyewitness memory at Iowa State University. Wells explained that eyewitness testimony is unreliable yet very persuasive to jurors. "You believe that person because they have no reason to lie," Wells explains. "The legal system is set up to kind of sort between liars and truth tellers, and it's actually pretty good at that. But when someone is genuinely mistaken, the legal system doesn't really know how to deal with that."

In a June 3 article in USA Today, journalist Yamiche Alcindor quoted Barbara Tversky, a professor of psychology at Stanford University. "At the time something happens, we are trying to make sense of it," Tversky said. "I'm not focusing on someone's shirt color or height. I'm focusing on what's happening and trying to make sense of what's going on."

"People," Tversky was quoted as saying, "are more influenced to what they think must have happened."

"All other things equal, earlier recountings are more likely to be accurate than later ones," Tversky was quoted as saying in an article in the Scientific American. "The longer the delay, the more likely that subsequent information will get confused with the target memory."

In a May 28 article in *The New American*, journalist Alex Newman quoted University of North Dakota forensic psychology professor Richard Wise. "To fill in gaps in memory, the eyewitness relies upon his or her expectation, attitudes, prejudices, bias, and prior knowledge," Wise explained. "Furthermore, information supplied to an eyewitness after a crime . . . by the police, prosecutor, other eyewitnesses, media, etc., can alter an eyewitness's memory of the crime."

In a May 26 article, Miami Herald journalist Frances Robles reported on the fragile nature of witness memory. "Studies show people who witnessed the same simulated event reported different memories depending on the language used by the questioner," Robles wrote. "People who were given false information about the simulated event often incorporated the made-up details into their own accounts."

According to Robles, Karen Newirth, an eyewitness identification expert with Innocence Project, told the Miami Herald that witnesses will fill in gaps in their memory. "Memory does not function like a videotape that records everything and can be replayed at will," Newirth told the Herald. "People remember pieces of events, and then fill in the blanks with what makes sense." Newirth calls the phenomena "memory contamination", and she explains that, in the killing of Trayvon Martin, "there is likely contamination coming from all over the place." Newirth explained that witnesses who only heard events are even less reliable than those who saw them.

Newirth explained that memory is best when it is fresh. "Memories do not improve over time," Newirth said. "In fact, they worsen over time and the worsening . . . begins very soon after the memory is created."

◈

Witness 1 was interviewed over the telephone by Sanford police investigator Chris Serino on March 1. The woman was making dinner when she heard a screaming noise behind her home. She thought it was children playing. She said it sounded like someone said either, "Nooooo!" or "Uhhhh!"

"They were running in the back," the woman told Serino. The woman said that she "peeped" out but couldn't see much because it was dark outside. "All I saw was arms flailing," she said. She still thought there were kids "roughhousing" outside.

Witness 1 couldn't hear any of the words. "It was really garbled," she told Serino. "You couldn't hear what the person was saying."

The woman explained that, at the same time that she looked out, her neighbor across the alley came outside and asked, "What's going on?" Still thinking there were children "playing around" outside, the woman went to turn off her stove. Then she heard the shot.

On March 20, FDLE Special Agent John Batchelor recorded an interview with Witness 1. The woman explained that she was cooking when she heard a noise that "sounded like a kid". Her window was half open. "They were making this weird noise," the woman told Batchelor, "so I looked out the window and I really couldn't see anything."

The woman went to the sliding glass door and could see "what looked like figures" but she couldn't "make out" if the figures were children or adults. "It looked like figures," she explained, "and it looked like arms."

Witness 1 explained to Batchelor that it is "really dark back there", and she told him, "[I]f there's no lights on in the back you can't hardly see." She recalled that her lights were on but her neighbor's lights were not.

The woman told Batchelor that her neighbor came outside and "was like, 'Yo, what's going on out there?'" "He said, 'I'm going to call 911,'" the woman explained. Her neighbor closed his door.

"By the time I came back to the stove to take [*sic*] it off," she said, "that's when the shot went off."

When Batchelor asked the witness if she could see any of the clothing worn by the "figures", she told him that it was too dark. "I couldn't tell you if they were black," she said. "I couldn't tell you if they were white. It was just so dark out there. I just saw movement."

Witness 1 told Batchelor that, after the shot, she looked outside again and saw a body on the ground, face down. She described  the body as being in a sort of "running position". She did not see anyone else. But when Batchelor asked about the clothing on "the body", the woman said that she thought the person on the ground was wearing gray sweatpants and a red jacket, consistent, at least in the jacket color, with Zimmer-man's clothing. Batchelor clarified that the woman was describing the clothes of the person who had been shot. "It was the body," she replied. "The only other person I saw was the cop."

Batchelor asked the witness how much time elapsed from when she first heard the voices outside to when she looked out and saw the body. The woman wasn't certain, but "it couldn't have been more than . . . sixty seconds."

◈

Witness 2, a young woman who lived with Witness 1, told po-lice that she was home the evening of the shooting. The two witnesses are sisters. On March 1, she told Serino, "I saw two guys running. Couldn't tell you who was in front, who was be-hind."

The woman was looking out her kitchen window. She went to the sliding glass door, looked out again, and saw the men fighting. "Just fists," the woman told Serino. "I don't know who was hitting who."

Serino asked the woman if she heard any arguing. "All I heard was, 'no, no,'" the woman explained. "That was it. And I heard the shot."

Serino asked the woman to show him about how far apart the running "guys" were when the witness saw them. He stepped away from her until she told him to stop. The woman and the investigator estimated the distance between them to be about ten feet.

However, on March 9, Witness 2 told Serino that she had taken her contact lenses out shortly before the shooting, and she wasn't wearing glasses. She also said that she had only got-ten a "glance" at what was taking place outside her home, and that she had been looking out an upstairs window, a marked change from her March 1 statement that she was looking out her kitchen window.

According to Serino, the woman said that "the chasing she saw was in the direction towards the 'T' where the sidewalk leads to either Retreat View Circle or Twin Lakes Lane." She "could not distinguish who was chasing whom" and could not "identify either of the persons she witnessed" that evening.

On March 20, Witness 2 was interviewed by FDLE Special Agent John Batchelor. During that interview, she recalled only seeing a glimpse of one person running. "I couldn't tell you if it was a man, a woman, a kid, black or white," the woman told Batchelor. "I couldn't tell you because it was dark and plus I didn't have my contacts on or glasses." She said it was just "a glance". The woman told Batchelor that what made her glance out the window was that she heard the sound of someone running. "The feet, running," she said. "That's what I heard."

"And what did you see when you glanced out?" Batchelor asked.

"Someone," the woman replied. "I just know I saw a person out there." She couldn't describe anything about that person.

Moments later, the witness heard someone yell "either 'yo' or 'no'." "By the time I got to the front room," Witness 2 explained, "I heard the shot." The woman explained that the shot sounded like it came from the front of the house. "We had the windows all open upstairs," she said, "so it sounded like it was from the front." She looked out the front window. The woman estimated that the shot rang out about fifteen seconds after she saw the person running.

Witness 2 thought that her sister dropped something until her sister came upstairs and told her that someone had been shot. Witness 2 went to the rear sliding glass door, looked out, and saw a body on the ground. "I want to say they were on their back," she told Batchelor. She described the clothing on the person as a light colored shirt, white sneakers, and sweatpants with one leg up and one leg down. "No hoodie or anything like that," she said.

"Did you see anybody else?" Batchelor asked.

"No," she replied. "Not until the cops came." When asked how long it was before police arrived, the woman said, "It seemed like immediately. Immediately the cops were here." The woman looked outside about thirty seconds after hearing the shot.

◈

"There's someone screaming outside," Witness 3 told the 911 dispatcher. "There was someone screaming. I just heard a gunshot!" The woman sounded panic stricken. "Hurry up! They're right outside my house!"

The dispatcher asked the woman if the person screaming was a male. The woman affirmed. "The guy on top had a white t-shirt," the witness told the dispatcher.

"What do you mean 'guy on top'?" the dispatcher inquired. "Did you see a fight?"

"I don't know. I looked out my window and there's a guy on top with a white t-shirt."

"A white t-shirt? Did you see what kind of pants?"

"No."

"OK, he's on top of what?"

"I couldn't see the other thing. I couldn't see . . . the person on the ground."

"But he's on top of a person?" the dispatcher clarified.

"Mmmhmm," the woman affirmed.

"OK, is he—the guy with the white t-shirt," the dispatcher inquired further. "Did he get up and run?"

"I didn't—I just immediately went to the phone and called you."

"OK, was he white, black, or Hispanic when you saw him?"

"Couldn't—couldn't—couldn't tell. It was completely dark."

On March 19, Batchelor recorded an interview with Witness 3, who told the investigator that she didn't know either Zimmerman or Martin. "I had my upstairs windows open," the woman told Batchelor, "because it was like a breezy night." From her upstairs office, the woman heard someone screaming for help. She "peeked" out her blinds and "saw a guy on top." She didn't see fighting, but she saw that the person on top was wearing a white t-shirt. "All I saw was white," she said, "because everything was dark." His back was to her.

"I couldn't see skin color. I couldn't see pants color. I couldn't see their head or hair," the woman told Batchelor. "I just saw this white shirt on top."

Witness 3 knew from the sound of the person screaming that something was really wrong. "I could tell," she said, "someone was scared."

"I was confused, though, because there was no one in a white shirt. Was there?" the woman said later in the interview. "That's what confuses me."

The woman went on to say that "the guy in the handcuffs had a hoodie on." The woman seemed to believe that Zimmerman was wearing a hoodie, but he wasn't.

"We're only concerned with what you indicated you thought you saw that night," Batchelor replied, stumbling for a moment on the words. Zimmerman was in red, Martin in dark gray.

Batchelor asked the witness if she heard the gunshot before or after she looked out the window. "After," she replied.

"Was this before or after or during you conversation with 911?" Batchelor asked.

"I am pretty sure it was during my conversation," she replied.[†]

◈

Witness 6 opened the back door to his home and saw Zimmerman and Martin on the ground struggling. The day of the shooting, he told Sanford police detective Chris Serino that he saw "a black man with a black hoodie" on top of a guy "with a red sweatshirt on". Martin was wearing a dark gray hoodie, Zimmerman a red jacket. According to Witness 6, Martin was on top.

"The one guy on top in the black hoodie was pretty much just throwing down blows on the guy kind of MMA style," the witness told Serino, referring to the aggressive, no holds barred mixed martial arts competition fighting style that has become a popular spectator sport in recent years.

"Like a ground and pound?" Serino asked.

"Yeah, like a ground and pound on the concrete at this point," the witness replied.

---

†    The shot is not heard on the recording of the 911 call; however, the publicly-released recording is heavily redacted at the beginning of the call.

Ground and pound. The Urban Dictionary describes the "ground and pound" as a "fighting style" in which one takes his "opponent to the ground" and establishes "a dominant position" from which to "reign down punches, elbows and forearm strikes to the downed fighter."

Serino's interview of Witness 6 lasted only three minutes.

When Witness 6 was interviewed by Orlando's Fox 35 News the day after the shooting, he said that Martin was "beating up" Zimmerman. "When I got upstairs and looked down," the witness said, "the person that was on top beating up the other guy was laying in the grass. And I believe he was dead at that point."

On March 20, Special Agent Batchelor recorded a forty-five minute interview of Witness 6. The man told Batchelor that, after he heard what he thought was a rock hitting a window, he ran upstairs and looked out the window. "[W]hen I looked down, I saw that the person that was actually on top at that point," the man explained, "was laying in my grass kind of in a sprawled position not moving."

The witness saw men with flashlights, and he saw Zimmerman standing with his hands in the air saying, "The gun's on the ground. I shot the guy in self-defense."[‡] Police were there, the witness said, within twenty seconds.

The man explained to Batchelor that Zimmerman and Martin were moving as they struggled. "As time went on," the witness explained, "it got closer."

"You keep referring to 'it was farther away,'" Batchelor said. "What was farther away?"

"If you hear someone yelling, and they're two blocks, three blocks down, it's going to be a faint sound," the man explained. "The sound just got louder." He wasn't sure, though, what direction the sounds were coming from.

"Could you tell if there was a hood up or down, or a hat or anything on the person on top?" Batchelor asked.

"Not really," the man replied, "because it was so dark. . . ."

---

[‡]   The gun was in a holster in Zimmerman's waistband according to both Zimmerman and the police officer who took it from him. It is unlikely that Zimmerman said that the gun was on the ground.

"Could you tell what race the person on top [was]?"

"When I first walked out there, the black guy was on top," the man said, "and the only reason I can tell that is because the guy that was on the ground under him at that point wrestling was definitely a lighter color." The witness later explained that he was seeing the back of the person on top.

"And this is the time you are looking out the window?" Batchelor clarified.

"Yelling at them, yes," the witness replied, "to stop."

"At this moment, the person on top," Batchelor asked, "how were they positioned?"

"The guy on top was on top of the other guy, vertically," the man explained.

"You're going to have to help with what you mean by vertically," Batchelor clarified. "Was he laying down?"

"Yeah, laying down, yeah," the man explained. "So like if I'm standing up and I lay down completely flat face first, it's pretty much like if you were on top of someone wrestling. They're on their back. . . He's on top of him."

"[W]hat is happening?" Batchelor asked.

"They're struggling," the man replied. "That's what I mean by wrestling at that point. I can't tell, you know, what is going on at that point. All I know is someone is on top of the other person, and I hear, 'Help! Help! Help!' yelled a couple times. . . ."

"Do you see anything in any of the two persons' hands?"

"No, I don't see anything in their hands. Not to say that there wasn't, but I really can't see anything in their hands at that point."

The witness explained that it looked like the man on the bottom was trying to get up. His back was off the ground. He also explained that, when he first went outside, the two were wrestling in the grass, but they moved onto the sidewalk. The guy in black was still on top of the guy in red.

"And that's why I made the statement that he was hitting him on top because," the witness explained, "that's what it looked like from where I was standing. It could've been him just trying to forcefully hold the guy down, or it could be hitting him."

When asked to clarify the reference he made to Serino about the fight looking like something out of mixed martial arts, Witness 6 significantly softened his description of what he had seen. On the day of the shooting, the witness told Serino that Martin had been "throwing down blows", but nearly a month later he told Batchelor that he wasn't sure if the teen was hitting Zimmerman or just holding him down. But he did tell the special agent that Martin—the guy on top wearing the dark hoodie—was "definitely in control".

Witness 6 did not hear any conversation or yelling between the two people wrestling behind his house, and he found it "odd" that, when he yelled at them, the person on top didn't stop what he was doing or say that "this guy's attacking me". The witness told Batchelor that he yelled "I'm calling 911" before going back inside.

"From the time you hear the sounds . . . initially to the time you hear the rock as you indicate against the glass door," Batchelor asked slowly and methodically, "how long do you think that was?"

"I truly couldn't even give an estimate," Witness 6 replied. He paused, then continued, "Maybe five minutes?"

On March 26, prosecutor Bernie de la Rionda recorded an interview with Witness 6. "[Y]ou described at some point that there was a man on top of another man," de la Rionda said.

"Correct," the witness replied.

"And from your perspective—you correct me if I'm wrong—you described the man on top either hitting or struggling with the man on the bottom," de la Rionda stated.

"Correct," the witness said.

"Is that correct?"

"Correct."

"Did you ever hear like this," de la Riondo asked, smacking his hand, "like a fist, like, you know, when—?"

"No," the witness replied.

"You've heard that before, I'm assuming, right?"

"Yes."

"Somebody actually striking somebody hard like I'm doing

right now?" The prosecutor struck his hand several times.

"Correct."

"Did you ever hear anything like that?" de la Rionda asked.

"No," the witness replied. "Did not hear a punch sound."

"Did you ever hear any sound like a head or another part of the body hitting concrete *hard* where it made a noise?"

"No, I did not."

"Did you hear it at all, any, like—?"

"Just the struggle sound."

◈

Sanford police did not obtain a recorded interview of Witness 12, a young mother who lived near the shooting scene. On March 20, she was interviewed by Agent Dale Crosby with the Florida Department of Law Enforcement, the state's version of the FBI.

"We heard someone yelling," she told Crosby. "It sounded like a dog at first." She described it as a "howl". Then she heard someone yell, "Help!" The sounds got louder, so she looked out the window, but didn't see anything. Then she heard a shot. She looked out the sliding glass door.

"I saw two shadows," she told the investigator. The woman explained to Crosby that it was dark behind her house. "Our porch light wasn't on," she said, "and I couldn't really see anything on the first glance. The second glance, that's when I saw the two shadows close to our backyard."

The witness said that she saw two people on the ground. One was on top of the other. "I don't know which one," she said. "All I saw while they were on the ground was dark colors." She couldn't describe their clothing.

The investigators asked Witness 12 if she could describe the positions of the two individuals on the ground, but she was uncertain and could only say that one was lying on the grass and the other was "on top". She did not know if the man on the grass was face up or face down. The woman did not see anything in the hands of the man that was on top.

On March 26, Witness 12 was interviewed by prosecutor Bernie de la Rionda. In that two-and-a-half minute recording, she told de la Rionda that she was certain it was Zimmerman who was on top. "I know after seeing the TV of what's happening," she told de la Rionda, "comparing their sizes, I think Zimmerman was definitely on top because of his size."

But by the time of the interview, most media outlets were showing pictures of Martin and Zimmerman that unfairly represented their sizes. Zimmerman's photo was from his 2005 arrest when he weighed nearly fifty pounds more than he did the day of the shooting, and Martin's most shown photograph was taken when he was twelve years old.

◈

On the day of the shooting, Serino recorded a three minute interview with Witness 13 who told the investigator that he heard the gunshot. His wife, Witness 12, looked outside and then told her husband that she thought someone just got shot. The witness went outside to see what was going on. He spotted Zimmerman, standing. He said the man, who looked "Puerto Rican", was wearing "an orange jacket".

"Man, I got blood on my face?" Zimmerman asked Witness 13.

"You got blood all over, man," the witness told Zimmerman.

"I looked over and he's got blood on the back of his head," the witness told Serino. He asked Zimmerman if he was "alright".

"The guy was beating up on me, so I had to shoot him," Zimmerman told the witness.

"And I go, 'Did you use a nine or a forty?'" the witness related to Serino.

"I used a nine," Zimmerman replied.

Zimmerman told the witness that he had already called police, and he asked the man to call his wife.

On March 20, Witness 13 was interviewed by an agent with the Florida Department of Law Enforcement. The man explained that he and his wife heard something that, at first, sounded like a dog. Then he heard someone yell, "Help!" His wife looked outside and saw two guys fighting. He told her to get away from the window. "Not a second later" the man heard what "sounded like a grunt" and a gunshot, although he wasn't sure if the grunt came before or after the shot. The whole episode took place in less than a minute.

"I went through the garage carrying a flashlight and my cell phone," the man explained. "I had my cell phone set for 911. All I had to do was push call on it."

"I shined my flashlight on him, and I said, 'Do I need to call 911?'" the witness told investigators. "He said, 'No, I just got off the phone with them.'" Zimmerman was on the sidewalk walking toward the witness.

Zimmerman turned away from the witness and "squatted down". The man could see "blood on the back of his head" and "grass stains".

"By that time, I kind of flashed my light down," the witness explained, "and there was this kid face down in the grass."

The police showed up. An officer handcuffed Zimmerman.

Zimmerman asked the witness to call his wife "and let her know what happened." The witness made the call and told Shellie Zimmerman that her husband was being held for questioning.

"Just tell her I shot somebody," Zimmerman told the witness matter-of-factly.

"[I]t looked like he just got his butt whipped," the witness told investigators, as if Zimmerman was "getting up from a fight." "[N]ot like he was in shock or anything," the witness explained, "not like, 'I can't believe I just shot someone,' but like, 'Just tell my wife I just shot someone,' like—like it was nothing."

The witness showed investigators several photographs he took with his cell phone, including photographs of Martin's body. It was the first time police learned of the images. He had deleted the photos from his phone, but had saved them on his laptop computer.

◈

Thirteen-year-old Austin McLendon was walking his dog between the two rows of buildings at Twin Lakes where Martin was killed. McLendon saw a man lying on the ground yelling for help. The dog got off leash, and the boy ran after his four-legged friend. Then he heard a shot. He told his eighteen-year-old sister who called 911.

"My brother said someone got shot behind our house," the frightened girl told the dispatcher.

The 911 operator asked the girl if she heard the shot. "I heard something, then my brother ran in the house," the girl replied.

"Is your brother there right now?" the dispatcher asked.

"He's next to me," the girl explained.

"OK, can you give him the phone?" The girl handed the phone to her brother.

"What exactly did you see?" the dispatcher asked McLendon.

"I saw a man laying on the ground that needed help that was screaming," the boy explained. "I heard a loud sound, and then the screaming stopped."

"Did you see the person get shot?"

"No."

Serino interviewed McLendon on March 5. McLendon said that he saw someone "lying on the ground that looked like they couldn't get up and they were yelling for help."

"Was he white or black?" Serino asked.

"I can't say," the soft-spoken boy replied.

"Did you see what he was wearing?" Serino asked.

"It looked like a red shirt," McLendon replied.

Serino clarified with McLendon that the person laying on the ground was yelling for help. McLendon only saw one person. "I only looked for a few seconds," the boy explained. McLendon didn't see anyone being chased, nor did he hear anyone arguing. The boy thought that the man on the ground "had fallen and broken his leg or something."

As the media maelstrom swelled in the weeks following the shooting, McLendon's mother, Cheryl Brown, accompanied by her attorney, went on MSNBC's *PoliticsNation* hosted by the Reverend Al Sharpton, one of the key figures in the ensuing protest about the refusal of Sanford police to arrest Zimmerman for the shooting. Brown complained that Sanford police never tried to talk with her son until March 2, five days after the shooting. She also alleged that investigator's led her son to say certain things during his interview.

"I just don't feel that it was done properly," Brown, who was present when her son was interviewed by Serino, said. I think there were some tactics used to maybe suggest some things to him." Brown explained that police asked her son what color clothing the person on the ground had been wearing. "[A]nd then they proceeded to give him options of what color that clothing could have been," Brown complained. "They suggested maybe it was black, maybe it was white, maybe it was red. I don't think that is information he would have been able to provide. . . ."

But, according to the audio recording of the interview, Brown's statement is false; Serino never suggested the color of the clothing. But even if he did at some point prior to the recording, by Brown's description, the investigator suggested colors that could have been worn by either Martin or Zimmerman. McLendon wouldn't have known which color to pick.

Oddly, Brown went on to tell Sharpton that the lead investigator in the shooting told her "that this was absolutely not self-defense." Brown claimed that the lead investigator told her there had been "some stereotyping" and told her "read between the lines" because he needed to prove that Zimmerman was not acting in defense of himself. Serino, the same person Brown accused of leading her son to say the person's clothing was red, was the lead investigator.[†]

On March 27, Assistant State Attorneys John Guy and Bernie de la Rionda and Investigator T. C. O'Steen from the special prosecutors office interviewed Brown and McLendon at their residence. The mother and son said that McLendon "may have been persuaded by police to say red hoodie." Shortly after the interview, O'Steen received a call; the caller's name was redacted from the memo. According to the caller, McClendon "felt obligated to say red hoodie since he had told police that

---

[†]   Serino had, in fact, wanted to charge Zimmerman with manslaughter, but was overridden by the upper echelon of the Sanford Police Department and State Attorney Norm Wolfinger.

during an earlier interview." But in his interview with Serino, McLendon said it was a red "shirt", not a red "hoodie".

While McLendon's testimony does little to prove that Martin was on top, it does even less to prove that Zimmerman was on top.

◈

Witness 18, known only as Jane, called 911 after hearing the shot. "[I]'m looking out my window, like my backyard," the woman told the dispatcher, "and someone's yelling and screaming 'help' and I heard . . . like a pop noise."

The dispatcher told the woman that other calls had already been received, and he told her that an officer is already at the scene. Hysterical, the woman stayed on the phone with the dispatcher for over fourteen minutes. Her emotions were strong. Tears were flowing. At one point, the woman said, "I'm too scared to live here."

"Why would this man just shoot him?" the woman asked. The thought of one person killing another terrified her.

Shortly after the shooting, Serino interviewed Witness 18.

"I thought I heard like loud voices outside," the woman told Serino. "I was upstairs in my bedroom reading and watching television." She wondered why people were outside "in the pouring rain."

"I think I didn't hear noise or any voices for awhile," the woman explained, "maybe ten minutes or so, and then I heard the loud voices again. I just kind of thought, 'Oh, brother. Who's out there talking that loud?'"

"I looked out my window," she continued, "but I couldn't see anything because I had my bedroom light on, and you can't see when the light's on." She turned off the light and opened the window. "When I looked, it looked like there were two men on the ground."

"For some reason in my head all I could think is like a heavier man on top, but I don't—"

"Can't say for sure," Serino added.

"I can't say for sure," the woman agreed.

"And then I heard someone desperately saying, 'Help!

Help!'" The woman realized the situation "was serious" so she reached for her phone to dial 911.

"I remember hearing a pop noise," she explained. "That's the only way I could describe it because I don't know what a gun sounds like."

The woman wasn't sure how many shots she heard. "I think I heard it more than once, though," she told Serino. She couldn't remember if she was still standing by her window when she was "calling 911 and panicking."

"All I remember seeing is a man, like a larger man," the witness explained, "standing like maybe a couple feet from where I saw just a person's body laying on the ground." She didn't see faces. She could only describe the man walking away as a "larger Hispanic man."

◈

Witness 19 also called 911. "Someone's yelling two doors down from me screaming, hollering, 'Help! Help! Help!'" the woman told the dispatcher. "I thought I heard like a gunshot."

"How many shots did you hear?" the dispatcher asked.

"One."

"How long ago was the shot?"

"Just like—when I heard that I picked up the phone and called you." The woman told the dispatcher several times that she thought the person she heard yelling might have been an elderly man that lives nearby.

Serino interviewed Witness 19 on March 10. The woman told Serino that she was about to walk her dog when she opened her door and saw someone lying on the ground moaning. She heard Witness 6 say that he was going to call 911. The woman went upstairs and was opening a window when she heard a "pop" sound. She told Serino that it took her about a minute or two to get upstairs after seeing the person on the ground until she heard the shot.

"I didn't see anybody except that gentlemen that opened the door," the woman explained, "and the kid laying on the ground."

"You didn't see any kind of fighting? You didn't see—?"

"I did not. I did not. I did not. I must've come in *after* the fact," the woman explained. "The only thing I can in my mind think that he was probably telling him, you know that . . . he was hurt, because he was moaning, the kid was moaning and groaning—"

"The one on the ground, correct?" Serino clarified.

"Right, when he was laying on the grass," the woman agreed.

"[C]ould you tell if he was black, white, or Hispanic?" Serino asked.

"I couldn't tell," the woman replied. She couldn't tell anything about the person on the ground. It was raining, it was dark, and the person was across the grass from her house.[†]

"I didn't see," she said. "I did not see it. OK, and I did not see anybody but, like I said, I assume it was a kid that was laying there, and I saw the guy sticking his head out the sliding glass door. . . ."

Later in the interview, Witness 19 told Serino, "I did not see anything happen. I heard it. I heard the guy say 911. I saw—it was the kid, crying out, he's hurt, whatever."

"Now I watched the news today, and I've been watching it when it comes on about all this—." Serino interrupted the woman.

"Could you do something a little bit different?" the detective asked. "Could I walk you up to point A to point B and time that? The reason being is that—I'm going to go ahead and pause this interview for a second." He stopped the recording at 1:40 p.m.

At 1:44 p.m., he started a second recording. He never finished explaining "the reason being". Serino had the woman reenact her movements from when she first looked out her door and saw someone on the ground to when she heard the shot. It took about sixty seconds.

---

†   There are two rows of buildings, the backs of which face toward the grass. A sidewalk runs down the center between the buildings. The distance across the grass from building to building is fifty feet. Serino estimated the distance from the witness's vantage point to where the person was lying on the ground was seventy or eighty feet. The woman agreed with that estimate.

"The calling out for help," Serino inquired. "How long do you think that lasted for? . . . Do you know how many times he called for help, or were the words 'help' used, or it was just a moan—?"

"It was very mumbled," the woman replied. "It was very mumbled and garbled. . . ." The woman said she "heard afterwards . . . that they were fighting." "I've heard so many different stories," she explained.

"I don't know who was beating up who," the witness explained. "I don't know because I did not see George at all. Like I said, I didn't know him until he came on the TV. I did not—he could have walked up to the door and I wouldn't have known him."

"I did not see anybody on the kid, fighting with the kid," she told Serino. "All I saw was a body laying on the ground there. . . . I thought it was the elderly gentleman that lives down that way."

◈

Witness 20 was in his home "laying on the sofa watching TV"; the sliding glass door was "wide open". He is the boyfriend of Witness 11, the 911 caller who heard the shot while reporting the she heard people screaming.

Witness 20 told Serino that the couple's back porch is screened in. "All the sudden, it kind of sounded like to the back left of the unit . . . we heard kind of a scuffle or kind of just ruffling around in the bushes," the man explained to Serino on March 2. "At the time we thought it was just a couple of drunk kids kind of just messing around." He later clarified that the "ruffling" was in the grass, not bushes. The sounds were coming from the left, toward the 'T' in the sidewalk.

"We were about ready to just tell them, you know, hey, shut up," the man told Serino, "but then from there we can kind of hear the tone of the voice kind of was a little more serious. Probably about twenty seconds later you started to hear more of a 'Ahh! Ahh! Ahh!' kind of tone in the voice, and you could hear how serious the voice was."

The witness "made it back to the kitchen", and then the

voice "started turning into more of a 'help' and you could just hear the distress in the voice." "In my mind, I was thinking it was somebody getting roughed up," the witness explained, "or getting jumped by a bunch of people. . . ."

"It sounded to me like it was a couple people roughing up one person," the man said. The man looked for a weapon in the kitchen and contemplated whether he was "going to run outside".

"After about twenty 'helps', at that point you just heard a pop," the witness told Serino. The man said his mind "just went a little nuts". He and his girlfriend ran upstairs.

"At that point, I think I heard somebody saying, you know, 'Oh, I've got a gun! I've got a gun!" the man explained to Serino. "You know, 'Take my gun away from me.' I don't know if it was a cop who was confronting him at that time or if it was a neighbor."

"I guess I couldn't tell who was saying the helps," he continued. "It's hard to tell . . . which person was saying 'help' or where that was coming from."

At one point in the interview, the man mentioned "the string of burglaries" that have occurred "in the neighborhood."

Agent Batchelor interviewed Witness 20 on March 19. "We heard 'helps' probably about twenty times," the man explained to Batchelor. "Once we heard the pop, we didn't hear anymore 'helps' after that."

"At any time from the time your heard the unknown sound to where it then became 'help' did you look out the window?" Batchelor asked in his slow, methodical manner.

"We couldn't see out the window," the witness replied, "We had a back porch light and we also have blinds that go over our screened porch there. It was also raining outside and when it's dark time . . . it's completely dark."

"From the time that you heard, as you described, the scuffle to the sound as you described of distress and then 'help, help'," the agent carefully crafted his question, "do you know how long that was before [your girlfriend] called 911?"

"I could not exactly say, but I can *guess* that it was maybe . . . fifteen seconds."

Batchelor asked the witness if he knew the people involved in the shooting. "I'm still not sure . . . who's who," the man replied.

◈

When Officer Timothy Smith took Zimmerman into custody, he placed the neighborhood watchman in handcuffs. "While I was in such close contact with Zimmerman, I could observe that his back appeared to be wet and was covered in grass, as if he had been laying on his back on the ground," Smith reported. "Zimmerman was also bleeding from the nose and back of the head."

◈

Witness 1 saw only figures. Witness 2 got a "glance" after taking her contacts out. Witness 3 said that the person on top was wearing a white t-shirt, but she also said that "the guy in handcuffs had a hoodie on." Witness 5, Mary Cutcher, didn't see anything until after the shot.[†] Witness 6 saw Martin on top either hitting Zimmerman or holding him down. Witness 11 didn't see who was on top. Witness 12 wasn't sure until after seeing the television coverage when she changed her story to say that she believed Zimmerman was on top. Witness 13 didn't see the struggle, but immediately afterward saw that Zimmerman had blood on the back of his head and grass on his back. Witness 14, Austin McLendon, saw a person in a red shirt lying on the ground but didn't see anyone else; he later claimed that he was pressured by police to say red "hoodie", but couldn't offer any testimony that suggested Zimmerman was on top. Witness 16, Selma Mora Lamilla, saw one man on top of the other but wasn't sure which one was on top. Witness 18 thought that the "heavier man" was on top, but she wasn't sure. Witness 19 said she saw a person lying on the ground moaning; she said it was "the kid", but she said during her 911 call and her interview with investigators that she originally

---

†    Cutcher saw Zimmerman straddling Martin after the shooting, a fact that is not disputed by Zimmerman.

thought it was her elderly neighbor having a heart attack. Witness 20 didn't see the struggle.‡

One said Zimmerman was on top. One said he was on the bottom. One said the guy in red was on the ground with nobody else around. One said the guy on top was wearing a white t-shirt. The only witness who definitively places either person on top is Witness 6, the one who had the best view because he stepped outside to ask what was going on and said he was calling 911. According to him, Martin was on top and was "definitely in control". And according to the first responding police officer, Zimmerman's back was wet and covered with grass.

And therein lies one of the greatest challenges to this case: the vast influence of the news media reporting with what some perceive as a bias in favor of Martin. By March, the public knew very little about the official findings in the case. As details of the investigation were made public, polls showed a marked shift in public perception in favor of Zimmerman.

But to the witnesses whose accounts were clearly affected by media coverage of the case, their recollection of events was molded at a time when media coverage most favored prosecuting the neighborhood watchman. That influence, when shown to a jury on cross-examination of witnesses whose accounts of the events changed over the weeks following the shooting, could prove damning to much of the prosecution's case. Had Sanford police conducted detailed interviews of these witnesses within days of the shooting, media influence on the witness testimony could have been drastically reduced, if not eliminated altogether. But Sanford police apparently failed to realize the

‡   As of this writing, no information has been released about Witnesses 4, 7, or 10. Witness 8 is Martin's girlfriend, DeeDee. Witness 9 is Zimmerman's cousin who was not present for the incident but called police anonymously to accuse him of being a racist; the woman, who is two years younger than Zimmerman, also claimed that he molested her while they were growing up. Witness 15 is the sister of Witness 14, Austin McLendon, who only called 911 when her brother ran inside and told her someone had been shot. Witness 17 is the wife of Witness 6; she was inside the house on crutches and wasn't able to see outside. Witness 21 is the president of the homeowner's association, but was not a witness to the shooting. Witness 22 is a former coworker who accused Zimmerman of harassment.

enormity of the case before them. It was a mistake that would cost them and the nation dearly.

---

*"The world is filled with violence. Because criminals carry guns, we decent law-abiding citizens should also have guns. Otherwise they will win and the decent people will lose."*

—JAMES EARL JONES

THERE ARE 963,512 CONCEALED firearm license holders in Florida according to the state's Department of Agriculture and Consumer Services. George Zimmerman is one of them. The neighborhood watch captain took a six-hour firearms safety training course on November 7, 2009. He paid by check, ninety dollars. The course is required to get the license.

Eighty percent of license holders are male. There are almost 318,000 license holders between the ages of fifty-one and sixty-five, over 261,000 ages thirty-six to fifty, nearly 207,000 over the age of sixty-six, and almost 178,000 ages eighteen to thirty-five, the group to which Zimmerman belongs. In Seminole County, with 422,000 residents, there are 17,052 concealed firearm license holders. Sanford is the county seat and its most populated city.

The Florida Concealed Weapon or Firearm licensing law allows those who attend the mandated training course and pass a background check to carry handguns and other weapons "in a manner that conceals them from ordinary sight of another person." Licensees must be citizens of the United States who are at least twenty-one years old, except that current or honorably-discharged military members may be younger. Felons and people who have been convicted of misdemeanor crimes of violence are ineligible. Substance abusers and people with documented mental health histories are disqualified. Anyone that has been dishonorably discharged from the military is also ineligible for licensing.

But Zimmerman was never in the military, he was never convicted of any crime, had no reported history of drug or alcohol abuse, and had no history of mental health problems. License holders are allowed to carry their firearm in most places within the state except in any place of nuisance, a police station, a school, an airport, or "any place where the carrying of firearms is prohibited by federal law". Florida concealed firearms license holders can carry their guns in thirty-five other states.

Zimmerman was carrying a Kel-Tec model PF-9 semiautomatic pistol. Black. Loaded with eight rounds of 9 mm Luger ammunition including one in the chamber. Nine-by-nineteen. A bullet nine millimeters in diameter in a cartridge case nineteen millimeters long. Loaded, the pistol weighs eighteen ounces. With a three-inch barrel, the gun is just shy of six inches long, slightly over four inches high, and less than an inch wide.

Kel-Tec CNC Industries, Incorporated, opened its doors in 1991 in Cocoa, Florida, one county away from Sanford. The initials 'CNC' stand for 'computer numerical control', an engineering achievement in which computer-controlled tools are used to manufacture all sorts of mechanical parts. Designers can submit computer models of needed parts and a CNC system will cut the piece with accuracy far greater than any human hands ever could.

Kel-Tec began building firearms in 1995. "Specializing in innovative rifle designs and handguns for concealed carry by law enforcement personnel and qualified citizens," the company's website says, "we are now one of the top five handgun makers in the US, making us one of the largest firearms manufacturers in the World."

The PF-9 has become a favorite among concealed carry customers. Designed "with maximum concealability in mind", the little pistol can easily be carried under clothing or in a pocket. The owner's manual claims that the pistol is "especially suited for plainclothes police officers or as a secondary weapon for military personnel." But the little pistol packs a punch. "Thanks to its locking dynamics and superior ergonomics," the manual

explains, "perceived recoil and practical accuracy are compara-
ble to much larger guns."

The powerful little pistol has no exposed hammer. It oper-
ates in double action only, which means that one need only
squeeze the trigger to fire it. There's no manual safety to disen-
gage, just point the pistol and pull the trigger.

As the convict-Zimmerman-now hype swelled, all sorts of
speculation about this pistol-packing vigilante was plastered on
the Internet. One blogger commented that he could "clearly
hear" Zimmerman cock his pistol before stepping out of his
truck. But the PF-9 can't be cocked. As has been the case with
many not-so-qualified commentators, fiction has become fact.[†]

Officer Timothy Smith took Zimmerman into custody. "Located on the inside of Zimmerman's waist band," Smith reported, "I removed a black Kel Tec 9mm PF9 semi auto handgun and holster." The pistol had six rounds left in the magazine
and one in the chamber. The eighth round had been fired. The
pistol had been filled to capacity. An inside-the-pants clip-on
type, the soft holster has no strap to hold the pistol in place. It
just slides out with a not-so-forceful tug.

Many bloggers and talking heads have speculated that Zimmerman, while lying on his back, straddled by Martin, could
not have pulled his pistol as claimed. But these would-be crime
scene analysts haven't gained an appreciation for just how simple it is to pull the Kel-Tec from a strapless, cloth, clip-on holster with absolutely no built-in retention features. As one blogger replied to a question on Yahoo! Answers, "Easy, he removed
it from the holster, and shot him." In fact, police officers and
military personnel train for just such a scenario, and then using
larger pistols and top-of-the-line security holsters. And even
while lying on top of the holster, the pistol can be pulled,

---

†    Other bloggers have suggested that they can hear sounds consistent with
    Zimmerman loading his gun. However, there were a total of eight rounds
    in the pistol when it was fired, the gun's maximum capacity. In order to
    load the pistol with eight rounds, Zimmerman would have to insert the
    magazine, rack the slide, remove the magazine, add another (loose) car-
    tridge, and reinsert the magazine, all while holding his cell phone and
    talking with the police dispatcher. The sounds required for that to hap-
    pen are not heard on the recording.

aimed, and fired.

Many, including the lead detective, questioned why Zimmerman got out of his truck carrying a loaded gun and argued that, if he had not done that, Martin would still be alive. A March 25 Tampa Bay Times piece quoted Sanford police civilian employee Wendy Dorival explaining what she told the Twin Lakes neighborhood watch group about their role in the ridding the community of crime. "I told them, this is not about being a vigilante police force," Dorival explained. "You're not even supposed to patrol on neighborhood watch. And you're certainly not supposed to carry a gun."[‡]

◈

Zimmerman's pistol was processed for latent fingerprints. One lift was obtained. A latent print analyst with the Seminole County Sheriff's Office determined that the fingerprint lift card contained no prints of value.

Getting fingerprints from a firearm is remarkably difficult, despite how easy it looks on Hawaii Five-O. Gun surfaces are typically textured. Pistols get slid in and out of holsters, carried under clothing, and handled in ways that are about as friendly to fingerprints as the Ku Klux Klan would be to Al Sharpton. They get wiped away, if they were ever deposited in the first place. Most people think that if someone touches something that something will have that someone's fingerprints on it. But that's simply not the case. Fingerprint transfer doesn't occur that easily, that neatly, that cleanly. In his book, *Practical Analysis and Reconstruction of Shooting Incidents*, criminalist Ed Hueske wrote, "Fingerprints are, contrary to television and the movies, elusive when deposited on firearms and ammunition components." Hueske explains that, in his experience, "identifi-

---

[‡]	Dorival's statement doesn't wholly make sense. If members of the neighborhood watch are not supposed to patrol, when would they be prohibited from a carrying a gun? Zimmerman explained that he was on his way to the grocery store, not patrolling; so far, the prosecution has not offered any evidence to the contrary. He had a permit issued by the State of Florida allowing him to carry a concealed firearm. Even if Zimmerman was patrolling while carrying a gun, at most he violated Sanford Police Department policy, not Florida law.

able fingerprints are found in fewer than 5% of the cases involving firearms examined to determine their presence."

But fingerprints aren't the only evidence that can prove that someone touched a gun. Today's technology provides another even better form of evidence: touch DNA. Skin cells left behind when a person touches an object. Forensic investigators swabbed the firearm's grip, trigger, and slide. They also swabbed the holster.

On March 26, FDLE DNA analyst Anthony Gorgone reported that the swabs from the trigger, the slide, and the holster "failed to give chemical indications for the presence of blood." No usable DNA profile was developed from the trigger. With regard to the swab from the slide, the analyst could only say that the results were "consistent with the presence of at least one male individual." According to the analyst, "[n]o determination can be made regarding the possible contribution of" Zimmerman or Martin because the DNA results were "limited". The swab from the holster contained mixed DNA. The major contributor was Zimmerman. As to the minor contributor, the analyst could neither include nor exclude Martin.

The swab from the grip "gave chemical indications for the presence of blood"; the analyst used the presumptive Kastle-Meyer test. Ethanol and the reagent are added to a swab of the possible bloodstain. Then hydrogen peroxide. An immediate pink reaction indicates that the sample is probably blood. A "mixed DNA profile" was obtained that "demonstrated the presence of at least two individuals. Zimmerman's DNA matched the profile of the major contributor, but the minor contributor remains unknown. Martin was eliminated. The only blood on the pistol was from George Zimmerman, not from Trayvon Martin.[†]

---

† The DNA report was released on May 17. It was on page 104 of a 183-page pile of documents that included the autopsy report and other FDLE crime laboratory reports. The news media made no mention of the DNA findings at that time. However, on September 19, the prosecution released another batch of public records, which included the DNA report again, along with a stack of other documents including the crime laboratory analyst's notes. The news media seized on the new document release incorrectly reporting the DNA report as "new evidence". Hundreds of

◈

Trayvon Martin was shot once in the chest. At autopsy, Volusia County Associate Medical Examiner Dr. Shiping Bao removed the pieces of the bullet. Located in Daytona Beach, the Volusia County Office of the Medical Examiner also serves Seminole County under contract. "Three fragments of projectile are recovered," Bao reported. "The lead core is recovered in the pericardial sac behind the right ventricle." The bullet struck Martin in the heart. "Two fragments of the jacket are recovered in the right pleural cavity behind the right lower lobe of the lung." Bao's wording suggests that six pieces were recovered, but, in fact, only four were. Those pieces were submitted to the FDLE crime lab in Orlando.

The Florida Department of Law Enforcement is the state's top law enforcement agency. With seven regional crime labs, the agency provides forensic analysis services to most of the local law enforcement agencies throughout Florida. Only a few of the larger law enforcement agencies in the state have their own crime labs.

On March 8, FDLE firearms analyst Amy Siewart reported on her examination of the pistol. She examined one "fired 9mm Luger caliber cartridge case", one "fired bullet jacket portion", two "fired bullet jacket fragments", and one "lead bullet core". She also examined one "9mm Luger caliber Kel-Tec model PF-9 semiautomatic pistol, serial number RJY08" on the frame above the backstrap. With the pistol were "one 9mm Luger caliber cartridge, one holster and one magazine containing six 9mm

---

news articles ran, many claiming that the DNA findings damaged Zimmerman's case. Time, for example, reported that the new document release did "not reveal much that was not already known from earlier discovery releases—with the exception of the DNA results." Also on September 19, the Orlando Sentinel reported the DNA results as "new evidence" but correctly pointed out that Zimmerman never claimed that Martin touched the gun. The September hype about the DNA evidence—with some in the media speculating as to how this "new evidence" might alter Zimmerman's defense—highlights how inaccurately the mainstream media have reported on this case, mostly because the reporters writing the stories don't really understand what they're writing about.

Luger caliber cartridges."[†]

The ammunition with the pistol bore the headstamp, "S & B 9mm Luger," the markings of Sellier & Bellot, a Czech ammunition company that has been in business since 1825. The ammunition cartridges Zimmerman was carrying have a 115 grain jacketed hollow point bullet that boasts 393 foot pounds of kinetic energy at a muzzle velocity of 1,237 feet per second—843 miles per hour. The bullet's hollow point means that it will expand in human tissue, slowing more quickly to do more damage and prevent the bullet from perforating the body only to pass through and hit someone on the other side. More tissue damage means the person who is shot is likely to be stopped more quickly, which is the goal of any self-defense shooter.

Siewart noted that the pistol was "dirty". She test fired one round "using the submitted magazine"; the pistol was "found to be functional." She also fired four rounds of laboratory ammunition. Siewart measured the trigger pull: between four-and-a-half and four-and-three-quarters pounds—the force one's finger must apply to squeeze the trigger to the point of discharge.

Siewart used acetone to clean the fired cartridge case that was found at the crime scene, standard laboratory procedure. She determined that the cartridge case—what many people incorrectly call a shell casing—was indeed fired through Zimmerman's pistol. "Images of a cartridge case fired in the pistol were entered into the NIBIN database and compared against images of evidence recovered in other incidents," Siewart reported. "No associations were made at this time." Siewart was referring to the National Integrated Ballistic Identification Network, a coast-to-coast database against which crime laboratories around the country can compare cartridge cases fired from known pistols to ones found at crime scenes in hopes of match-

---

[†]    Some, including Martin family attorneys Benjamin Crump and Natalie Jackson, have suggested that Zimmerman fired two shots—a warning shot and a kill shot—because two loud sounds are heard on the recording of Witness 11's 911 call. However, eight witnesses reported hearing only one shot, and the physical evidence supports this testimony. Police found one fired cartridge case on the ground, one live round in the pistol's chamber, and six live rounds in the magazine. The pistol has a maximum capacity of only eight rounds.

ing the pistol to other crimes. Zimmerman's pistol, however, hadn't been used in any other reported shooting.

The barrel of the pistol is rifled, which means that grooves in the barrel make the bullet spin as it passes through the barrel much like a quarterback spins the pigskin when passing it to a wide receiver. The spin stabilizes the bullet to keep it from tumbling end-over-end out of control. Siewart noted the pistol's rifling as "6R"—six right—which means the bullet rotates halfway around clockwise while traveling down the handgun's three-inch barrel. One rotation for every six inches of barrel.

Siewart cleaned the four fragments of the bullet by soaking them in isopropanol for ten minutes. Examining the pieces for marks imparted by the rifling, the analyst determined that the "bullet jacket portion" recovered from Martin's body was also fired through the gun. But the "two fragments could neither be identified nor eliminated as having been fired from the same unknown firearm" as each other or from the Kel-Tec pistol "due to damage and a lack of class and individual characteristics." The lead core, Siewart reported, "does not display class or individual characteristics and was not further examined." The weight of all four fragments totaled 115 grains, which means that the medical examiner recovered the entire projectile.

Class or individual characteristics. Firearms examiners use specific information about fired bullets and cartridge cases to link them to the gun that fired them. Class characteristics categorize the items based on certain properties: diameter, weight, material, design, caliber, twist. The list of possible weapons is narrowed from every firearm in the world to only certain makes and models. But the analyst's goal is not just to narrow the possibilities, it is to determine which firearm was used to the exclusion of all others.

When a firearm is suspected in a crime, it is test fired using either the ammunition that was recovered with it or ammunition kept in the laboratory. Bullets are fired into water so they can be recovered without damage, preserving the marks made as the projectiles passes through the pistol's barrel. The bullets are viewed side-by-side in a microscope. The marks on the test fired bullet—the individual characteristics—are compared to the marks on the evidence bullet. If they match, the analyst knows that the bullet from the crime scene was fired from the suspected gun. The same process is used for fired cartridge cases.

Sometimes the gun is never found. In those cases, fired bullets and cartridge cases at the scene of a shooting are compared to one another to see if collectively they were fired from a single firearm or if more than one were used. Cartridge cases can be matched to cartridge cases, bullets matched to bullets, but they cannot be matched to one another. The marks are different, made by different parts of the firearm. But that isn't an issue in this case. In this case, there's no doubt, not even a dispute. George Zimmerman fired one round from his Kel-Tec pistol that struck Trayvon Martin in the chest, killing him.

# *Hoodie*

*"This wound is consistent with a wound of entrance of intermediate range."*

—DR. SHIPING BAO, ASSOCIATE MEDICAL EXAMINER

TRAYVON MARTIN WAS WEARING a dark gray hooded sweatshirt. Fifty percent cotton, fifty percent polyester. Fruit of the Loom. A "hoodie" as it's called in pop culture, many would come to view the ubiquitous piece of clothing as, in many ways, the centerpiece of the racial profiling controversy.

Fox News's Geraldo Rivera told a live *Fox and Friends* audience that Martin's hoodie drove Zimmerman's suspicions of the teen. "I believe that George Zimmerman, the over-zealous neighborhood watch captain, should be investigated to the fullest extent of the law," Rivera said, "and if he is criminally liable he should be prosecuted."

"I am urging the parents of black and Latino youngsters particularly not to let their children go out wearing hoodies," Rivera continued. "I think the hoodie is as much responsible for Trayvon Martin's death as much as George Zimmerman was."

"What's the instant identification?" Rivera asked. "What's the instant association?" He explained:

> It's those crime scene surveillance tapes. Every time you see someone sticking up a 7-11, the kid is wearing a hoodie. Every time you see a mugging on a surveillance camera or they get the old lady in the alcove, it's a kid wearing a hoodie. You have to recognize that this whole stylizing yourself as a gangsta, you're gonna be a gangsta wannabe? Well, people are going to perceive you as a menace. That's what happens. It is an instant reflexive action. . . . When you see a black or Latino youngster,

particularly on the street, you walk to the other side of the street. You try to avoid that confrontation. Trayvon Martin's you know, God bless him, he's an innocent kid, a wonderful kid, a box of Skittles in his hand. He didn't deserve to die. But I'll bet you money, if he didn't have that hoodie on, that —that nutty neighborhood watch guy wouldn't have responded in that violent and aggressive way.

Rivera's comments were not well received in news media or by the public, but the television personality later explained that his comments were a "repugnant . . . reality". Rivera, writing in Fox News Latino about teens wearing hoodies and "low slung pants", quoted then-presidential-candidate Barack Obama who, in 2008, told a Georgia high school crowd, "Maybe you are the next Lil Wayne, but probably not, in which case you need to stay in school." As Rivera explained, "If you dress like a hoodlum eventually some schmuck is going to take you at your word."

Rivera's own son, Gabriel, was disappointed by his father's comments. "[H]e just told me that for the first time in his life he's ashamed of what I wrote," Rivera explained. He apologized for his comments saying that he had "obscured the main point that someone shot and killed an unarmed teenager." But despite all the criticism, Rivera said that he had received much support. "In the avalanche of criticism," Rivera explained, "how interesting that most minority moms back me because they want their sons to live long and prosper."

In May, Rivera debated the issue with Martin family attorney Benjamin Crump. "The reason I mentioned . . . the hoodie was the surveillance video from the 7-11," Rivera explained. "It's such a contrast what Trayvon really looked like that night as opposed to the little boy pictures that were released initially, that's the only reason. If he had taken that damn hood off his head, if he and Zimmerman had only spoken . . . don't you think that could have avoided this awful tragedy?"

Crump argued that Facebook founder Mark Zuckerberg often wears a hooded sweatshirt. "You mean to tell me if Mark Zuckerberg was walking through the gated community, he could be profiled by George Zimmerman?" Crump said. "What's the difference between the two?"

"The difference is in the eye of George Zimmerman, isn't it?" Rivera said. "Isn't that the only subjective viewpoint, when you're talking about self-defense and why the encounter was initiated, isn't that what counts?"

But Crump was incredulous. "You can't profile people and act on it," Crump responded. "It would be one thing if you profile and call the police and let the police deal with it, but you can't act on it. Because then, you give a license to everybody to say if a black man is walking in his neighborhood, going to the store with his hoodie up, you can shoot him."

"[Y]ou're embarrassing your son again with these statements," Crump chided Rivera.

Rivera's comments may not have resonated well in America, but some understood the connection he was trying to make, as explained by writer Patrick Jonsson in a piece for the Christian Science Monitor. "While some have criticized Rivera's view of the hoodie as a symbol of criminality," Jonsson wrote, "he does put his finger on the populist nuances of the broader Trayvon Martin debate." The writer explained that "thousands of Americans donned hoodies to protest both what they believed was a case of racially motivated profiling and racial injustice." At the same time, "an entrepreneur quickly sold out of a stockpile of gun targets depicting someone, presumably Martin, in a hoodie."

While not expressly mentioning the hoodie, the probable cause affidavit charging Zimmerman with second-degree murder claims that Martin was "profiled by George Zimmerman." According to the affidavit, Zimmerman "assumed Martin was a criminal. Zimmerman felt Martin did not belong in the gated community and called police."

On May 30, CNN legal analyst Mark NeJame, an Orlando attorney, wrote a column in which he explained that the legal case wasn't about "racial profiling". NeJame noted that prosecutors have only alleged profiling saying nothing about race. "This allows the state to keep such a claim open-ended," NeJame explained, "likely knowing early on that it couldn't sustain the burden of proving racial profiling."

"There's a difference of opinion about whether racial profiling was actually involved," NeJame wrote, "but a key question that is often overlooked is the distinction between profiling by a citizen and profiling by a member of law enforcement. That distinction is likely to be crucial in determining the direction the case may go."

"Zimmerman was not a law enforcement agent," NeJame explained. "He was a civilian, operating under different legal standards than those applied to the police. Merely because he was a neighborhood watch captain does not attach law enforcement status to him. . . . A civilian, as offensive as it may be, is allowed to personally act on biases or prejudices, whereas a law enforcement officer is prohibited from doing so."

On March 26, Law professor and former federal prosecutor Paul Butler wrote a column in The Daily Beast in which he explained that he "became a prosecutor because of Trayvon Martin." "I used to be him, black, baby-faced, and 17," Butler explained. "The times I wasn't being harassed by police and security guards, I was being harassed by young African-American men. Stopped and patted down by the former, robbed of my lunch money by the latter."

"The black prosecutor lives at the intersection of crime control and racial profiling," Butler wrote. "I think that many fail to make the difference that they hope to because their tool—locking people up—is too blunt an instrument. In the adversarial system of American criminal justice, prosecutors are forced to choose a side. So they end up defending the police and locking up a lot of black people." Butler's sentiment sums up how many black Americans view the case against Zimmerman, and how they view Martin and his hoodie. "Black prosecutors are still black," Butler explained, "which means they have stories about being racially profiled."

But as Zimmerman faces his fate in court, Martin's hoodie will play less of a role as an instrument of racial prejudice and more of a role as a piece of forensic evidence that may well sway the jury's decision. The hoodie, after all, was what stood between Zimmerman's gun and Martin's chest.

◈

Martin's body was placed in a blue body bag and secured with seal number 0000517. The medical examiner's case number was 12-24-043. The year 2012, district twenty-four, body number forty-three. Dr. Shiping Bao performed the autopsy.

"The body is that of a normally developed, black male appearing the stated age of 17 years," the doctor reported. "The body presents a medium build with average nutrition, normal hydration and good preservation." As part of the external examination, Bao reported on Martin's general physical condition and attributes. "Short black hair covers the scalp. The face is unremarkable. There is average body hair of adult-male-pattern distribution." The doctor inspected Martin's mouth. "The oral cavity presents natural teeth with fair oral hygiene."

Bao noted a one-inch by one-half-inch scar on Martin's right shoulder, and another equally-sized scar on his right hand. He had two tattoos, one on his right arm, the other on his left wrist. A cardiac monitor pad was still attached to the teen's left rear side, the flank as it is referred to in medical terminology.

The doctor thoroughly examined Martin's body. But for a gunshot wound to the chest, he was perfectly healthy.

"The entrance wound is located on the left chest," Bao reported, "17½ inches below the top of the head, 1 inch to the left of the anterior midline, and ½ inch below the nipple." The bullet did not exit Martin's body. The doctor described the gunshot wound. "It consists of a 3/8 inch diameter round entrance defect with soot, ring abrasion, and a 2 x 2 inch area of stippling."

"Further examination demonstrates that the wound track passes directly from front to back," Bao reported, "and enters the pleural cavity with perforations of the left anterior fifth intercostal space, pericardial sac, right ventricle of the heart, and the right lower lobe of the lung. There is no wound of exit." In other words, the bullet passed between Martin's fifth and sixth ribs, ripped through his heart, and then tore through his right lung. Both sides of his chest cavity filled with blood—nearly two-and-a-half liters, about one third of the blood in his body.

His lungs collapsed.

Although shot in the heart, Martin would not have died instantly. He wouldn't even have been immediately incapacitated. According to an August 17 article in the Orlando Sentinel, Dr. William Anderson, formerly the deputy chief medical examiner for neighboring Orange County, said that Martin would have remained conscious for a short period of time. "You're talking about minutes, at least, for him to survive," the doctor said.

According to the Sentinel, Dr. William L. Manion, a forensic pathologist from New Jersey, believed that Martin would have remained conscious for about twenty to thirty seconds.

Despite Hollywood's best efforts to dramatize the effects of bullets on human bodies, gunshot wounds do not necessarily stop a person instantly, even hollow point bullets fired into the chest. "Physiologically, no caliber or bullet is certain to incapacitate any individual," wrote Urey Patrick in *Handgun Wounding Factors and Effectiveness*, "unless the brain is hit."

Vincent DiMaio, a reknowned forensic pathologist and expert on gunshot wounds, wrote in his text *Gunshot Wounds: Practical Aspects of Firearms, Ballistics, and Forensic Techniques*, that a bullet will stop a person "dead in his tracks" when "the bullet injures a vital area of the brain, the brain stem, or the cervical spinal cord. . . . Aside from areas in the central nervous system, while a bullet may produce rapid incapacitation, there is no guarantee that it will produce instant incapacitation."

The lethality of most gunshot wounds is due to blood loss, which is unlikely to result in immediate incapacitation because the brain can continue to function without oxygen for a short period of time; the amount of oxygen deprivation is dependent on the amount of blood flow to the brain, which, unless all blood flow to the brain is shut off, may not drop to incapacitating levels until the wounded person has lost a considerable amount of blood. "The fact that an individual can be mortally wounded, yet still capable of aggressive actions and a threat, sometimes for a prolonged amount of time," DiMaio explained, "is not appreciated by the public whose concepts of shootings [are] derived from television and the movies."

In the autopsy report, the associate medical examiner reported his opinion of the distance from which Zimmerman fired the shot that tore into Martin's body. "This wound," Bao wrote, referring to the hole in the teenager's chest, "is consistent with a wound of entrance of intermediate range."

Intermediate range. These two words touched off a storm of news coverage that came at the peak of anti-Zimmerman sentiment, and after these two words were heard on virtually every cable news analysis show from coast to coast, few in the public were any the wiser about what this single sentence really said of the killing of Trayvon Martin. Speculation swirled. Some claimed it meant that Martin was executed, others that Zimmerman acted in self-defense. But almost nobody knew that another piece of evidence analyzed by another forensic scientist would be the key that unlocked the mystery of how Martin was shot.

A gunshot produces residue. The trigger is pulled. The firing pin strikes the primer, a small piece of shock-sensitive metallic compound that ignites the gunpowder packed inside the cartridge. The gunpowder rapidly combusts, gases expand forcing the walls of the cartridge case to spread releasing the bullet, and the building pressure pushes the projectile through the barrel sending it on its deadly mission. But the bullet isn't the only thing propelled out the barrel. As forensic firearms expert Brian Heard wrote in *Handbook of Firearms and Ballistics*, "a great volume of incandescent . . . gaseous material is produced."

"The gaseous material is mainly the combustion products from the propellant and consists of carbon dioxide, carbon monoxide, water as steam and oxides of nitrogen," Heard explained. "In amongst this vast cloud of gases are also partially burnt and unburnt propellant particles and combustion products from the priming compound." As Heard explained, these tiny solid particles make up what is known in the world of forensic science as gunshot residue, commonly referred to by the three initials "GSR".

Gunshot residue is deposited on the skin of a victim if the muzzle of the firearm is sufficiently close. Sometimes soot is seen, sometimes stippling, sometimes nothing. Soot particles from combustion are light and resistant to travel through air. When they are seen on skin it is because the muzzle was very close, within inches. Also known as powder tattooing, stippling on skin is a pattern of punctate abrasions caused by particles of unburnt and partially burnt gunpowder pummeling the skin from the pressure of the blast. These are actual injuries. Soot wipes off; stippling does not.

The particles that leave the muzzle of the pistol form the shape of a cone which, when the gun is fired perpendicular to the surface of the skin, forms a circular pattern of stippling on the body. The further the muzzle is from the skin, the larger the circle.

Just how far the powder particles will travel is dependent on both the pistol and the ammunition. Shorter barrels make for a more open cone, longer barrels a tighter one. Different ammunition cartridges have different types of powder, the grains of which may have different sizes, different shapes, different weights. Some particles pass through air better than others just like a baseball flies farther than a feather. The pressures produced by various cartridges also vary; the greater the pressure, the farther the particles will travel.

The day the autopsy report was released, I appeared on CNN Headline News with Jane Velez-Mitchell. "When this autopsy report . . . says that George Zimmerman shot Trayvon Martin at 'intermediate range'," Velez-Mitchell asked, "what exactly are they talking about?"

"With intermediate range," I explained, "based on that gunshot residue, the pathologist is able to tell that the gun is not in contact with the skin—so at least several inches away—but it was close enough to have deposited that soot, the stippling, and the gunshot particles."

"[W]hat's the outside range?" Velez-Mitchell inquired. "How far away can it be and still be intermediate?"

"With most firearms of this type, about three feet is where you would be at your maximum," I answered. "After that, you wouldn't see any of this gunshot residue."

"OK, because I thought that was distant," Velez-Mitchell commented.

"Distant would mean that there's no presence of any type of gunshot residue," I explained. "So at that point, you know it would have to be beyond the three feet, but you wouldn't know how far beyond it."

The same day, Dr. Larry Kobilinsky, professor of forensic science at John Jay College of Criminal Justice, appeared on CNN's Anderson Cooper 360 discussing the evidence in the newly released documents.

"Intermediate range, what does that mean to you?" Cooper asked.

"Well, there's several possibilities," Kobilinsky explained. "There's a contact wound, where the muzzle is right up against the target. There's a close-in distance from zero to six inches. Then there's the intermediate distance, which is about six inches to roughly 1.5 feet. And that's what the pathologist is talking about." Kobilinsky described the range as "consistent with a struggle."

There are several categories used to classify gunshot wounds based on the presence or absence of gunshot residue, but those categories are not set in stone in the world of forensic science. Some pathologists use more categories than others. Some use different terms. Some cite different distances. But what's important to understand is that the term 'intermediate range' is not a distance but a category for describing a wound. Dr. Bao's description follows what DiMaio wrote in his monumental text on the topic. "An intermediate-range gunshot wound," DiMaio wrote, "is one in which the muzzle of the weapon is away from the body at the time of discharge yet is sufficiently close so that powder grains emerging from the muzzle strike the skin producing powder tattooing." DiMaio describes the stippling or powder tattooing as the *sine qua non* of intermediate range wounds: without which, there is nothing. Without that stippling, without the presence of any gunshot residue on the skin or on the clothing covering it, the gunshot falls in the distant category which only means that the muzzle was too far away to leave residue on the victim. How far away, though, cannot be determined from gunshot residue alone.

Bao classified the range of fire as "intermediate", but others, including me, would, based on his qualitative description of the wound, classify the range as "close". The distinction is in the soot. While stippling may be present out to several feet—as much as five feet with some handgun and ammunition combinations—soot will not. Soot will generally not be present beyond one foot, often less.

"As people try to understand this case," Velez-Mitchell asked me, "what does it say that even the experts can't definitively say what intermediate range means? And my understanding is that there will be tests done probably on the actual weapon that was used with the ammunition that remains to determine exactly down to the final, final dot how far George Zimmerman was away."

"There are actually notations in the autopsy report about the size of the stippling pattern and the fact that there's a presence of soot," I explained. "Intermediate range is a fairly wide range. When you have the soot and you have the actual size of the stippling, then with that test you can narrow it down to within an inch or two of what the actual distance is between the muzzle of the firearm and the gunshot wound."

The distance is dependent on many factors, ammunition being the most prevalent. Different types of powder create stippling on skin at different distances. "In centerfire cartridges," DiMaio explained, "powder tattooing extends out to greater ranges with ball powder . . . than with flake powder, because of the shape of the powder grains. The sphere was a better aerodynamic form than a flake; thus, ball powder can travel farther retaining more velocity, enabling it to mark the skin at a greater range." That's why if you want to throw a piece of paper at someone, you ball it up first.

In the initial release of documents, there were no reports indicating that any range of fire testing had been done with regard to the stippling pattern on Martin's skin. In other words, police knew only that the shot was fired from intermediate range but hadn't narrowed that range down by test firing the pistol at various ranges and then comparing those results to what was noted in the autopsy report. But even without that testing, the presence of soot and the small diameter of the stippling pattern—about two inches—indicates that the distance between the muzzle of Zimmerman's pistol and Martin's skin was probably no more than six inches. There's no mention in the autopsy report of burned skin, which happens when the muzzle is closer than that, so three to six inches is the likely range.

While some in the media spoke in terms of feet, referencing the textbook definition in which intermediate range can extend out to three feet or so, nobody in mainstream media or even Internet blogging were talking about another report that was in the stack of documents released along with the autopsy report: a March 22 report by FDLE's Amy Siewart, the same analyst who had examined Zimmerman's pistol.

Siewart examined Martin's clothing. She received two exhibits: one "light grey Nike sweatshirt" and one "dark grey Fruit of the Loom hooded sweatshirt". Siewart noted the gunshot hole. "The sweatshirts each display a hole located in the upper left chest area," the analyst reported. "The areas around these holes were microscopically examined and chemically processed for the presence of gunshot residues."

There have been discrepancies in reports regarding exactly what Martin was wearing that evening. Surveillance video from the 7-11 convenience store show him wearing a long sleeved, dark colored hooded sweatshirt and beige pants. The first arriving Sanford police officer, Timothy Smith, reported that Martin was wearing "a gray sweater, blue jeans, and red/white sneakers"; however, another police officer, Sergeant Joseph Santiago, reported that Martin was wearing "a grey sweatshirt and light colored shorts and white tennis shoes." The Medical Examiner's Office logged Martins clothing as "shoes, undershorts, socks, pants, tee shirt, hoodie, [and a] black plastic watch." No colors or further descriptions were noted.

Siewart noted that the hole in the hoodie was "L-shaped", about two inches by one inch in size. There was "very light sooting directly surrounding the hole" on both the outside and inside of the dark gray sweatshirt. She indicated that there was singeing or burning of the "fibers around [the] hole". There was a "slight orange discoloration surrounding [the] hole out to" about six inches, a discoloration that tested positive for blood. Using a microscope, the analyst determined that the gunpowder was of the flattened ball type, a hybrid between ball and flake.

The analyst performed the Griess test, a chemical examination in which a piece of filter paper dampened with a solution is pressed against the fabric in an effort to visualize a gunshot residue pattern. If the particles are there, the analyst will see a reaction with the inorganic nitrites present in the gunpowder. "Propellant particles and many of the sites where they have impacted a surface contain traces of nitrites . . . and nitrates," write Michael and Lucien Haag in the second edition of their textbook, *Shooting Incident Reconstruction*. The father and son forensic firearms experts explain that, while nitrates are "common in nature and can be found in a number of materials", nitrites "are neither common nor particularly stable in the environment and *are* present in readily detectable amounts in nearly all smokeless and black powder residues following discharge." Siewart saw "no visible pattern".

The FDLE analyst used another chemical, sodium rhodizonate, a reagent that reacts with lead. She noted "vaporous [lead] immediately surrounding" the bullet hole.

Beneath the now-infamous dark hoodie, Martin was wearing a light gray Nike sweatshirt, long sleeved, with no hood. Seventy percent cotton, thirty percent polyester. It had one hole seven inches below the shoulder seam and seven-and-a-half inches from the left sleeve seam that corresponded in location to the hole in the hoodie. Siewart measured the size of this hole at two inches by one-and-a-quarter inches. She noted "light sooting directly surrounding the hole" with "heavier sooting inside the sweatshirt". The analyst also noted "stellate tearing" and burned or singed "fibers around the hole" and a few flattened ball powder flakes she found using a microscope. Again, no visible pattern, "just a few particles directly above and below the hole on both [the] inside and outside of [the] sweatshirt."

Tearing of the hole. Soot. No powder pattern. Vaporous lead around the hole. "Both holes display residues and physical effects consistent with a contact shot," Siewart reported. The muzzle of Zimmerman's pistol was touching Martin's hoodie when the neighborhood watch captain fired the shot that ripped through Martin's chest.

◈

Almost nobody in mainstream media reported on the FDLE analyst's findings.[†] Apparently, the bloggers missed it, too. The focus was on Bao's use of the term "intermediate range" and just exactly what that meant. But while many sought to villainize Zimmerman claiming that intermediate range was too far away from Martin to justify a claim of self-defense—especially since Zimmerman claimed that Martin was on top of him when he fired—the critics' claims were quietly controverted by a crime laboratory report almost nobody in the public had read, even though it was released in the same batch of documents as the widely publicized autopsy report. And they weren't that far from one another in the 183-page digital document; Siewart's report on the hoodie was at page 122, the autopsy report at page 125. The media most likely missed it because they had no idea what they were looking at.

Forensic pathologist Vincent DiMaio appeared on the NBC's *Today* offering his opinion that the shot was most likely fired from a distance of two to four inches. Fox News reported that former New York City chief medical examiner Michael Baden said that intermediate range was one to eighteen inches away. But both knew that Martin was clothed in the infamous hoodie,

---

[†] A May 26 article in the Miami Herald did report that the "FDLE tests on Trayvon's shirt show he was shot at very close range." Published nine days after the release of the documents, the article did not elaborate further. Also, on August 22, NBC News published a story on how other countries would handle a case like this one. Experts on criminal law in five different countries were given the facts of this case with names changed. As part of his set of facts, journalist Ian Johnson reported that the "range of the shot is disputed" and wrote that "the gun is either in contact with Jones' clothing or was fired at 'intermediate' range." While Johnson did reference Siewart's report, he clearly did not understand that both pieces of information are simultaneously accurate. The muzzle was in contact with the clothing, but the loose-fitting clothing—and, therefore, the muzzle—was not in contact with the skin.

which would have acted as an intermediary target between the pistol and Martin's wound. No opinion as to distance would be reasonable without examining the clothing.

Dr. Larry Kobilinsky told CNN's Anderson Cooper that he believed the FDLE report somehow contradicted the autopsy report. "The ballistics people that looked at the clothing are saying it's contact," Kobilinsky said, "but it's very inconsistent with what the autopsy report shows." Kobilinsky, too, appears to have missed the fact that, if stippling was present on the skin beneath the hoodie, then either the hoodie wasn't there or the muzzle was in contact with the hoodie with space between the hoodie and Martin's skin. Siewart's report confirms the latter.

There was also no information included in the document release as to the results of any range of fire testing. Categories for range of fire such as the term "intermediate range" are qualitative descriptions, not quantitative. Intermediate range for one firearm may not be intermediate range for another. Even the same firearm can have different distances associated with a given range when different ammunition is used. To quantify the distance, forensic scientists fire the pistol and ammunition from various distances in an effort to match the residue pattern seen on the actual wound. But none of that testing was known to the news media on the day that the autopsy report was released. When the firearms analyst's notes were released weeks later, there was no mention of testing being done with respect to the stippling on Martin's skin. The only testing Siewart did was to duplicate the contact shot to the two sweatshirts.

◈

On March 26, FDLE crime laboratory analyst Anthony Gorgone reported his findings with regard to DNA on Martin's clothing. Gorgone examined the "[h]oodie jacket represented as being from Trayvon Martin" and the gray Nike sweatshirt Martin was wearing under the hoodie. On the Nike sweatshirt, Gorgone found five possible bloodstains on the front of the garment near the bottom. He labeled the stains "A" through "E" and checked each one using the Kastle-Meyer test. Stains "A", "B",

"D", and "E" "gave chemical indications for the presence of blood" but stain "C" did not. Gorgone's analysis showed that stain "A" had Zimmerman's DNA and stains "B" and "E" had Martin's. Stain "D" had the DNA of "at least two individuals", and both Martin and Zimmerman were included as possible contributors. Gorgone also swabbed each cuff and sleeve below the elbow. No DNA "foreign to Trayvon Martin" was found on the right sleeve. On the left, Gorgone found DNA from "at least two individuals." "Assuming Trayvon Benjamin Martin . . . is a contributor to the mixture," Gorgone wrote, "foreign DNA results were obtained." But the analyst found that the data were "insufficient for inclusion purposes." He could not determine if Zimmerman's DNA was in the mixture.

When Gorgone examined that hoodie, he found that it was "very damp" and had a "strong odor". He speculated in his notes what the odor could have been: "Mold? Ammonia?" Whatever it was, the evidence had not been thoroughly dried before being packaged, a cardinal sin in the world of forensic investigations. Someone at the medical examiner's office had made a serious mistake. Failing to dry clothing before packaging it promotes the growth of mold and bacteria that can degrade biological evidence and render the clothing unusable for reconstruction and court presentation. But Gorgone managed to examine it anyway. Had it languished in storage for much longer, it may not have been of any use.

Gorgone found three possible bloodstains, two of which tested presumptively positive for blood, and only one of which yielded results for DNA. Gorgone determined that the DNA was from Martin, not Zimmerman. Again Gorgone swabbed the cuffs and lower sleeves for DNA but found only Martin's.

On May 9, Gorgone reported on his examination of Zimmerman's clothing. The analyst examined a shirt and a jacket "represented as being from George Michael Zimmerman". The shirt was a gray "Layer 8 Performance" with long sleeves, size large. Gorgone examined sixteen possible bloodstains, fourteen of which tested positive, at least presumptively, for blood. All of the stains had only Zimmerman's DNA.

Gorgone described Zimmerman's jacket as "gray [and] orange" and noted that it was a "Free Country" brand, extra-large. Gorgone saw seventeen bloodstains, twelve of which "gave chemical indications for the presence of blood." Using an alternate light source—a very high-tech light that can be fine-tuned to specific colors—the analyst found fourteen more possible bloodstains. Using the Kastle-Meyer test, Gorgone found that only three of those stains were probably blood. Zimmerman's DNA was found in most of the stains, Martin's in only one. Two of the stains had mixed profiles, and Martin could not be excluded as a possible donor. Another stain with mixed DNA included Martin "as a possible contributor".

The DNA results led to much speculation in the media with many suggesting that the findings were harmful to Zimmerman's defense. But how can they be? They are anything but clear-cut, and where doubt exists, the defense has an advantage. The pundits seem to forget that the State of Florida has the burden of proof, and if reasonable doubt exists, the jury must find Zimmerman not guilty.

The DNA findings prove that, at some point, Zimmerman and Martin were in close quarters, close enough to get each other's DNA on their clothing. But the DNA results say nothing about when that transfer occurred. Some have suggested that too little DNA has been transferred for the struggle to have taken place the way Zimmerman has claimed, but such speculation has no scientific basis. There is no literature on how much DNA should be found on a neighborhood watchman struggling with an unarmed teen in the rain. The amount of DNA found is a direct result of the amount searched for, and while Gorgone examined the clothing quite extensively, he did not take DNA samples from every square inch of all four garments he examined. Absence of evidence is not evidence of absence, at least not necessarily.

The same holds true for gunshot residue found on Zimmerman. On March 28, FDLE crime laboratory analyst Stephen Krejci reported that gunshot residue was found on the swabs taken from Zimmerman's hands, but on the same day Siewart reported that only one particle of lead was found on Zimmerman's jacket, a fact that some have argued means that Zimmerman couldn't have shot Martin as claimed. But Zimmerman's jacket wasn't even collected from him until after he was taken to the Sanford police headquarters and photographed. Gunshot residue is short-lived evidence, and normal activities can wipe it away. Being rained on certainly doesn't help, either. If the claim is that Zimmerman's arm must have been outstretched when he fired, therefore preventing gunshot residue from being deposited on the body of his jacket, then why wasn't any found on his lower right sleeve? The one particle that was found was on the back of the upper right sleeve, not in a place that would make sense for any conceivable scenario, which means that the particle was most likely transferred there after the fact.

◈

The evidence of the contact shot to the hoodie adds a new dimension to the reconstruction of the shooting: it means that, while the pistol was touching the sweatshirt, there was some distance between the sweatshirt and the skin. Explaining that discrepancy could be key to using physical evidence to determine just how the shooting took place and figuring out who was on top of the fatal fracas.

Trayvon Martin.

Trayvon Martin at the 7-11 just minutes before he was killed.

Photograph of George Zimmerman taken by Sanford police.

The Retreat at Twin Lakes.

The location where the shooting took place.

Police photograph of the shooting scene.

George Zimmerman's Kel-Tec pistol.

Zimmerman's pistol, holster, and magazine.

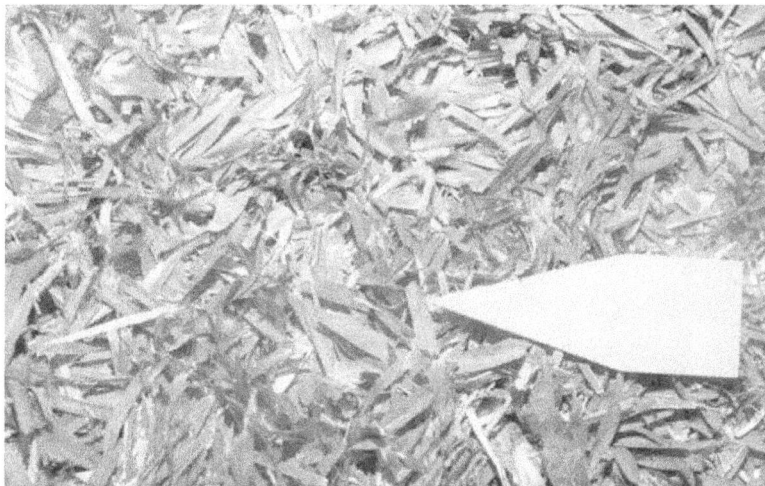
Cartridge case from Zimmerman's pistol.

The cartridge case from Zimmerman's pistol. It has been moved from its original position for this photograph.

Zimmerman's keys and flashlight.

Trayvon Martin's cell phone.

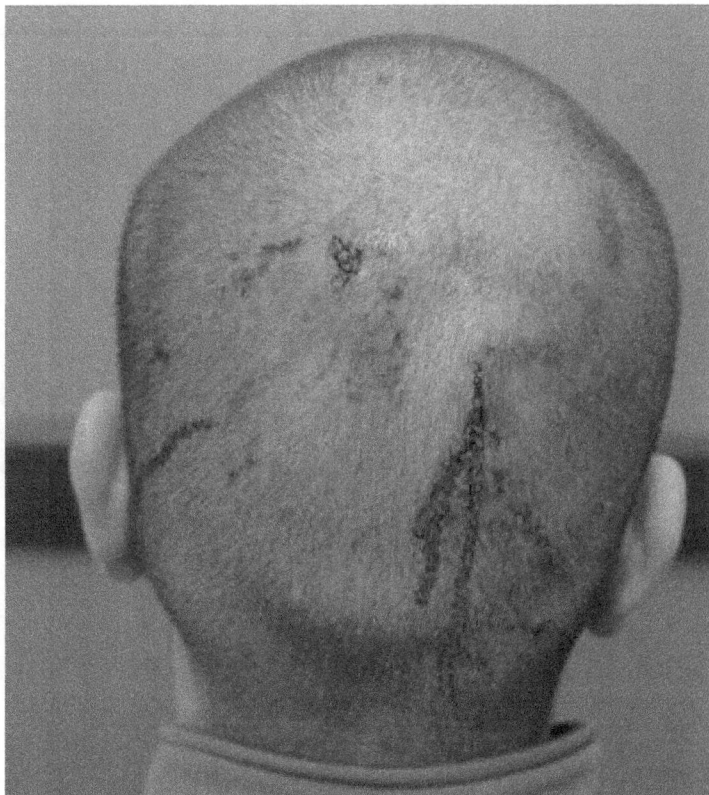
Injuries to the back of George Zimmerman's head.

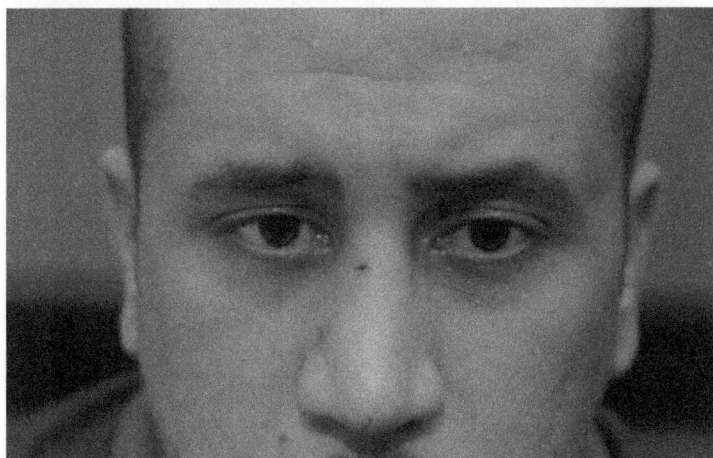
Zimmerman's nose.

Zimmerman during his videotaped walk-through interview.

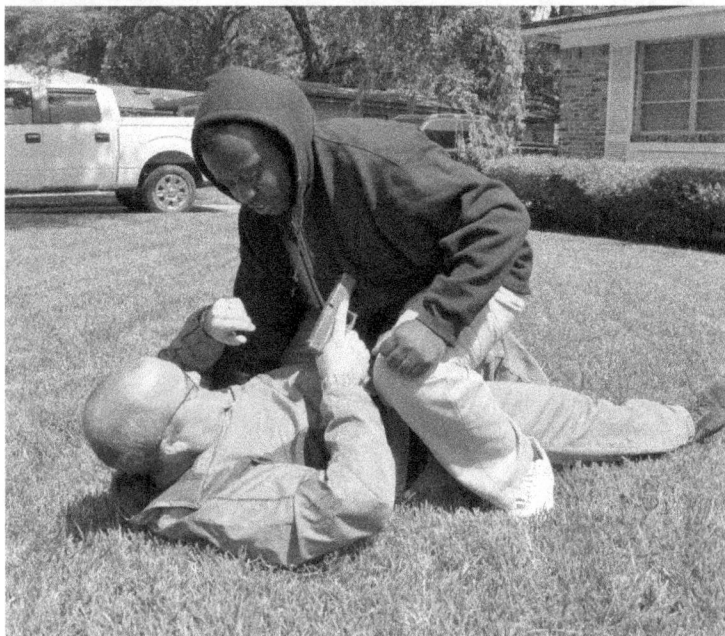
The author and an assistant reenact the shooting.

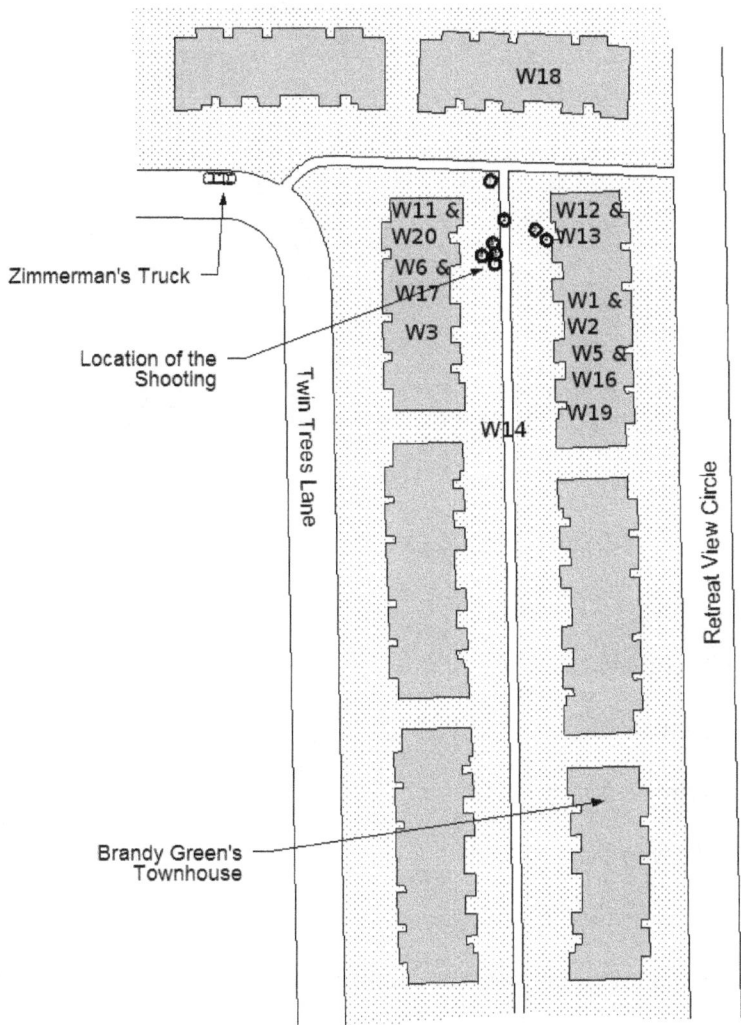

Diagram of the scene showing Zimmerman's truck, Brandy Green's Townhouse, the location of the shooting, and the locations of key witnesses.

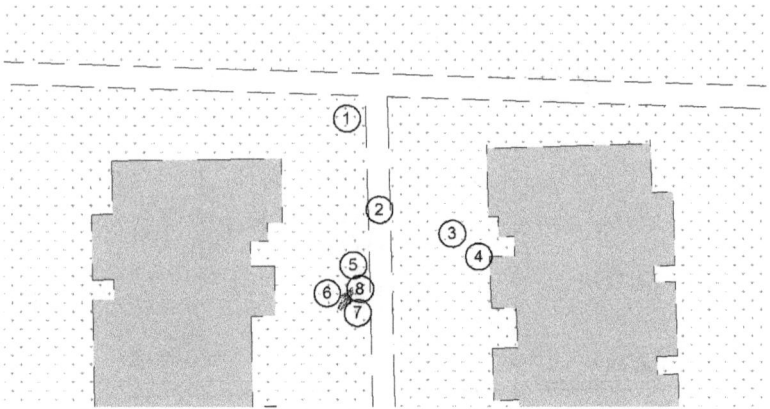
Close-up diagram showing the evidence at the scene.

1 = George Zimmerman's keys and flashlight

2 = Plastic 7-11 bag

3 = Plastic WalMart bag

4 = First aid kit

5 = Witness 13's flashlight

6 = Trayvon Martin's body

7 = Trayvon Martin's cell phone

8 = Fired cartridge case from Zimmerman's pistol

# Lynch Mob

*"All of our reasoning ends in surrender to feeling."*

—BLAISE PASCAL

IT's DIFFICULT NOT TO get emotional when thinking about a seventeen-year-old kid walking home from the store with a bag of Skittles and a can of Arizona Iced Tea getting shot and killed by a man who thought the teen was a "real suspicious guy". Something about that scenario sets a person on his heels and makes him wonder just what could have been going through the mind of, as Geraldo Rivera described him, that "nutty neighborhood watch guy".

Many, including civil rights leader Jesse Jackson, reflected on the 1955 murder of Emmett Till, a black fourteen-year-old Chicago boy who was brutally murdered while visiting relatives in the Mississippi Delta after he spoke to a twenty-one-year-old white woman, the wife of a local merchant. His killers, the woman's husband, Roy Bryant and his half brother, J. W. Milam, dragged Till to a barn, beat him, gouged out one of his eyes, and then shot him before throwing his body into the Tallahatchie River, a seventy-pound weight tied around his neck. "Bryant and Milam were acquitted of Till's kidnapping and murder," a Wikipedia article on the killing explains, "but months later, protected against double jeopardy, they admitted to killing him in a magazine interview." Till's mother insisted on having an open-casket funeral so that the whole world could see what was done to her son.

Writing for NewsOne, editorial director Leigh Davenport expressed her dismay at the fact that Sanford police didn't try harder to find Martin's parents to tell them that their son was dead. "Despite Trayvon having a cell phone on him that had his family's phone numbers in it," Davenport wrote on March 21, "the police made no effort to notify his parents that he had been brutally shot and murdered in the neighborhood complex where his father lived. Instead he was taken by the medical examiner, tagged and listed as 'John Doe.'"

As with many of the editorials about this case, Davenport's description of events isn't quite accurate. Martin's father didn't live in the complex; his fiancée, Brandy Green, did. Martin was staying with Green and her son while his father attended a conference in Orlando. But Martin's body *was* tagged as "John Doe". It wasn't until the next morning when Tracy Martin reported his son missing that police knew who he was. In addition to Davenport's claim that police could have used Martin's phone to find his family, critics argued that Sanford police should have knocked on every door in the complex in an effort to identify the dead teen. While knocking on all 263 doors in the complex may have been an option[†], police were unable to access Martin's phone because it was protected with a password, one that even his later-located family didn't know. Between a dead battery, finding an expert to access the data, and cracking the password, it took police days to get access to the teenager's phone.

To Davenport, Martin's death was analogous to Till's murder. "Here we are more than 50 years later and the story reads almost exactly the same," she wrote. "Two little Black boys go to the store, two little Black boys never come home. They are brutally murdered and the only crime committed is that their bodies exist. Their flesh is used as target practice for men full of hatred and loathing and then disposed of like trash. Racism is too slight a word to describe brutally killing children in cold blood. Evil sounds more appropriate to me."

"Why does Trayvon's death evoke the most-traumatic sentiments of brutality against Black men?" Davenport asked. "It is because Trayvon was gunned down by a civilian. While we've been consistently enraged at the police brutality leveraged against our Black men over the years, to be reminded that any White male civilian can murder a little Black boy without

---

[†]   At an average of five minutes per residence, it would have taken Sanford police just shy of twenty-two person hours to knock on every door.

repercussions terrifies us."

But not all black Americans saw the killing this way. Conservative black author, columnist, and Stanford University senior fellow Shelby Steele wrote an opinion column in the Wall Street Journal on April 6 in which he accused civil rights leaders Jesse Jackson and Al Sharpton of exploiting Martin's murder. "His death was vindication of the 'poetic truth' that these establishments live by," Steele wrote, referring to America's civil rights establishments. "Poetic truth is like poetic license where one breaks grammatical rules for effect. Better to break the rule than lose the effect. Poetic truth lies just a little; it bends the actual truth in order to highlight what it believes is a larger and more important truth."

"The civil rights community and the liberal media live by the poetic truth that America is still a reflexively racist society, and that this remains the great barrier to black equality," Steele wrote. "America has greatly evolved since the 1960s. There are no longer any respectable advocates of racial segregation. And blacks today are nine times more likely to be killed by other blacks than by whites."

To Steele, Trayvon Martin's murder was not a poignant representation of the second-class status of black Americans, but a shocking rarity in a nation besieged by murders of black males by black males. "If Trayvon Martin was a victim of white racism," Steele explained, "his murder would be an anomaly, not a commonplace. It would be a bizarre exception to the way so many young black males are murdered today. . . . Black teenagers today are afraid of other black teenagers, not whites."

Steele also saw a marked difference between the murder of Emmett Till and the killing of Trayvon Martin and suggested that making any such connection was a feeble attempt at perpetuating racist ideals in an attempt to avoid moving forward. "[T]he idea that Trayvon Martin is today's Emmett Till," Steele wrote, "suggests nothing less than a stubborn nostalgia for America's racist past."

Steele was not alone. Walter Williams, a black economist and professor at George Mason University, posted an editorial

on May 22 on CNS News in which he lamented the fact that
ninety-four percent of the 7,000 blacks murdered in the United
States each year are killed by another black person.[‡] "A much
larger issue is how might we interpret the deafening silence
about the day-to-day murder in black communities compared
with the national uproar over the killing of Trayvon Martin,"
Williams wrote. "Such a response by politicians, civil rights or-
ganizations and the mainstream news media could easily be interpreted as 'blacks killing other blacks is of little concern, but
it's unacceptable for a white to kill a black person.'"

Civil rights leader Jesse Jackson spoke to reporters from Orlando's News 13 at the Democratic National Convention in
Charlotte on September 4 demanding justice for Trayvon Martin. "We just want the one who killed him to pay the price of
justice as a deterrent from it happening again," Jackson said.
"There is simply too much violence, too much racial violence.
We as a nation must become more civil and more caring, but I
do want us in the process to remain nonviolent, and disciplined
and focused."[†]

Williams quoted T. Willard Fair, the president of the Urban
League of Greater Miami, who asked, "Wouldn't you think to
have 41 people shot [in Chicago] between Friday morning and
Monday morning would be much more newsworthy and deserve much more outrage?"

On March 19, WGN News in Chicago reported on the violent weekend in the nation's third most populated city. Forty-six
people shot, nine dead. The youngest murder victim was six
years old. WGN quoted Father Michael Pfleger as saying, "This
is something that should be talked about in every school today,

---

‡    Williams' figure is backed up by a report by the Bureau of Justice Statis-
     tics based on homicide data from 1980 through 2008.

†    According to the Bureau of Justice Statistics, during the period from
     1980 through 2008, 93% of black homicide victims were killed by other
     blacks, 84% of white victims by other whites. During every single year of
     that period, black-on-white homicides outnumbered white-on-black
     homicides. According to data from the Tuskegee Institute, between 1882
     and 1968, 3,446 blacks were lynched by whites, a little more than half
     the number of blacks that, in recent years, have been killed by other
     blacks in the United States each year.

in every one today, in every church today."

But people nationwide weren't talking about the shootings in Chicago; they were talking about one killing in Sanford, Florida. The nation was going on red alert over a death that so many viewed as a heinous racially-motivated slaying of an innocent black teenager for doing nothing more than walking home with a bag of Skittles and a can of iced tea. But while so many in the nation declared, "I am Trayvon Martin," nobody seemed to care about a seven-year-old-girl named Heaven Sutton, who, on June 27, was shot and killed outside her home on Chicago's West Side. She was killed while selling candy outside her home, something her mother had arranged to keep the neighborhood children close at hand because there had been so many shootings in the area.

"She looked forward every day to opening up the candy store," the little girl's mother, Ashake Banks, told the Chicago Tribune, "and for somebody just to come take her life, it's not right." Banks was planning to take her daughter to Disney World the following month. The little girl had never been.

While arguments of the injustice of the acquittal of Till's killers may be strong, Sanford, Florida, in the year 2012 is far from the Mississippi Delta in 1955. But strong views of the impending injustice of allowing George Zimmerman to get away with Martin's murder brewed on the black American consciousness. "With the whole world watching, what will happen to George Zimmerman?" Leigh Davenport asked. "If brought to trial, how will our nation react if he is tried and acquitted by a jury of his peers? And if so, what will that mean for our Black boys and all of us who love them?" Davenport, writing before Zimmerman was even charged with a crime and before the public knew much of anything about Martin's death, was already pondering the racial implications of Zimmerman's acquittal. In other words, it didn't matter what really happened that night. Apparently all that mattered was that an unarmed black teenager was shot and killed by a non-black man because beyond that fact, almost nothing was publicly known about the shooting.

Early on, George Zimmerman was spoken of as white. Then

it was learned that he was born to a white father and a Peruvian mother. Then he became, in the media's phrasing, a "white Hispanic", a nonsensical description that somehow set about to change America's longstanding cultural belief that black is black, white is white, and Hispanic is Hispanic.‡ In this new description, black was still black, but white and Hispanic were no longer different. Somehow George Zimmerman's status had been elevated from minority to majority—an "honorary white" as Manhattan Institute scholar Heather MacDonald called him. Zimmerman, whose father was away in the military during much of his childhood, was raised by his Peruvian mother and grandmother. Spanish was his first language, English his second.

Former CBS News correspondent and Fox News analyst Bernard Goldberg appeared on *America Live* with Megyn Kelly expressing his dismay at news media handling of the case. "While no decent person is happy about what happened, no matter what your politics, there are some people whose purposes are served by what happened," Goldberg said. "And I'll tell you about the two: The national media. The national media doesn't do stories about black-on-black crime. It doesn't interest them. They don't do stories about black-on-white crime, which happens in far, far greater numbers than white-on-black crimes. They don't do those stories either. But this is like a movie script handed to them from Hollywood. Oh my goodness! A white guy—or, in this case, a white Hispanic guy—shoots an unarmed black kid. Perfect story."

"He's only a white Hispanic," Goldberg explained, "because they need the word 'white' to further the storyline, which is 'white, probably racist vigilante shoots unarmed black kid.'"

On March 28, National Review Online editor-at-large Jonah Goldberg commented on a New York Times column by Charles Blow, in which Blow claimed that "the burden of black boys" is racial stereotyping and said that official handling of Martin's killing "can either ease or exacerbate it." "No doubt, white—

---

‡    A March 22 article in the New York Times, for example, referred to Zimmerman as "a white Hispanic". Reuters and other media outlets also used the term.

and 'white Hispanic'—prejudice is a problem for young black men," Goldberg wrote, pointing out the disparity between white-on-black crime and both black-on-white and black-on-black violence, "but the notion that it is the singular or chief 'burden of black boys in America' is nonsense."

Mediaite columnist Tommy Christoper pointed out that 'white' and 'black' are racial designations, while 'Latino' or 'Hispanic' are ethnic designations. Even the U.S. Census Bureau and the FBI follow such designations. But as Erik Wemple pointed out in the Washington Post on March 28, the New York Times' use of the term was "rare". In fact, according to Wemple, New York Times standards editor Phil Corbett admitted that the terms "white Hispanic" and "white and Hispanic" are "not very commonly used." Corbett denied that the paper was "trying to make some larger point", and he explained that they dropped the term in their coverage of Martin's killing because "[s]ome readers seemed to find them distracting or confusing". "To suggest that our coverage of this story or our description of Mr. Zimmerman is intended to serve an agenda or push a political view," Corbett said, "is simply ridiculous. It's just false."

Zimmerman's supporters, too, made outlandish accusations. One photograph showing a bare-chested teen proudly displaying both middle fingers was widely circulated as being a social networking photograph of Trayvon Martin. The problem was that it was the wrong Trayvon Martin. This one was from Georgia, not Miami, and anyone looking at his face should have quickly recognized it wasn't the same person. But one photograph of the real Trayvon Martin taken from his Twitter page showed the teen displaying one middle finger, and Zimmerman supporters made it a point to circulate the picture. While some would argue that the photograph debunked the angelic image of Martin portrayed by the five-year-old photos most of the media had been publishing, others would claim that the more current middle finger picture was nothing less than an attempt to smear Martin's reputation and paint him as a young black thug who deserved to die.

But much of the nation saw the shooting as nothing less than an unjustifiable murder of an unarmed teenager who was profiled for being black and wearing a hoodie. Protests began. Million hoodie marches were organized. Congressional representatives donned hoodies while speaking from the House floor. Sanford's police chief lost his job. The FBI launched a civil rights investigation. The Seminole County State Attorney was forced to step aside. A special prosecutor was appointed, and, ultimately, George Zimmerman was arrested and charged with second-degree murder.

"The unlawful killing of a human being, when perpetrated by any act imminently dangerous to another and evincing a depraved mind regardless of human life," Florida law reads, "although without any premeditated design to effect the death of any particular individual, is murder in the second degree . . . ." The maximum sentence is life in prison.

While Zimmerman's actions that February evening may well constitute second-degree murder, his fate, in many ways, has already been tried in the court of public opinion. Released on bond and restricted to living in Seminole County, Zimmerman was forced to reside as a recluse for fear of his own safety. Rumors swirled of rewards offered to any private investigator who could uncover his hideout.

The amount of misinformation spread in the social and news media about the killing has exposed the tendency of so many in the public to believe almost anything, however outlandish it may be, as long as it jibed with their preconceived notions about what happened at Twin Lakes. Martin family attorneys Benjamin Crump and Natalie Jackson appeared before reporters to claim that Zimmerman fired two shots. Jackson mistakenly believed that a loud sound heard on Witness 11's 911 call was actually a warning shot fired by the neighborhood watch captain several seconds before he killed the teenager. "You hear a shot, a clear shot," Jackson said, "then you hear a 17-year-old boy begging for his life then you hear a second shot."

On March 20, Orlando Sentinel reporters Rene Stutzman and Bianca Prieto wrote, "Those statements fueled a great deal of anger and frustration among those following the case in cyberspace. Twitter, Facebook and other social media exploded with news that two shots were fired." Although Jackson and Crump would later learn the truth, such blatant and uniformed speculation undoubtedly tainted public perception of the case. While the attorneys were quick to make unsubstantiated claims, they were not so quick to admit they were wrong. When questioned by Sentinel reporters about evidence contradicting the attorneys' claims, Jackson and Crump responded with a prepared statement. "Regardless of how many times George Zimmerman pulled the trigger that night," the statement read, "unfortunately for Trayvon Martin, it only took a single bullet to end his life."

While Zimmerman fired one fatal bullet into Martin's chest, Crump fired volley after volley of inaccurate and misleading information into the center of public discourse on the killing. He paraded witnesses Mary Cutcher and Selma Mora Lamilla before reporters to have Cutcher publicly state her opinion that Zimmerman had not acted in self-defense, despite the fact that the woman admitted she hadn't seen anything take place until after the shot was fired. Cutcher claimed that the "crying" voice she heard had to have been that of "the little boy" because it stopped after the shot. But Cutcher's logic is about as scientific as a flip of a coin. Although restricted to a boolean choice, at least a coin toss gives a random result. Cutcher's claim, on the other hand, was clearly influenced by her undeniable bias, so much so that she concocted an elaborate story of what she thinks happened when Zimmerman confronted Martin. But the truth is, she has no clue.

As an attorney, Crump had to know that Cutcher's claims would never be heard inside a courtroom. Fact witnesses can testify to what they saw, what they heard, what they smelled. They cannot testify to their opinions about what happened or their speculation about how events they didn't witness may have taken place. They can testify to what they know about the case, not what they learned later from neighbors or news media.

Bloggers from all over have opined on what they believe took place that night. Zimmerman couldn't have reached for his pistol while lying on the ground. A man in white referred to by witnesses must have been Zimmerman's friend, Frank Taaffe, who was an accomplice to the shooting. Witness 6, the 911 caller who stepped oustide and told the two he was calling 911 must have been a Zimmerman confederate, presumably because he claimed to have seen Martin on top of Zimmerman "throwing down blows" in what he described as a "ground and pound". Liars became truth tellers; truth teller became liars.

This case, in many ways, epitomizes the ubiquitous phrase, "rush to judgment." It's not about whether Zimmerman did or didn't commit a crime, whether he should or shouldn't have been arrested and charged. It's about being right for the right reasons. The right answer, if reached for the wrong reasons, is still wrong.

At the root of so much of the misinformation surrounding this case is the fact that so few in the public, including those who reported on it and speculated about it in the media, have any real appreciation for how one goes about reconstructing a shooting such as this one. Speculation isn't allowed in a court of law. A witness's opinion that the shooting was not in self-defense will never be heard by a jury, especially when that witness admits she didn't even see the shooting happen. And while prosecutors will likely argue that he did, no witness will be allowed to testify that George Zimmerman in any way profiled Trayvon Martin, racially or otherwise. The jury will hear the facts, they will hear the arguments of the attorneys, and *they* will decide whether to find Zimmerman guilty of a crime. Finding the facts, then, is at the center of the case against George Michael Zimmerman.

Arguing a case on fake facts is a surefire way of losing in court. When the facts are proven wrong, the argument falls apart. In the prosecution of a crime, it is particularly important for the State to stay within realistic boundaries of what the evidence proves. The farther a prosecutor strays from the truth, the more he or she dances with the devil. When the jury sees through it, the defendant goes free.

One of the biggest mistakes that many people make with regard to reconstructing a crime scene is the overuse of inductive reasoning. Crime scene reconstruction is a process of logic.

It is the assemblage of scientific and investigative data into a coherent representation of past events. The pieces are put together; the picture is formed, at least enough of the picture that the missing pieces may be interpolated. Logic is at its root. The crime scene reconstructionist must strive to apply proper logic and well-founded reason that is as free from bias as is humanly possible.

"The use of correct reasoning processes," wrote Charles and Gregory O'Hara in their text, *Fundamentals of Criminal Investigation*, "must be learned by conscious application, and constant vigilance against the pitfalls of false premises, logical fallacies, unjustifiable inferences, ignorance of conceivable alternatives, and failure to distinguish between the factual and the probable."

Crime scene reconstruction employs both deductive and inductive reasoning to answer questions associated with the commission of a particular crime. Deductive reasoning is the process of moving from the general to the specific. A deductive statement might read as follows: "Fingerprints can only be deposited on an item if the donor touches that item. The suspect's fingerprints are on the window; therefore, the suspect touched the window." As long as the base principle is valid, the conclusion is likewise valid. Inductive reasoning, however, moves from the specific to the general. Inductive reasoning, while necessary and useful for crime scene reconstruction, must be carefully employed, and it generally leads to statements of probability rather than certainty. In their text, *Criminal Investigation: A Method for Reconstructing the Past*, James Osterburg and Richard Ward explain: "[C]onsider the man who notes that of the 10 species of bird he observed, all are able to fly. When he induces from this observation that all birds fly, he will be incorrect." In fact, there are numerous species of birds that do not fly.

To make scientific study of criminal matters a valid fact-finding tool, it must be based on a proper understanding of the underlying physical, physiological, and psychological phenomena. Supposition must be replaced by critical study of the evidence. To accomplish this type of analysis, practitioners rely on substantive research. That research, unfortunately, is not always readily available.

A committee of the National Academy of Sciences issued a report that was, in many ways, strongly critical of the current state of forensic science. One of the committee's major criticisms was the paucity of research on which forensic science has relied. "The simple reality is that the interpretation of forensic evidence," the committee wrote, "is not always based on scientific studies to determine its validity."

The committee does, however, clarify one issue important to crime scene reconstruction: that the value of forensic evidence is directly proportional to the context in which the evidence is viewed. "In evaluating the accuracy of a forensic analysis, it is crucial to clarify the type of question the analysis is called on to address," the committee writes, referring to identification evidence. "Thus, although some techniques may be too imprecise to permit accurate identification of a specific individual, they may still provide useful and accurate information about questions of classification."

This concept is equally true of crime scene reconstruction. Precise evidence leads to precise conclusions; imprecise evidence leads to imprecise conclusions, but not useless ones. This distinction is critical to the understanding of crime scene reconstruction as a process. Practitioners need not be limited by the constraints of definition. Unknowns have been dealt with in science for millennia, yet scientific progress has not slowed. Successful scientists have embraced the unknowns, understood their effect on analysis, and used them to define the limits of the science and guide scientists in pushing the envelope.

◈

In the months following the shooting, many have opined on Zimmerman's guilt, and others, albeit in fewer numbers, have opined on his innocence. Some have questioned Zimmerman's account; others have concocted elaborate stories of what they think happened. But the lynch mob sentiment that swelled in the wake of the killing isn't what will be heard in court. When the forensic evidence is presented, the six jurors deciding Zimmerman's fate will know about facts that few in the public have heard.

# Stand Your Ground

*"My head felt like it was going to explode."*

—George Zimmerman

"In August of 2011 my neighbor's house was broken into while she was home with her infant son," George Zimmerman wrote in a statement to police. Writing on an official Sanford Police Department form, the neighborhood-watch-volunteer-turned-gunman explained what led him to kill Trayvon Martin.

He wrote in cursive, skipping every other line. His full name is written at the top of the page: George Michael Zimmerman. His address has been blacked out on the redacted form, sanitized for public release. His date of birth, Social Security number, telephone number, height, weight, eye color, and hair color have also been blacked out. Zimmerman's name is written differently on each page. On the first page, his full middle name is written out. The third page has only his middle initial. The second and fourth pages, no middle name at all. At the bottom of each page, there is a handwritten notation: "Suspect Statement". The same handwriting appears at the top of each page where the date and a simple label of "shooting" are written. It is not Zimmerman's handwriting, though. And each page is signed at the bottom by Detective Doris Singleton, ID number 5011.

"The intruders attempted to attack her and her child," Zimmerman continued. He correctly spliced together two independent clauses using a semicolon, the conjunctive adverb "however", and a comma. "SPD reported to the scene of the crime and the robbers fled."

Zimmerman explained his concern over the burglaries that had been occurring at Twin Lakes. "My wife saw the intruders running from the home," Zimmerman explained, "and became scared of the rising crime within our neighborhood." Zimmerman explained that he and several neighbors formed the now-infamous Retreat at Twin Lakes neighborhood watch.

"We were instructed by SPD to call the non-emergency line if we saw anything suspicious," Zimmerman wrote, "[and] 911 if we saw a crime in progress."

"Tonight, I was on my way to the grocery store," he continued, "when I saw a male approximately 5'11" to 6'2" casually walking in the rain looking into homes." Zimmerman explained that he stopped his truck and called Sanford police, using the non-emergency number as instructed. It wasn't, after all, a crime in progress.

"I told the dispatcher what I had witnessed," Zimmerman wrote. "The dispatcher took note of my location [and] the suspect fled to a darkened area of the sidewalk. As the dispatcher was asking me for an exact location the suspect emerged from the darkness [and] circled my vehicle." Zimmerman didn't write out the word "and" but instead used a common adaptation of the ampersand.[†]

"I could not hear if he said anything," Zimmerman continued. "The suspect once again disappeared between the back of some houses. The dispatcher once again asked me for my exact location. I could not remember the name of the street so I got out of my car to look for a street sign."[‡] Zimmerman was on Twin Trees Lane, a road that runs across the middle of the complex from the front entrance to the back of the neighborhood. Retreat View Circle wraps around the perimeter of the complex, encircling Twin Trees. Zimmerman lived on the west side of Retreat View; Martin was staying with Brandy Green, who lived on the east side of the circle.

---

[†]   Where Zimmerman used an ampersand, the symbol has been replaced by the spelled-out word set off in brackets.

[‡]   Zimmerman claimed to have been looking for a street sign; however, many have challenged that notion as unbelievable. There are only three named streets in the complex. Zimmerman was a neighborhood watch volunteer in the community who would be expected to know the names of the streets. Furthermore, police photographs and video show that street signs are only present at the intersections between two streets; the nearest street sign, therefore, was behind Zimmerman near the clubhouse where he was when he first dialed police. The altercation with Martin occurred in the opposite direction, away from the street sign.

"The dispatcher asked me for a description and the direction the suspect went," Zimmerman wrote. "I told the dispatcher I did not know but I was out of my vehicle looking for a street sign [and] the direction the suspect went. The dispatcher told me not to follow the suspect [and] that an officer was in route [*sic*]."†

Zimmerman's written account jumps from the point where the dispatcher told him not to follow Martin to where the physical altercation began. At least two minutes passed between that portion of his conversation with the dispatcher and the beginning of his encounter with Martin.

"As I headed back to my vehicle," Zimmerman wrote, "the suspect emerged from the darkness and said, 'You got a problem'." Zimmerman did not use any punctuation to indicate if Martin was asking a question or making a statement, but Zimmerman wrote that he said "no", indicating that he took Martin's words as being a question. According to Zimmerman, Martin then said, "You do now."

Zimmerman tried to find his phone to call 911. Martin, Zimmerman claimed, punched him in the nose. "I fell backwards onto my back," Zimmerman wrote. "The suspect got on top of me. I yelled 'Help' several times. The suspect told me to 'shut the fuck up'.

"As I tried to sit up right [*sic*]," Zimmerman continued, "the suspect grabbed my head and slammed it into the concrete sidewalk several times." Zimmerman described how the fight continued.

"I continued to yell 'Help'," Zimmerman wrote. "Each time I

---

† Zimmerman's claim does not comport with the recording of his call to police. The only time the dispatcher asked about the direction Martin went was immediately after Zimmerman said, "Shit, he's running." The dispatcher asked, "He's running? Which way is he running?" Zimmerman replied, "Down towards the other entrance to the neighborhood." The dispatcher inquired, and Zimmerman clarified that Martin was running toward the back entrance of the complex. "Are you following him?" the dispatcher asked. "No," Zimmerman replied. At the time that he wrote the statement, Zimmerman did not have the benefit of hearing the recording of his call to police. Whether intentionally deceptive or just a faulty recollection, Zimmerman's written account of what was said was incorrect.

attempted to sit up, the suspect slammed my head into the side
walk. My head felt like it was going to explode. I tried to slide
out from under the suspect and continue [*sic*] to yell 'Help'."

Zimmerman claimed that Martin tried to smother him. "As I
slid," the neighborhood watchman wrote, "the suspect covered
my mouth and nose and stopped my breathing. At this point I
felt the suspect reach for my now exposed firearm and say
'Your [*sic*] gonna die tonight Mother Fucker'."

Zimmerman responded with deadly force. "I unholstered
my firearm in fear for my life as he assured he was going to kill
me and fired one shot into his torso," Zimmerman explained.
"The suspect sat back allowing me to sit up and said 'You got
me'. At this point I slid out from underneath him and got on
top of the suspect holding his hands away from his body."

While Zimmerman was holding Martin's hands, a neighbor
spoke to him. "An onlooker appeared and asked me if I was
OK," Zimmerman explained. "I said 'no'. He said 'I'm calling
911'. I said I don't need you to call 911. I'd already called
them. I need you to help me restrain this guy."

Police arrived quickly. "At this point a SPD officer arrived,"
Zimmerman wrote, "and asked 'who shot him'. I said 'I did' and
I placed my hands on top of my head and told the officer where
on my person my firearm was holstered. The officer handcuffed
me and disarmed me. The officer then placed me in the back of
his vehicle." Zimmerman wrote nothing else about the shooting
that night.

◈

The day of the shooting, Investigator Doris Singleton recorded
a twenty-six minute interview of Zimmerman at Sanford police
headquarters. "I'm going to read you your Miranda rights," Singleton told Zimmerman, "because obviously you're here and
you're not free to go because we've got to figure out what's going on."

"You have the right to remain silent," Singleton admon-
ished Zimmerman, "and you don't have to talk to me, OK?"
Singleton continued with the well-known warning: anything
you say can be used against you; you have the right to an attor-

ney; if you cannot afford an attorney, one will be appointed to represent you.

"Do you understand these rights?" Singleton asked.

"Yes, ma'am," Zimmerman replied.

"And do you want to talk to me?"

"Yes, ma'am."

Singleton told Zimmerman to tell his story. Zimmerman explained that there had been "crimes" in the community and he had started a neighborhood watch program in response.

Zimmerman said that he didn't know who Martin was. "I'd never seen him in the neighborhood," Zimmerman explained. "I know all the residents."

As Zimmerman was telling his story, he was interrupted when Singleton was called by another investigator inquiring about video surveillance in the neighborhood. Zimmerman said that there were cameras there, but last he knew they weren't working.

Singleton asked if Zimmerman had contact information for management at the gated complex. Zimmerman did. Kent Taylor with Leeland Management in Orlando. But he didn't know the phone number. It was in his cell phone, but police took his cell phone when they brought him to the station. Singleton left the room to go find Zimmerman's phone.

When the interview resumed, Zimmerman explained that he had called police in the past to report suspicious people who he thought had been associated with the burglaries in the neighborhood.

"I had called before, and the police had come out," Zimmerman  told Singleton, "but these guys know the neighborhood very well. They would cut in between buildings and lose —"

"You're saying 'these guys'," Singleton interrupted. "Who are these guys?"

"The people committing the burglaries," Zimmerman replied.

"So you've seen more than one person like looking suspicious and doing these burglaries?"

"Yes, ma'am."

"But you never had seen *this guy* prior to tonight, or you don't know?"

"I don't recall. I have called a few times. You guys probably have the records. I've probably called a half a dozen times."

Zimmerman explained that he was headed to the grocery store when he saw Martin near a house the neighborhood watch leader had called police to before. He explained that the owner of the residence "leaves his doors unlocked and stuff."

"He was walking leisurely and looking at the houses," Zimmerman explained, speaking about Martin. "So I just pulled me car to the side, and I called the non-emergency line."

"Were you armed at this point?"

"Yes, ma'am."

"You were already armed."

"Yes, ma'am."

"OK."

"I called the non-emergency line, and I just reported that there was a suspicious person in the neighborhood. The dispatcher—whoever answered the phone—asked me where they went. And I said I wasn't sure because I lost visual of him when he went in between houses. And he said, well, can you tell what direction he went, and I said not really. And then all of a sudden I see him circling my car, and then he goes back into the darkness."

"You pull out of your house and you're heading . . . down the road as you're looking at him."

"Yes, ma'am."

"You're on the phone, and he dips between two houses? Is that what you mean?"

"Yes, ma'am."

"Because you lose sight of him."

"Correct. And then he comes back out and circles my car while I'm on the phone with the police."

"OK, is he saying anything to you?"

"I couldn't hear him. My windows were up. As soon as I saw him coming up, I rolled up my windows and I stayed on the phone with dispatch."

"Your car was running?"

"Yes."

"The lights were on?"

"Yes, ma'am."

"So he knew somebody was in this car?"

"Yes, ma'am."

"Is he walking completely around the car?"

"Yes, ma'am."

"OK."

"And dispatch asked me where he went. I didn't know the name of the street that I was on."

"So you had come off your street and gotten to another street?"

"Yes, ma'am, that goes and cuts through the middle of my neighborhood. I didn't know the name of the street or where he went, so I got out of my car to look for the street sign and to see if I could see where he cut through so I could tell the police."

"So, after he circled your car he disappeared again?"

"Yes, ma'am."

"OK."

"Then the dispatcher told me, 'Where are you?' And I said I'm trying to find out where he went. And he said, 'We don't need you to do that.' And I said, 'OK.' He said, 'We already have a police officer enroute.' And I said, 'Alright.' I had gone . . . through the dog walk where I normally walk my dog and walked back through to my street, the street that loops around. And he said, 'We already have a police officer on the way.' So, I said, 'OK.'"

Zimmerman explained how Martin confronted him as he walked back to his truck on the other side of the dog walk. "So I was walking back through to where my car was," Zimmerman explained, "and he jumped out from the bushes. And he said, 'What the fuck's your problem, homey?' And I got my cell phone out to call 911 this time. And I said, 'Hey, man. I don't have a problem.' And he goes, 'No, now you have a problem.' And he punched me in the nose. At that point, I fell down. I tried to defend myself. He just started punching me in the face. I started screaming for help. I couldn't see. I couldn't breathe.

Then he started taking my head—"

"And you're still standing at this point?" Singleton asked.

"No, ma'am. I fell to the ground when he punched me the first time."

"OK."

"It was dark. I didn't even see him getting ready to punch me. As soon as he punched me, I fell backwards into the grass. Then he grabbed—he was wailing on my head. Then I started yelling help. When I started yelling for help, he grabbed my head and started hitting my head into the—I tried to sit up and yell for help, and then he grabbed my head and started hitting it into the sidewalk. When he started doing that, I slid into the grass to try and get out from under him so that he would stop hitting my head into the sidewalk and I'm still yelling for help. And I could see people looking and some guy yells out, 'I'm calling 911.' And I said, 'Help me! Help me! He's killing me!' And he puts his hand on my nose and on my moth. And he says, 'You're going to die tonight.' And I don't remember much after that. I just remember I couldn't breathe and then he still kept trying to hit my head against the pavement or I don't know if there was a sign or what it was. So, I just—oh, when I slid, my jacket and my shirt came up. And when he said, 'You're going to die tonight,' I felt his hand go down on my side, and I thought he was going for my firearm. So I grabbed it immediately, and as he banged my head again, I just pulled out my firearm and shot him."

"OK," Singleton said. "And then what happened? You're both on the ground and he's on top of you?"

"I'm on my back. He's on top of me. He's mounted on top of me, and I just shot him and then he falls of and he's like, 'Alright. You got it. You got it.'"

"Does he fall to the side and he stays laying on the ground or does—"

"I don't remember."

"OK."

"My vision was blurry, and—"

"You didn't feel him fall toward you? He somehow ended up to one side or the other or you don't know?"

"I don't remember. I think when I shot him it might have pushed him back, but I remember I didn't know what he was hitting—it felt like he was hitting me with bricks. So I remember . . . once I shot him, I holstered my firearm and I got on top of him and I held his hands out because he was still talking. And I said 'Stay down. Don't move.' Then somebody comes out, and I couldn't see. There was a flashlight on my head, so I asked if it was a police officer. And he said no, it was a witness, but he was calling the police. And I said, 'The police are on their way. They should be here already because I called.'"

◈

Just after midnight, Serino recorded a six-minute interview with Zimmerman at the Sanford police station.

"What's your date of birth, sir?" Serino asked.

"10/5/83," Zimmerman replied.

"Highest level of education?"

"Associate's degree."

"In what?"

"Criminal justice." Zimmerman's answer wasn't quite accurate. Although in his final semester at Seminole State College, he had not yet graduated. Documents released in April, the New York Daily News reported, showed that Zimmerman "was a mediocre college student" who earned a C in a class called "Evil Minds, Violent Predators", a D in each of two other criminal justice classes, and failing grades in two algebra classes. Zimmerman did earn an A in "Criminal Litigation" and a B in "Criminal Investigation". Zimmerman didn't earn his degree, though; in the wake of the shooting, Zimmerman, who was on academic probation at the time, was kicked out of school.

"You been read your rights correctly?" Serino asked.

"Yes, sir," Zimmerman replied meekly.

"You understand that you're not quite free to go because we're in the process of [investigating] but you're not quite going to jail—that kind of stuff?"

"Yes, sir."

"I got the gist of it all. I'm going to ask you a quick question. This photograph that I'm showing you right here—"

"Yes, sir."

"Do you recognize that face?"

"No, sir."

"OK, this is the person that . . . had the incident with you today?"

"Yes, sir."

"Uh, I don't know who he is," Serino said with a sigh. The sound of a slap on the table is heard. "Real briefly, let me tell you what I got, OK? You were going to the store?"

"Yes, sir."

"And you saw somebody who [you] felt to be suspicious?"

"Yes, sir."

"This suspicious person you—because of the break-ins in the neighborhood you decided to call 911?"

"No, sir. The non-emergency line."

"You called non-emergency?"

"Yes, sir."

"OK, the 665-6650 or—"

"The 5199."

"OK, so you did non-emergency?"

"Yes, sir."

"You reported a suspicious person?"

"Yes, sir."

"You followed this person?"

"Yes, sir."

"You lost visual on this person?"

"Yes, sir." Zimmerman was almost whispering in stark contrast to Serino's booming voice.

"Where did this whole thing start at?"

"Retreat View Circle in the—"

"OK, tomorrow," Serino interrupted. "Tomorrow morning in the daylight hours. Do you work?"

"Yes, sir."

"Where?"

"Digital Risk Maitland."

"When do you get off of work?"

"Five p.m."

"When do you start work?"

"Nine a.m."

"Nine a.m.? OK, five p.m. tomorrow when you get off work and you get home, can you call me?"

"Yes, sir."

"So we can go ahead and walk through the scene entirely."

Zimmerman told Serino that he had a class. He was working on his Bachelor's degree. He could skip the class, though.

"I want to retrace your path—exactly what happened. . . . I want to videotape this," Serino explains. "The difference between statutes and homicide and justifiable homicide, use of force—you're aware of them. You have a degree. You're familiar with what we're talking about here, right?"

"Yes, sir."

"OK, you follow this person. . . . You lose sight of this person. You're walking in the darkness out there. [Did] you have a flashlight?"

"It was dead. I had one, but it was dead."

"You have to hit it a couple times. It's on right now, so—"

"Oh, is this it?"

"Yeah. It's probably like the one I have. You've got to smack it around a couple times," Serino explained. "This person . . . jumped you from somewhere?"

"Yes, sir."

"From the darkness?"

"Yes, sir."

"Did he say anything to you?"

"Yes, sir."

"What did he say to you?"

"When he came up to me, he said, 'You got a problem?' I said, 'No.' And then I went to reach for my phone to find my phone to call 911 instead of non-emergency."

"OK."

"And then he punched me—he said, 'You have a problem now,' and then he punched me in the face."

"OK, he punched and you fell?"

"Yes, sir."

"And you got injuries? Where did he punch you, in your face or your chest or where?"

"In my face. My head—I mean, all over my head."

"OK, you've cleaned up already, because Officer Smith said that you were pretty much battered when—?"

"Yes, sir."

"He mounted you basically?"

"Yes, sir."

"And he started to beat up on you?"

"Yes, sir."

"At what point did you draw your weapon?"

"After he hit my head against the concrete several times, uh, yelled out for help and then he tried to smother my mouth —"

"Who yelled for help?"

"I did."

"OK, at which point he did what?"

"He smothered my mouth and my nose."

"OK."

"And when he did that, I tried to slide out and squirm and I realized . . . my shirt came up and I felt him slide his hand towards my right side and he said, 'You're going to die, mother fucker.' And that's when I grabbed it. I—I don't know if it was away from him or, you know, I just unholstered."

"So he was going for your gun?"

"Yes, sir."

"What kind of gun was it?"

"A PF—a Kel-Tec PF-9."

"Nine millimeter?"

"Nine millimeter."

"Semi-automatic?"

"Yes, sir."

"What kind of ammunition?"

"I think it was hollow point."

"What happened then?"

"I *shot* him." Zimmerman emphasized the word "shot".

"Were you able to unholster entirely? You cleared the holster?"

"Yes, sir."

"One time?"

"One time."

"When you shot him, what happened?"

"He kind of sat up and he said, 'You got me.' And so I—I don't remember if I pushed him or he fell but somehow I got out from under him, and when he was hitting me I don't know what he was hitting me with. I thought he had something in his hands. So I grabbed his hands when I was on top of him and I spread his hands away from his body because he was still talking." Zimmerman couldn't remember what Martin was saying.

Serino told Zimmerman that he "was going to have anxiety over" the shooting "and nightmares". He relayed briefly his understanding of what the neighborhood watchman had told him.

"So in your mind's eye this person was committing no good over there," Serino said. "You followed in good faith to see what he was doing. He jumped you. He attacked you. OK, he reached for your gun. You discharged. You got off of him. You only shot once. Police arrived. You surrendered, and here you are."

"He told me he was going to kill me."

"Exactly. He said he was going to kill you."

"Yes, sir."

Serino asked Zimmerman if there "was anything else" that he wanted to add. That was it. Zimmerman had told his story.

◈

On February 27 at 5:20 p.m., less than twenty-four hours after the shooting, Zimmerman participated in a videotaped walk-through of the events with investigators from the Sanford Police Department. Zimmerman showed the detectives where he first saw Martin between two buildings about a block from the neighborhood watchman's house.

"Right here," Zimmerman explained. "Right in front of this house."

"Right in front of 1460?" a detective asked.

"Yes, sir," Zimmerman replied. "He was walking like in the grassy area . . . between these two poles. Like I said, it was rainy. He wasn't—he was just leisurely looking at the house."

"I left for the grocery store," Zimmerman explained, "and I

just felt like something was off about him. . . . There's been a history of break-ins in that building, and I called previously about this house." Zimmerman pointed to the two adjacent buildings where he first saw Martin. "When the police arrived at this house when I called the first time," Zimmerman continued, "the windows were opened and the doors were unlocked, and the police came and secured it. So I said, you know what, it's better to just call, I kept driving. I passed him, and he was— he kept staring at me and staring around, looking around to see who else was—I don't know why he was looking."

"Did he walk off from there," the detective inquired, "or did he stop there last night?"

"He stopped," Zimmerman replied, "and he like looked around. That's why—that's what threw me off. It's raining. I didn't understand why somebody would be just stopping in the rain especially—it wasn't like somebody was trying to run to get out of the rain, and I'd never seen him before. It didn't look like he was exercising."

"Where did he—where was he standing at when you— when he stopped?" the detective inquired.

"Right there," Zimmerman said, pointing at one of the homes. "Right in front of 1460."

"On the sidewalk, or in the grass area?"

"No, in the grassy area." The camera panned to show the area where Zimmerman first saw Martin.

"I drove past him," Zimmerman continued, "and I went to the clubhouse." Zimmerman showed the investigators where he parked in front of the clubhouse.

"This is where you got out?" a detective asked.

"No," Zimmerman replied. "This is where I just stopped to call. . . . Then he walked past me and he kept looking at my car —still looking around at the houses and stuff."

Zimmerman continued his explanation of what took place. "[The] dispatcher said, 'Where did he go? What direction did he go in?' and I said, 'I don't know.'" Zimmerman explained that Martin turned right onto Twin Trees Lane and he lost sight of him.*

---

*    No such conversation took place during Zimmerman's call to police. The

According to Zimmerman, the dispatcher asked, "Can you get to somewhere where you can see him?"

"So I backed out," Zimmerman explained.[†]

The detective backed the car out from the parking space in front of the clubhouse and continued on Retreat View Circle the short distance to Twin Trees Lane. Zimmerman directed the detective to turn right on Twin Trees and then follow the road around to the left as it winded toward the cut-through near where Zimmerman got out of his truck.

"I parked right about where that sign is in the yard," Zimmerman explained. He described Martin's direction of travel. "And I saw him walk through that way and then cut through the back of the houses."

"He looked back and he noticed me and he cut back through the houses," Zimmerman explained. "I was still on the phone with non-emergency. And then he came back and he started walking up towards the grass and then came down and circled my car and I told the operator that."[‡]

"He was circling my car," Zimmerman continued. "I didn't hear if he said anything, but he had his hand in his waistband. I think I told the operator that, and they said, 'Where are you?' And I could not remember the name of this street because I don't live on this street."

Zimmerman said that the dispatcher asked for an address. "He goes, 'We need an address,'" Zimmerman explained, "and I said, 'I don't know an address.' I think I gave them my address."[†]

---

only time the dispatcher asked him about Martin's location or direction of travel was after Zimmerman said, "Shit, he's running."

[†]    Zimmerman said he backed out, but there are only two times in the recording that he can be heard moving the vehicle's gear selector—once to put it in drive and a second time to put it in park.

[‡]    Zimmerman never told the dispatcher that Martin was circling his vehicle; however, he did say, "[H]e's coming to check me out." He says this in between the two sounds of him moving his truck's gearshift suggesting that he was still driving as Martin began to circle his truck.

[†]    Zimmerman provided directions to where his truck was parked, but not at the request of the dispatcher as he claimed in his walk-through inter-

"And then I thought to get out and look for a street sign," Zimmerman went on to explain. "So I got out of my car and I started walking."

The detective had Zimmerman get out so they could walk Zimmerman's path of travel. As they walked, Zimmerman said, "I was still on the phone with non-emergency and I started walking down this way." Zimmerman walked toward the sidewalk that runs between Twin Trees Lane and Retreat View Circle, toward the area where the shooting took place.

"I didn't see a street sign here," Zimmerman explained, "but I knew if I went straight through that that's Retreat View Circle and I could give him an address because he said, 'Just give me the address of the house you're in front of.'" Walking on the sidewalk, Zimmerman could only see the backs of the houses and couldn't see any house numbers.[‡]

As Zimmerman approached the "T" intersection in the sidewalk, he told the detectives that he turned to look for Martin. "I got to about here, and I had a flashlight with me," Zimmerman said. "The flashlight was dead, though. And I looked around. I didn't see anybody, and I told non-emergency, I said, 'You know what? He's gone.'

"I still thought I could use their address," Zimmerman explained, pointing toward a home on Retreat View Circle. "I actually walked all the way to the street, and I was going to give them this address, and they said, 'Well, if he's not there, do you still want a police officer?' and I said, 'Yes.'"

"They said, 'Do you still want a police officer?' and I said, 'Yes'," Zimmerman repeated. "And they said, 'Are you following him?' Oh, I'm sorry, back there, they said, 'Are you following him?'" Zimmerman turned and pointed back toward the "T", the direction from which he had come. "And I said, 'Yes,' because I was, you know, in the area. And he said, 'We don't need you to do that,' and I said, 'OK.' So I—that's when I walked

---

view. He did not give the dispatcher his address. Later in the call, the dispatcher asked for his address.

‡   Again, Zimmerman's claim is not accurate. The dispatcher asked Zimmerman for the address he was parked in front of after Zimmerman got out of his vehicle and followed Martin.

straight through here to get the address so that I could meet
the police officer."

Zimmerman said that the dispatcher asked where he
wanted to meet the officer. "I said, 'You know what? Just tell
him to meet me at my truck,'" Zimmerman explained. His silver
Honda Ridgeline was parked near the cut-through. He walked
the detectives back toward the "T". As they passed, he told the
investigators that he looked to his left down the sidewalk between the two rows of buildings and didn't see anything that
caught his eye.

"[W]hen I got to right about here," Zimmerman explained
just steps after passing the "T" in the sidewalk, "he yelled from
behind me to the side of me. He said, 'Yo, you got a problem?'
And I turned around and I said, 'No, I don't have a problem,
man.' And—"

"Where was he at?" a detective interrupted.

"He was about there, but he was walking towards me,"
Zimmerman replied. The detective stood in the approximate
spot where Martin was when Zimmerman saw him, about ten
feet away. "Like I said, I was already passed that, so I didn't see
exactly where he came from. . . ."

"I went to go grab my cell phone," Zimmerman explained,
"but my—I had left it in a different pocket. I looked down at
my pant pocket, and he said, 'You got a problem now,' and then
he was here." Zimmerman held his left hand out in front of him
demonstrating how close Martin was. "And he punched me in
the face."

Zimmerman wasn't certain exactly where he was when
Martin punched him, but he knew it was close to the "T". "I
think I stumbled," Zimmerman said, "and I—I fell down. He
pushed me down. Somehow he got on top of me."

"On the grass or on the cement?" Serino asked.

"It was over—more over like here," Zimmerman replied as
he walked away from the "T" adjacent to the sidewalk that
runs between the two rows of buildings. "I think I was trying to
push him away from me and then he got on top of me somewhere around here."

Zimmerman paused for a moment. "That's when I started

screaming for help," Zimmerman continued. "I started screaming, 'help, help,' as loud as I could. . . . I tried to sit up, and
that's when he grabbed me by the head and tried to slam my
head down."

Serino asked Zimmerman if he was on the cement or on the
grass when Martin tried to slam his head down. "No, my body
was on the grass," Zimmerman replied. "My head was on the
cement."

"He just kept slamming and slamming," Zimmerman said,
motioning with his arms. "I kept yelling, 'help, help, help,' as
loud as I could. . . . He put his hand . . . on my nose and his
other hand on my mouth. He said, 'Shut the fuck up!'" Zimmerman demonstrated using his right hand in the air to cover an
imaginary nose, his left hand to cover a mouth.

"Then I tried squirming again," Zimmerman continued, "because all I could think about was when he was hitting my head
against it it felt like my head was going to explode and I
thought I was going to lose consciousness. . . . He only had a
small portion of my head on the concrete so I tried to squirm to
get off the concrete, and when I did that, somebody here
opened the door, and I said, 'Help me! Help me!' And they said,
'I'll call 911.' I said, 'No, help me! I need help!'"

The person, apparently Witness 6, did not help. "And, I
don't know what they did, but that's when my jacket moved
up," Zimmerman said, running his right hand up his side starting at his waist. "I had my firearm on my right side hip. The
jacket moved up, and he saw it. I feel like he saw it. He looked
at it and he said, 'You're going to die tonight, mother fucker.'
And he reached for it." Zimmerman bent his right arm, lowered
his elbow to his hip, and slid his left hand across beneath his
right elbow demonstrating for the detectives what Martin was
doing. "Like I felt his arm going down my side and I grabbed it
and I just grabbed my firearm and I shot him—one time."

"After you shot him—keep on going—what did he say?"
Serino asked.

"After I shot him, he sat up—"

Serino interrupted to clarify that Zimmerman's head was
still toward the sidewalk and the rest of his body was out in the

grass.

"He was on top of me like this," Zimmerman said, bending his knees mimicking a crouching position, "and I didn't think I hit him because he sat up and he said, 'Oh, you got me.' You got it, you got me, you got it—something like that. So I thought he was just saying I know you have a gun now. I heard it. I'm giving up."

Zimmerman explained that he got Martin off of him. "I don't know if I pushed him off me [or] he fell off me, either way I got on top of him and I pushed his arms apart." Zimmerman demonstrated by moving his hands away from each other, elbows locked, arms straight.

"You kind of flipped him over," Serino asked, motioning with his hand.

"I don't remember how I got on top of him," Zimmerman replied. "I'm sorry."

"That's fine," Serino said.

"But I got on his back and I moved his arms apart because when he was repeatedly hitting me in the face and the head," Zimmerman explained, moving his hands in alternating punches, "I though he had something in his hands. So I just—I moved his hands apart."[†]

"So you had him face down then?" Serino asked.

"Yes," Zimmerman replied. "Face down and I was on his back. Then somebody came with a flashlight and I thought it was a police officer. So I said, 'Are you the police?' I still had my handgun out and I told him, 'Are you the police? My gun's right here. And he goes, 'No, no I'm not. I'm calling the police.' I said, 'Don't call the police. Help me restrain this guy!' And he said, 'I'm calling the police. I'm calling the police.' And I said, 'I already called. They're on their way. They—their coming. I need your help.'"[‡]

---

[†]  Ironically, the testimony of Mary Cutcher—the woman who went on the news claiming that Zimmerman profiled Martin and had not acted in self-defense—corroborates Zimmerman's account. After hearing the shot, she looked and saw Zimmerman on top of Martin.

[‡]  The man Zimmerman referred to is most likely Witness 13 whose testimony, although not identical to Zimmerman's statement, does tend to

"Then's when the police officer came around," Zimmerman said. "I saw the police officer so I stood up and I holstered my weapon. And he said, 'Who shot him?' And I said, 'I did.' And I put my hands up." Zimmerman raised his hands demonstrating. He explained that he turned his back to the officer and leaned his body, lifting his shirt to expose his pistol.

"I said, 'My gun's right there,'" Zimmerman said. "And he goes, 'OK, I understand. I just need you to keep your hands up.' And he put the handcuffs on me and then he took my firearm from me." After only fifteen minutes, the walk-through interview ended.

◈

After concluding the walk-through interview, Zimmerman and the investigators went to the Sanford police station for a video-taped interview and voice stress analysis. He was taken to an interrogation room with a simple table, a few basic chairs, two large mirrors that were almost certainly the two-way kind that are so ubiquitous on episodes of *Law and Order*. Before the CVSA began, a forensic investigator swabbed the inside of Zimmerman's cheeks to collect samples of his DNA.

Zimmerman explained to Investigator Doris Singleton that he went to his place of employment to tell his supervisor that he had been involved in the shooting. Zimmerman explained that he learned of news media reports that someone had been murdered in the Twin Lakes complex and that the suspect was in custody. He was concerned that if he did not see his supervisor in person, a rumor that he was in jail would circulate.

"I went to the doctor," Zimmerman explained, "and my psychologist, and I think the psychologist is the one that hit me the hardest." Zimmerman's voice reflected a build-up of emotion. After a moment, Zimmerman whispered, "But what are you going to do?"

Zimmerman asked Singleton, "Have you ever had to shoot anybody?"

---

support what the neighborhood watch volunteer claimed. Witness 13 said that he asked Zimmerman if he needed to call police, but Zimmerman told him he had already called.

"No," Singleton replied.

"Good for you," Zimmerman said quietly.

Zimmerman told Singleton that she had a commanding presence.

"My wife's a mess," Zimmerman said. Singleton asked Zimmerman how his wife learned of the shooting. He explained that the police officer wouldn't let him call his wife, so he asked the man with the flashlight to call her. "So she knew within five minutes," Zimmerman said.

Singleton asked Zimmerman if he had undergone an MRI or CT scan. Zimmerman explained that his doctor said that, since it wasn't done immediately after the shooting, there wasn't any need in doing it the next day when he went for treatment. "My doctor said that if they didn't do it then that I should just be cautious if I start vomiting or get nauseous or any loss of vision or blurriness," Zimmerman said.

Zimmerman explained to Singleton that he had been "cleared" at the scene and was told it was his choice whether or not he wanted to be taken to a hospital—at his expense. "Those things add up quick," Zimmerman said. Singleton asked him if he had any insurance; he said that he did, but that it was the "bargain basement" type with a high deductible that only paid a portion of the his medical expenses. The two had a discussion about health insurance with Singleton explaining how expensive her City of Sanford employee coverage was compared to a Blue Cross and Blue Shield of Florida plan she had that covered her whole family, but only for hospitalization and surgery.

Zimmerman told Singleton a story about how, as a retired Army veteran, his father had very good insurance benefits. One time as a kid, Zimmerman used a form that allowed him to obtain a bunch of over-the-counter medications and supplies. "I was a young kid and I took the form and I just started checking stuff off," Zimmerman explained. "I was like, 'I want that. I want that. I want that.' And I turned it in and they gave me a bag full of stuff and I went all excited to my dad, 'Dad, look! All this stuff was free!' I'll never forget he said, 'None of this is free, George. I paid for this with my service.' And I felt like garbage."

When Sanford police investigator William Ervin came into the room, he did so with a certain measure of bravado, slinging his computer case onto the table and speaking with a commanding voice, in stark contrast to Singleton's laid back, soft-spoken, I'd-rather-be-anywhere-but-here manner. Ervin asked Zimmerman if he was on any medications. Zimmerman said he takes something for his stomach.

"Any narcotics?" Ervin asked.

"I think Adderall is considered [a narcotic]?" Zimmerman replied.

"Adderall? OK. I'm not worried about Adderall."

"And Temazepam."

"Temazepam, OK. Do you got ADHD or something?"

"Yes, sir."

Ervin explained to Zimmerman that he was the "senior CVSA operator for the City of Sanford", referring to the computerized voice stress analysis system that he was about to use to verify if Zimmerman's statements to police were true. "I've been doing this for quite a long time," Ervin said. The investigator explained that the system is a "computer-aided truth verification" tool similar to the more commonly known polygraph. "This is basically the latest and greatest in truth verification," Ervin explained.

After having Zimmerman sign a consent form, Ervin explained the purpose of the CVSA interview. "The reason why we're here is yesterday you got into a situation," the investigator said, "a very bad situation and we are here to talk about that, OK?"

"Yes, sir."

"I will tell you up front, for me to be able to do this effectively I know very little about what's going on in your case."

"OK."

"I mean very, very, very little," Ervin emphasized. "All I know there was an incident last night. I probably know a little bit more than what the news says, but not a whole lot. I know a little bit more now because as far as I know the news doesn't even know who you are yet."

"Thankfully," Zimmerman said.

"Thankfully, yes," Ervin replied. "So your first name is George?"

"Yes, sir," Zimmerman said, speaking softly.

"And your last name is Zimmerman?" the left-handed investigator said as he wrote on a piece of paper on the table next to his computer.

"Yes, sir," Zimmerman affirmed again.

"I served on submarines with a Zimmerman," Ervin said.

"My father was Army," Zimmerman said. The investigator wasn't listening; he was trying to remember where the Zimmerman he knew during his submariner days was from.

"What's your date of birth?" Ervin asked.

"10/5/83," Zimmerman replied.

Ervin explained how the CVSA works. It's a Dell computer. Nothing special. "What's special about it," Ervin said, "is the program." Ervin explained that the software has "the ability to read the tonals on your voice."

Ervin used a radio frequency analogy telling Zimmerman that a normal voice has two ranges, which he called AM and FM. Ervin explained that the AM "rides on top of" the FM, and that, during normal speech, the FM dominates. But under stress, the FM diminishes. "You can't change it. You can't alter it. There's nothing you can do about it," Ervin explained.

Knowing little about the case, Ervin said, he would let Zimmerman tell him about the shooting and together they would develop nine questions that would be used for the voice stress analysis.

Ervin asked Zimmerman to rate his stress level on a one-to-ten scale. "Six, maybe seven," Zimmerman replied.

"Are you nervous about sitting here talking to me at the station?"

"Not necessarily, no."

"You came here on your own free will, no doubt, right?"

"Yes, sir."

"Investigator Serino didn't say, 'You're going to come down here or I'm going to thump you,' or anything like that?"

Zimmerman chuckled, "No, sir."

"Or 'I'm going to burn your eye out with a cigarette'?"

"No, sir."

"Well, he does that," Ervin said in a dryly humorous way. "You've got to be careful with him." He was trying to calm Zimmerman so that the CVSA could do its job.

Ervin told Zimmerman to explain the shooting in his own words from start to finish. "I'm not going to interrupt you, I hope, for the most part" Ervin said.

"I have one question," Zimmerman said. "I can't really breathe out of my nose, so I have to breathe out of my mouth. Is it OK if I drink water during the deal?"

"You can drink as much water as you want," Ervin said. "Did you get your nose broken."

Zimmerman, taking a drink of water, nodded his head then lowered the cup, swallowed, and said, "Yes, sir."

Zimmerman offered few new details beyond what he explained to Serino and the other investigators during the walk-through interview. He told Ervin he was on his way to buy groceries for the week.

"What store did you go to?" Ervin asked.

"Target," Zimmerman replied. "I was leaving my neighborhood when I saw this guy walking slowly in front of a house looking towards the house and I knew he didn't live there." Zimmerman explained that it was raining and Martin wasn't trying to get out of the rain. He didn't look like he was a "hard core" type that would be exercising in the rain. "He just looked out of place from what they've taught us in the neighborhood watch."

Zimmerman again explained that he drove past Martin and called the non-emergency number from the clubhouse. "As I was on the phone with the non-emergency line," Zimmerman said, "he walked past my car and I lost visual contact of him." He told Ervin that the dispatcher asked what direction Martin was headed, so Zimmerman pulled out and "drove adjacent to the clubhouse."

"I was unfamiliar with the street name," Zimmerman explained. "The operator asked me what street I was on, and it's not the street that I live on. It's a side street that cuts through the neighborhood. And I told him I didn't know." Zimmerman claimed that the dispatcher said that he needed to know what house Zimmerman was in front of.[†]

Just as he had explained to the other investigators, Zimmerman told Ervin that Martin, with his hand in his waistband, walked around Zimmerman's truck. Martin then "disappeared back through a cut-through between the houses."

"While he was doing that," Zimmerman said, "the operator asked me, they said, 'We need to know what exact address you're at.'" Zimmerman said that he got out of his truck to try to find a street sign so that he could at least know what street he was on.

"I saw him walk through the cut-through and then make a right behind other houses," Zimmerman explained. "I knew if I went straight and I didn't cut through where he went that was the street that I lived on—Retreat View Circle." Zimmerman said that he knew that if he got to his street he could give the dispatcher the street name and an exact house number where he was.

"So as I walked through, I looked to my right where he had gone through," Zimmerman explained. "The operator said, 'Are you following him?' and I said, 'Yes.' They said, 'We don't need you to do that,' and I said, 'OK.'" Zimmerman said that he "walked through to the other end of the street" to give the dispatcher the address. He told the dispatcher that Martin was gone.

Zimmerman told Ervin that the dispatcher asked if he still wanted a police officer to respond. He affirmed and told the dispatcher that he would meet the officer at his truck.[‡]

---

†   While Zimmerman was consistent in this account with what he told investigators earlier, it was incorrect. No such exchange took place during his call to police. When Zimmerman drove to follow Martin along Twin Trees Lane, he did so of his own volition, not at the request of the dispatcher. In fact, he never even told the dispatcher that he was following Martin.

‡   Zimmerman didn't explain why he never actually provided an address on Retreat View Circle, his claimed intent in walking through to that street in the first place. If Zimmerman's intent was to provide an address that the police could find, it certainly didn't make sense to turn around from that point and go back to his truck that was parked on another street, the

"So I walked through again," Zimmerman explained, "and as I was about half way through, he appeared out of nowhere."

"Were you still on the phone?" Ervin asked.

"No," Zimmerman replied, "I hung up. . . . I hung up and I put my phone away."

Zimmerman explained how his encounter with Martin took place. "I heard him say, 'You got a problem?',", Zimmerman explained, "and I turned around and I saw him and I went to go for my phone . . . and call 911 instead of non-emergency this time." Zimmerman demonstrated by moving his hand down to his right side as he sat in the chair across the table from Ervin. He moved his hand as though he were drawing his phone from a holster. He also began to say a word with a "shhh" sound, what some have asserted was a Freudian slip from a man who was about to say "shoot".

"But I—I guess I didn't have my phone in the pocket that I thought I had it in," Zimmerman said. "I had it in my jacket pocket and I reached for my pocket and I was looking for my phone and he just punched me in the nose." Zimmerman explained that he fell and ended up on his back with Martin on top of him. "He just kept punching my face and my head and I was screaming for help."

Just as he had in his walk-through interview, Zimmerman explained how Martin grabbed his head and slammed it into the concrete several times. "[E]ach time it felt like my head was going to explode more than the last," Zimmerman said. He thought he was going to pass out, so he screamed for help louder than before. Again, Zimmerman explained how Martin covered his nose and mouth. "I couldn't breathe. I was suffocating."

Zimmerman explained that he tried to squirm his way off the concrete so that his head wouldn't explode when Martin was slamming it down. He shifted. His jacket slid up. His pistol was exposed. "And that's when he said—he like sat up and looked and said, 'You're going to die tonight, mother fucker,'" Zimmerman explained, "and I felt him take one hand off my mouth and slide it down my chest and I just pinched his arm

---

name of which he didn't know.

and I grabbed my gun and I aimed it at him and fired one shot."

Zimmerman explained again how Martin reacted after getting shot, how he pushed Martin off of him, how he got on his back and held his hands out believing that Martin had been hitting him with something in his hands. He again spoke of the witness who approached and said he was calling 911. He again explained how the police officer approached him, handcuffed him, and took his pistol. Zimmerman said that paramedics arrived and treated Martin. Eventually they came to him and poured peroxide on his head to clean his wounds. They felt his nose. Zimmerman heard one of them tell somebody that his nose was broken and that he would need one or two stitches on the back of his head.

Zimmerman explained that an officer said the police were going to take him down for questioning. Another officer asked if they should take him to the police station first or take him to Central Florida Regional Hospital. The decision was made: take him to the station first.

When asked by Ervin if there was any communication between Zimmerman and Sanford police at the time of the struggle, Zimmerman told the investigator that he was not talking to the dispatcher but he recalled a bystander looking out at him and Martin. "I said, 'Help me! Help me!' and I think he said, 'I'm calling 911.'"[†]

Ervin clarified some of the details of Zimmerman's account. "He said, 'You got a problem?'" Ervin asked.

"Yes, sir," Zimmerman answered.

"At that point you went for your phone?"

"Yes, sir."

"And he punched you in the face?"

"I answered him. I said, 'No, I don't have a problem.' And that's when I went for my phone and he punched me in the face."

"And then you guys exchanged . . . some punches?"

"I didn't hit him at all. I mean, I was trying to defend my-

---

† Zimmerman is apparently referring to Witness 6, the man who told police that Martin was on top "throwing down blows".

self, but every time he punched me in the nose, it felt like my head was going to explode."

"OK, was it that time you pulled out your gun?"

"No," Zimmerman answered quickly, adamantly.

"No? At any time prior to did you pull out your gun?"

"No."

"So this possible bystander that you told to call 911 or help, he should be able to tell us that your gun was still in your holster."

"Yes, sir," Zimmerman replied. Again his answer was quick, direct, and firm.

"Or didn't see the gun?" Ervin asked.

"Correct."

Ervin asked Zimmerman if he knew that person who said he was calling 911 during the fight. "You don't know this guy?"

"No."

"Why did you try to maintain such close proximity to him?" Ervin asked, referring to Zimmerman following Martin.

"To tell the police where he—what direction he was headed in," Zimmerman replied.

"Didn't you feel that you put yourself in danger?"

"No because I—where I was parked my headlights were . . . illuminating and I saw him turn down [between the buildings] —and by the time I was on the phone with the non-emergency. By the time I got to where he was at I felt like he had already made his way—"

Zimmerman interrupted his train of thought and began explaining. "I've called non-emergency probably a dozen times," Zimmerman explained, "and they—these guys are known just to run. As soon as they get suspicious, they run and they know the neighborhood back and forth and they just disappear between houses within seconds." These assholes, they always get away.

"So I kind of walked and I looked around the corner and he was gone," Zimmerman continued. "That's why I told non-emergency, 'He's gone.'"

Ervin asked what Martin was wearing. Gray hoodie. Either gray pants or stonewashed denim jeans. Zimmerman wasn't sure.

"When you were laying on the ground, you were laying on your back, correct?" Ervin asked.

"Yes, sir."

"That's when your jacket came up and he saw . . . your gun, right?"

"Yes, sir."

"Your gun on your left side [or] right side?"

"My right side."

"OK, so your gun's on your right side. Where were your hands then?"

"Trying to keep his hands away," Zimmerman said, moving his hands in the air as though guarding against Martin's hands.

"And then you felt—what did you feel next?"

"His hand slide down my chest. He took—he had one hand on my mouth and one hand on my nose and he took one off and that's when he said, 'You're going to die, mother fucker.' And I felt his hand going down the side of my chest. "

"So you felt something like this."

"Yeah, a brushing, and to be honest with you the whole time I forgot that I had the gun. When he said that I was going to die and I felt him brushing I—it automatically clicked that he was going for my—"

"Your hands are out here defending yourself," Ervin said holding his hands up near his face. "His hand was going down."

"Yes, sir."

"Were both your hands on the weapon?"

"No, sir."

"OK, where was his hands when you went to retrieve the weapon?"

"One hand was going towards the gun. He took it off my mouth."

"Right."

"And I was trying to get his hand—he was suffocating me so I was trying to get his hands off of my face."

"Mmmhmm."

"So when I felt his hand—he let go of my mouth so I wasn't

trying to do anything again with my right hand," Zimmerman said, slapping his right side, "so I grabbed my gun and I don't know if he did at the same time or what the case was but I got to it first."

"OK, and then how did you come to fire upon him from that position because you're laying down like this, OK, on your back, right?"

"Yes, sir."

"And then you just bring it out of the holster and straight up like this?" Ervin motioned with his right hand near his hip. Zimmerman had to lean to look around Ervin's computer to see what the investigator was showing him.

"Yes, sir."

"OK, you didn't like try to . . . push it into him or anything? You just fired almost like from the hip?"

"I think I made sure that it wasn't—because my hand was in the way. I made sure it was past my hand because his other hand was still on my face."

"OK, was it that far away or were you right up under—"

"No, he was—he was like putting all his weight on my nose and my mouth trying to suffocate me."

"Uh-huh."

"So he was like creating a crevice with his body then he like —when he slid to go for my gun—"

"Did he go for your gun with his left hand or [his] right hand?"

Zimmerman sighed. Quietly, he said, "I don't recall. I don't recall which hand he used."

"One of the hands went?"

"Yes, sir."

"What was on your mind?"

"That's when it clicked that I had my gun and when he said —"

"But the hand that was on your mouth, it went to—it went to your gun?"

"Yes, sir."

"When you got it, it went out like this?"

"I think I went far enough to where I could make sure it

was past my other hand and in his general area."

"From what you've described to me, he's not that far away from you?"

"No, he's on me."

"He's on *top* of you?"

"Yes, sir."

"There's not a whole lot of distance between you and him."

"Correct."

"So you can't really extend your arm."

"Correct."

"Then you've got a gun sticking out. What kind of gun was it?"

"A Kel-Tec nine millimeter."

"A Kel-Tec nine?"

"Yes, sir."

"OK, so it's probably only about that long, right?"

"Shorter."

"Maybe a little bit shorter? That's a little tiny gun. But still I mean—I mean you—you don't have hardly any play—"

"No, sir."

"Before that gun's directly aimed at his chest?"

"Correct. I was on him. I knew I was—"

"As soon as the round went off he stopped trying—attacking you?"

"Yes, he sat back and he said, 'You got me' or 'you got it.' Whatever."

"I'm sure it all happened just that quick, too," Ervin said.

"It felt like an eternity," Zimmerman replied. "And I thought the police were there—they were going to be there. It felt like it took forever."

◈

After letting Zimmerman use the restroom and get some more water to drink, Ervin called Serino on his Nextel two-way to get the case number. Zimmerman mentioned that his employer had asked for the case number also. Ervin said it wasn't any of their business.

Ervin asked Zimmerman what color the walls were in the

interview room.

"Green," Zimmerman replied.

"OK, remember that. We agree that the walls are green." Ervin was setting up a control question for the CVSA. Ervin typed out a series of questions on his computer.

"What do you call the guy? You call him the kid you call him—?" Ervin asked.

"The guy," Zimmerman replied.

Ervin continued typing.

"So this is what we're going to do. I told you there's going to be nine questions. Didn't lie to you. There's going to be nine questions." Ervin explained that he was going to start with a series of benign questions to determine what Zimmerman's stress level was when telling the truth. "Is your name George? Is today Monday? Is this the month of February? Are we in the city of Sanford? Am I wearing a watch?" Then Ervin said that he wanted Zimmerman to lie to two control questions to determine what his stress level looked like on the CVSA when he was untruthful. First, Ervin wanted Zimmerman to answer 'no' when he asked, "Is the color of the wall green?" Then the investigator asked Zimmerman to recall a time when he was stopped by police for speeding. He told Zimmerman to recall that "oh, shit" feeling he had when he saw the police car's lights. Then he instructed Zimmerman to answer "no" to the question, "Have you ever driven over the posted speed limit?"

Then Ervin told Zimmerman what the relevant questions would be. "Were you in fear for your life when you shot the guy? Did you confront the guy you shot?"

Ervin directed Zimmerman to turn a chair toward the wall and have a seat. He handed the neighborhood watchman a microphone and told him to clip it to his shirt. "Both feet on the floor. Sit straight up," Ervin instructed. He told Zimmerman to answer simply "yes" or "no".

When Ervin asked Zimmerman the two key questions—was he in fear and did he confront Martin—the shooter answered "yes" to the former and "no" to the latter. He was in fear. He didn't confront Martin. In his report, Ervin classified Zimmerman's performance on the test as "no deception indicated".

Ervin determined that Zimmerman "told substantially the complete truth."

A June 27 USA Today piece reported Zimmerman's performance on the lie detector. The writers quoted Jacksonville criminal defense attorney and former prosecutor Randy Reep who said that, although the test may not be admissible in court, knowledge of the results may contaminate a potential jury pool. "It makes it harder for the state to get an impartial jury," Reep said. "It certainly supports the Sanford police department's determination not to make an arrest."

But not everyone agreed that the test's results were conclusive. The USA Today article quoted former FBI agent Ron Greiner, an expert in lie detection. Greiner believed that Ervin's questions were vague because he didn't clearly define what he meant by "confront". The former FBI agent also said that Zimmerman's psychological state could affect the results. "He may have convinced himself that he was in fear of his life," Greiner said, "but whether or not he was is not definitive." Greiner proposed what he believed were clearer, more direct questions: "Did Trayvon Martin attack you and knock you to the ground? Was Trayvon Martin on top of you hitting you before you shot him?"

Former FBI agent and St. Leo University instructor Joe Navarro was also quoted in the USA Today article. "You have to ask precise questions," Navarro explained. "You want to know at what point [Zimmerman] feared for [his] life."

◈

On February 29—three days after the shooting—Serino and Singleton again interviewed Zimmerman, this time for over an hour.

Serino asked Zimmerman if he had ever heard of "Murphy's Law". Zimmerman answered, "Yes."

"OK, that's what happened. This person wasn't doing anything bad," Serino said. He asked Zimmerman if he knew the name of the person that died.

"Trayvon Martin," Zimmerman replied.

"Trayvon Benjamin Martin," Serino said. "He was born in

1995. February the fifth. He was seventeen years old, an athlete. Probably somewhere someone who was going to be in aeronautics, a kid with a future, a kid with folks that care. In his possession we found a can of iced tea and a bag of Skittles and about forty-two dollars in cash. Not the goon."

Serino asked Zimmerman if he had any prior training in law enforcement. Just college courses, Zimmerman told the investigator, for his "AA" degree. He also described a talk given by the Sanford Police Department on the neighborhood watch program.

"But if you guys continue a neighborhood watch typically speaking at nighttime," Serino replied, "the garb is black-on-black-on-black with a black hoodie. Now this guy had on a dark gray hoodie, it was dark, but his pants were beige, not quite your prime suspect type."

"I listened to the phone call that you made to the non-emergency line," Serino said. "You sound—well, tell me, what was going through your head at the time?"

"Two or three weeks prior to that I had seen somebody looking in the window of the house that he was in front of," Zimmerman explained.

"Was he white or black?" Serino asked.

"Black," Zimmerman replied. "The guy that lives there I know he's active in the neighborhood watch and he's Caucasian."

For the next three minutes, Zimmerman explained to Serino that he had called police about the suspicious person he had seen at the residence, the same place where he would later see Martin. When the police arrived they checked the residence and found all of the windows open as well as the front door. A week later, another nearby house was broken into and a laptop was stolen. The suspect in that case was later arrested.

Zimmerman saw Martin standing near and looking into the same residence he had called about two or three weeks earlier. Zimmerman was suspicious of Martin because the teenager didn't appear to be getting out of the rain.

"You know, you're going to come under a lot of scrutiny, correct? OK, the profiling aspect of the whole thing," Serino asked. "Had this person been white, would you have felt the same way?"

"Yes."

"OK. Gotta ask that."

"Like I said, this child has no criminal record whatsoever," Serino said. "A good kid, a mild mannered kid. Part of what I've been doing the last couple days is trying to get into his head—a psychological profile—and find out what his likes are, dislikes are, his hobbies were—that stuff. And one of his hobbies happens to be the videotaping of everything he does."

Serino explained that the police were in the process of analyzing the phone but the battery died. "There's a possibility that whatever happened between you and him is caught on videotape," Serino told Zimmerman. "This is going to be our final interview. I'm not talking to you anymore. After this, we're good."

"There's a very strong possibility that what's on there is either going to help you or, you know, not help you," Serino said, "and that's why I've got to clarify a few things about what happened out there."

"How tall are you?" Serino asked. "How much do you weigh?"

"Five-eight, one ninety."

"OK, Trayvon was about six foot, a hundred and fifty pounds," Serino said. He flips through some pages. "That's him. That's the gunshot you put in him—went right through his heart." Serino described Martin as a "skinny kid".

Serino tells Zimmerman that Martin was unarmed in an attempt to get Zimmerman to say something because it may have been captured on video. "I pray to God that someone videotaped it," Zimmerman said, "or the neighborhood had put up a camera that I didn't know about or something."

Serino covers Zimmerman's account of being punched twenty-five or thirty times. "I have consulted with a lot of people. Not quite consistent with your injuries," Serino tell Zimmerman. "You do have injuries, however."

Serino asked Zimmerman how Martin managed to slam his head into the concrete. "I was on my back when he first punched me," Zimmerman replied. "I don't know if I immediately fell down,  he threw me down—I  was stumbling. I ended up on my back and he was on top of me, mounted. He kept punching me, and then when I started yelling for help, that's when he grabbed my head and started to slam it."

"Grabbed your head by your ears, by—hard to say?"

Zimmerman couldn't recall. He didn't remember how many times Martin punched him in the nose either.

"OK, you never got a chance to hit him? You have no defense wounds here?" Serino asked.

"No, sir."

"Any bruising on your body at all?"

"No."

"No broken ribs? No fractured ribs? None of that?"

"No."

Serino showed Zimmerman a picture. "Is that what he looked like the night this happened?"

"Pardon?"

"Did you see his face like that the night this happened?"

"No, sir."

"OK. He's young—young and skinny. Seventeen. There he is again. I'm showing you this because I have to some day meet his family . . . and they have a *lot* of questions, obviously, and I want to prepare you for that because, like I said, I'm basically out of it after this. . . ."

Serino told Zimmerman that he was "not trying to torture" him  but wanted him to see what he had done before he saw it "anywhere else."

"The court of public opinion is going to beat up on you a lot, OK?" Serino told Zimmerman.

"Yes, sir," Zimmerman replied.

"A lot of people don't think that your injuries are consistent with getting in a life threatening thing," Serino explained. "It's a matter of perception. I understand that."

Serino showed Zimmerman another picture. "That right there is the only injury to his hands that we could document," Serino explained.

Serino touched on Zimmerman's cries for help. "It's a matter of perception. Like I said, there's no doubt in my mind that you were in fear," the detective said. "But the question comes into play is that what enraged him so badly besides the fact he felt he was being profiled. He's from a bigger city. I don't know. He can't talk. I wish he would have ran away."

Serino claimed that he had received a phone call from an anonymous witness who recounted "a different version of events." Serino alleged that the person said Zimmerman attempted to detain Martin and that there was arguing back and forth. "I'm hoping that whatever they tell me doesn't come out on here," Serino said, "and then all of sudden you're looking at something you never *dreamed* that you'd be looking at."[†]

Serino talked about the cuts on Zimmerman's head. "These have been interpreted as capillary type cuts or whatever," Serino said. "Lacerations, not really coinciding with being slammed hard onto the ground. That's skull fractures happen with that. I have seen them all, you know." Serino told Zimmerman that he reserved judgment on the neighborhood watch volunteer; the investigator's job, he explained, was to remain neutral.

"It's kind of a good shoot, bad shoot type thing," Serino said. "The only thing that you don't have is the authority to go ahead and do the stop legally. . . . You're working under the authority of a absolutely private citizen. But then again you can make citizen's arrests all day long . . . for felonies. Problem was that this child wasn't committing a felony at the time. He was just walking."

Serino talked about Zimmerman's defensive wounds. On the audio recording, it sounds like the detective is showing photographs to Zimmerman. The detective tells Zimmerman his defensive wounds were "essentially non-existent" because he is looking for "bruising and scraping" but doesn't see any. "You faired pretty well," Serino said, "probably because you had long sleeves on. I'm thinking I could write that up pretty easy."

"Do you have any problems with black people?" Serino

---

[†] As of this writing, no information has been released about any witness making such claims. This was likely a ploy by Serino to get Zimmerman to admit to having attempted to detain Martin.

asked.

"No, sir," Zimmerman responded in a shaky whisper, emotion slipping through his voice.

"Had you told this child that you were neighborhood watch and you were just wondering what the hell he was doing when he came up to your car, we probably wouldn't be here right now," Serino told Zimmerman. "Did it ever occur to you to go ahead and actually ask this person what he was doing out there?"

"No, sir," Zimmerman replied.

"Was it fear, precaution, safety, all of the above?" Serino asked. "Tell me what was going through your head?"

"I didn't want to confront him and risk losing my job," Zimmerman said.

"Your job's not to really do anything at all when it comes to that kind of—it wasn't your job to monitor him either," Serino said. "From our vantage point you've had two opportunities to identify yourself as somebody who was actually not meaning to do him harm. The problem being, in his minds-eye—which I can't get into because he's passed—that he perceived you as a threat, OK? He perceives you as a threat. He has every right to go and defend himself, especially when you reach into your pocket to grab the cell phone."

Serino wanted Zimmerman to explain why Martin became enraged and snapped. He told Zimmerman that Martin wasn't a violent kid. He wasn't on drugs. "What do you think his mindset was?" Serino asked.

"The other thing was when he walked up to my car," Zimmerman replied, "he reached into his waistband and held his hand there."

"He was probably holding his iced tea," Serino said. "Did he say anything?"

"It was raining so I had my windows up and I was on the phone," Zimmerman answered. "I didn't hear."

"How close to your car did he get?"

"Maybe a car length?"

"What do you think set him off?"

Zimmerman paused, thinking. "I don't know," he replied.

"Had he been a goon, a bad kid, two thumbs-up, you know. No. . . . He does not fit the profile of what occurred, which is another unfortunate thing that we got going on here."

Singleton asked Zimmerman why he didn't confront Martin.

"I guess fear," Zimmerman replied. "I didn't want to confront him."

"You were afraid of him?" Singleton asked.

"Yes, ma'am," Zimmerman replied.

"Then do you say, 'He ran'?"

"Yes."

"Then you get out of your car and run after him?"

"I didn't run after him, no," Zimmerman replied. "I—I walked to find the street name or a street sign, and he had already run—cut out between the houses so I knew that if I walked straight through that little sidewalk, I knew that that was my street that I lived on."

"Retreat View," Singleton said.

Serino asked Zimmerman why he didn't know the names of the three streets in the complex. "How do you not know the names of the three streets in your neighborhood you've been living in for three years?" Serino asked. "I don't know how to answer that, and I'm trying to speak for you."

"To be honest with you," Zimmerman says, "I have a bad memory anyway. That's why I gave—"

"Is that documented anywhere as far as having the bad memory?" Serino interrupted.

Zimmerman told Serino that he has been diagnosed with ADHD since childhood and takes Adderall for it, twenty milligrams, twice a day.‡

---

‡   Sanford police would later be criticized for not having obtained a blood sample from Zimmerman the night of the shooting to test for the presence of drugs such as the Adderall he had been prescribed. Without a court order, the police had no authority to obtain such a sample unless Zimmerman consented. There is no indication in the police reports, however, that investigators ever asked for such consent. Al Sharpton said, "Now if you want to discuss something relevant, discuss what Zimmerman might have had in his system. Discuss his past. Mr. Zimmerman was not tested. Trayvon was. Let's examine why we had a test on the victim

"What kind of holster did you have?" Serino asked.

"It was just one I bought at a gun show," Zimmerman replied, "like a nylon inner waistband—"

"Like an Uncle Mike's with a—with a nylon—the retainer?"

"It did not have a retainer."

"So, it's an unsecure holster, basically?"

"Yes, sir."

"No locking mechanism? No safety feature? Nothing?"

"No, sir."

"It was inside your pants?"

"At what point were you able to free your waist side to go ahead and pull out your weapon?" Serino asked.

"When he—he was mounted on me but he had pressure on my nose and my mouth suffocating me," Zimmerman explained, "and when he let go of my mouth and started reaching down my side, he said, 'Your gonna die tonight, mother fucker.' I didn't need my hand anymore because he let go of my mouth. I don't know if I was still screaming or not. That's when I grabbed his hand and I grabbed my—my firearm and fired."

"How long did he suffocate you for, approximately?" Serino inquired.

"It felt like hours," Zimmerman said, "but I don't—I don't know."

◈

Serino and Singleton went over Zimmerman's call to Sanford police step-by-step, playing the recording for the neighborhood watchman, pausing it along the way to ask questions.

*. . . There's this real suspicious guy . . .*

"Real suspicious guy," Serino said. "One more time. Why

---

rather than the one that was aggressive." Toxicology examinations are routinely done on victims of homicide and other non-natural deaths. Ultimately, it's a non-issue. If Zimmerman had tested positive for a prescribed, mood-altering medication, it would likely be used to help the defense, not the prosecution. There's no indication that Zimmerman was under the influence of alcohol or any illicit drug.

suspicious?"

"It was raining," Zimmerman explained. "He was looking into the houses, looking behind, looking at me. He wasn't walking quickly to get out of the rain. It didn't look like he was, like, trying to head home. He didn't look like a hard-core athlete that wanted to, like, train in the rain or anything. He just looked out of place."

*. . . This guy looks like he's up to no good or he's on drugs or something . . .*

"On drugs, why?" Serino asked.

"Oh, because he just kept looking around, looking behind him, looking—just kept shifting where he was looking."

*. . . Now he's just staring at me . . .*

"When you explained it to me," Singleton questioned Zimmerman, "you said you had pulled over initially at the clubhouse, correct?"

"Yes, ma'am."

"OK, but it seems so fast, and then I thought you told me—and you can correct me if I'm wrong—I thought you said they asked you can you still see him and you told them you couldn't . . . and they said, well, get to where you could see where he's at and you told me it was at that point you moved."

"Yes, ma'am."

"Now, you're saying he's coming up to your car. Does that mean you've already—at this point in the tape you're already on Twin Tree, the street you didn't know the name of at the time?"

"No, I was on—I called when I was at the clubhouse."

"OK, but he's walking up to your car now, right?"

"Yes, ma'am."

"Because you're saying he's walking up."

"Yes, ma'am."

"You're talking about when you've already left the clubhouse and now you're around the corner?"

"No, ma'am. I'm at the clubhouse."

"So you're still at the clubhouse when he does this?"

"Mmmhmm."

"OK."*

*. . . He's got his hand in his waistband . . .*

"Where are you at now?" Singleton asked. "Are you still at the clubhouse?"

"I think I'm still at the clubhouse."

*. . . He's got a button on his shirt . . .*

"Has he moved yet?" Singleton asked.

"I don't think so," Zimmerman replied. The investigators apparently missed the sound of Zimmerman shifting the truck into gear.

"You're still in front of the clubhouse?" Singleton asked.

"I think so."

"On Retreat View Circle?"

"Yes, ma'am. I don't remember even saying he had a button on his shirt."

*. . . Something's wrong with him . . .*

"Something's wrong with him," Serino said. "What's that statement supposed to mean?"

"I don't know," Zimmerman replied, confusion apparent in his voice.

*. . . I don't know what his deal is . . .*

"And where are you at now?" Singleton asked. "Are you still in front of the clubhouse?"

---

\* The clubhouse is about half way between the building where Zimmerman first saw Martin and the area where the shooting took place. Martin would have walked past Zimmerman while the neighborhood watch leader was at the clubhouse talking to the police dispatcher.

"I don't remember," Zimmerman said, half under his breath. He was growing confused. The recording of the conversation was different than his recollection.

*. . . These assholes, they always get away . . .*

"That statement," Serino said. "These assholes. What's behind that?"

"People that victimize the neighborhood," Zimmerman said meekly.

"Didn't you just tell us from there that a week earlier they made an arrest?" Singleton challenged Zimmerman.

"Yes, ma'am."

"They don't all get away."

"No."

"Good point," Serino added.

*. . . When you come to the clubhouse you come straight in and make a left . . .*

"What's happening now?" Serino asked. "Are you guys walking now? Is he walking?"

"No," Zimmerman answered. "I was parked where I could see him now."

"So you're definitely not in front of the clubhouse anymore," Singleton added.

"No," Zimmerman agreed.

"So you're ahead of him?" Serino asked.

"No, I was behind him," Zimmerman replied.

"So he walked to your car and then walked—went his path and you were behind him?" Serino asked.

"Yes, sir."

"OK."

"When I was at the clubhouse he walked—"

"Were you driving slowly or something?"

"No, I pulled over and stopped before I called."

*. . . Shit, he's running . . .*

"OK, full sprint, full on flight, jogging, trotting—describe the run," Serino said.

"I don't remember. I just—because I was on the phone. It happened so quickly."

"Well, I understand that, George, but like I said it's—if it was a bicycle theft I could say OK, but it's kind of important. I mean, was he running as to evade you? Get away from you? Maybe he got tired of getting wet in the rain? What kind of run was it? I mean, it sounds like he's running as to get away from you."

"I don't know why he was running," Zimmerman said slowly, quietly.

"But what kind of run was it? Can't say?"

"I don't remember," Zimmerman says under his breath.

*. . . He's running? Which way is he running? . . .*

"Is that you getting out of the car?" Serino asked.

"Yes," Zimmerman replied without hesitation.

"So as soon as he runs," Singleton added, "you're getting out of the car to follow him."

"When he says which way are you running, I turn off the ignition."

*. . . Down toward the other entrance of the neighborhood. . .*

"At that point, you're out of the car?" Serino asked.

"I think so," Zimmerman replied.

"OK, so you basically jumped out of the car to see where he was going?"

"Yes, sir," Zimmerman answers quietly but without hesitation.

"That's not fear. You know what I mean? That's one of the problems I have with the whole thing."

*. . . The back entrance. . .*

"It sounds like you're running," Singleton said.

"I wasn't running," Zimmerman replied.

*. . . These fucking— . . .*

"What was that you whispered?" Serino asked. "These fucking what?"

"Punks," Zimmerman replied. His voice was certain. He did not hesitate.

"These punks," Serino said. "He wasn't a fucking punk."

*. . . Are you following him? . . .*

"At the point where he said, 'Are you following him?' . . . what went through your mind?" Serino asked.

"He's right," Zimmerman said.

"So you should have stopped and went back to your vehicle."

"I still wanted to give him an address."

*. . . He ran. . .*

"He said 'he ran' again," Serino stated. "Is this because you don't see him?"

"Correct."

"So at this point he has to be hiding from you."

"I don't know where he is. I don't think—"

"Well, the laws of physics says that he's hiding from you at this point. He could not have made it home and came back to attack you in that time."

Serino began to go back over Zimmerman's account of what took place at that point on the recording.

"I wasn't following him," Zimmerman said. "I was just going in the same direction he was."

"That's following," Serino said, laughing.

"The other day," Singleton chimed in, "you told me you got out of the car because dispatch was asking your location and you wanted to orient yourself. You did not tell me that you said, 'Oh, shit. He's running,' and then got out of the car and went in that same direction at the same time. See where the problem is?"

"Yes, ma'am."

"You told me that the reason you got out of your car was to get an address."

"Yes."

"But you decide to get the address a fraction of a second after you say, 'Oh, shit. He's running.' And then it *sounds* like you're running, too."

"Because it was fast walking, maybe?" Serino asked.

"No, it was just windy," Zimmerman replied.

"It was," Serino said.


*. . . Tell them to go straight past the clubhouse . . .*


"What are you doing right now?" Serino asked.

"Walking back to my car."

Serino timed part of the recording. "That's eighty-four seconds," Serino said. "From the point where you were walking back to your car from Retreat View to Twin Tree, basically. . . . Did you stop at the "T"?"

"No, I walked through. I stopped on Retreat View Circle."

"That's where you were standing?"

"Yes, sir."

"But you didn't get back into your car?"

"No, sir."

"Why not?"

"I was—"

"You're in the rain. You're getting wet. You're on the phone."

"Because I was waiting—I had light there where I was at and I was trying to hit my flashlight. I didn't want to walk back through without light."

"OK, a minute and twenty seconds. You're in the rain getting wet. You've wrote this guy off basically. You're going to meet the police, OK? You see where the obstacle is here?"

"Yes, sir."

"I want you to think about that. I am speaking for you. . . . It doesn't sound like you're saying—well, it doesn't sound like you quite recall exactly what happened at that point."

"My concern is also this," Singleton added. "Oh, shit, he's running and I'm getting out of my car—in an instant to make sure I don't lose sight of this guy. That's what it sounds like. Are you following him? Because that's what it sounds like you're doing. That's why he asked you the question. It sounded to the dispatcher likely that you were running, and that's why he asked you that question, are you following him, and your answer is yes, OK? But then you get to the other side and you're concerned about walking past this guy when you've already been chasing him, essentially. And he's telling you to go back to your car, and now you want to pretend—or, not pretend—you want us to believe that you're concerned about having a flashlight to move back where you just ran? You're trying to catch up to him."

"You're looking for him," Serino chimed in.

"No, I wasn't," Zimmerman said.

"It sounds like you're looking for him, OK?" Serino added.

"You brought a flashlight with you," Singleton said.

"Yes, ma'am," Zimmerman replied.

"You wanted to be able to see him," Singleton said, pressing Zimmerman for a response.

"You wanted to catch him," Serino said. "You wanted to catch the bad guy. Fucking punk, can't get away. Listen, we're outside the interrogation room, OK? We are in a whole different area right here. . . . This is why I took you out of there, so you can hear this. So I can recall your memory and let you see if . . . you say you walked back to car or you stood outside your car . . . they're not going to believe anything I have to say. . . . Is there anything that you need to clarify right now? Did you pursue this kid? Did you want to catch him?"

"No," Zimmerman replied, dragging out the no and dropping the pitch of his voice as he spoke. He was certain, adamant. No.

"OK, it's not you? It's not what you're about?" Serino asked.

"No," Zimmerman replied. Again, the emotion was strong

in his single-word response.

"Why did you tell them never mind just have them call me when they get here and I'll tell them where I'm at?" Singleton asked.

"I was frustrated that I couldn't think of the street name," Zimmerman answered.

"But you were going to be back in your car from *that* distance in less than fifteen or twenty seconds," Singleton said, "so why would they need to call you?"

"I felt like I didn't give them an adequate description of where I was from the clubhouse," Zimmerman replied. He didn't hesitate. He didn't stop to think about his answer.

"Just know what the impression would be is that you're going to continue to look and when they get here you'll just tell them where you're at at that point," Singleton explained. "You see what I'm saying? No, never mind. Just tell them to call me when they get here and *I'll* tell them where I'm at meaning I might not be at my car where I just told them I would be."

"We're here working for you," Serino told Zimmerman. "We've got to open your mind, and if there's anything that needs to be changed, this is it."

The investigators began playing the 911 call from Witness 11, the call that captured the desperate cries for help.

"You hear that voice in the background?" Serino asked.

"No, sir," Zimmerman replied.

"That's you. Are you hearing yourself?"

"That doesn't even sound like me," Zimmerman said.

"It's you," Serino said. The detective played the 911 recording until the shot was heard. Zimmerman screamed right before the shot. "I can't pinpoint where you were smothered. That's the problem I'm having, and nobody's saying they saw him smothering you."

"When we're listening to the screaming," Singleton added, "it doesn't sound like there's a hesitation to the screaming. It sounds like it's continuous." She tells Zimmerman that if someone covers his mouth while he's screaming, the screaming's going to stop. "But we don't hear it stop."

"We don't hear him at all, either," Serino said. "Is he being quiet? Is he whispering to you or something?"

"He's telling me to shut the fuck up," Zimmerman said.

"Is he calm?" Serino asked.

"No," Zimmerman said, dragging out the word, "he's like *angry.*"

"I don't hear him, though," Serino said.

"Is he shouting it or is he—?" Singleton inquired.

"No, he's on top of me. He's telling me to shut the fuck up."

"And then when he saw you had a gun at that point," Serino began to ask a question but shifted gears to make a slightly different inquiry. "Do you think he might have saw you had a gun when you guys were standing before he punched you?"

"No," Zimmerman answered quickly but softly.

"No way, no how?" Serino asked.

"No, sir."

"Was it totally concealed under that jacket?"

"*Totally* concealed."

"He couldn't have gotten a glimpse of it accidentally?"

"I walk around in Wal-Mart all the time and no one has ever seen it."

"What was the provocation for him punching you other than you following him that you can think of? Why was he so mad at you?"

"I've gone through it a million times and I have no idea."

◈

On March 25, Serino called Zimmerman on the phone to arrange an interview with the newly-appointed special prosecutor. Zimmerman agreed, but said he was about fifteen hours away. Serino called again on March 26 and the two agreed that Zimmerman would be interviewed in Jacksonville on March 28. But that interview never took place.

◈

On July 18, Fox News talk show host Sean Hannity interviewed Zimmerman and his attorney, Mark O'Mara. The interview aired that evening during the show's regular nine o'clock hour. It was the first time anyone in the news media got to interview the embattled neighborhood watch leader.

"Your gun was legal," Hannity said, prefacing a question. "You had a legal weapon in the state of Florida. Why did you feel the need to carry a gun? . . . Did you carry it at all times?"

"I carried it at all times except for when I went to work," Zimmerman explained.

"A lot of this case, legally, . . . has to do with 'Stand Your Ground,'" Hannity said. "You've heard a lot about it, and I was just curious prior to this night, this incident, had you even heard [of] 'Stand Your Ground'?"

"No, sir," Zimmerman said, shaking his head with a sort of half-grin.

"You said in that tape, 'Something's wrong with him. He's checking me out. I don't know what his deal was.' So it's almost from the very beginning you felt—are you saying on that 911 tape that *you* felt threatened at that moment when you said that to the dispatch?"

"No, not particularly." Zimmerman described Martin's "demeanor" and his "body language" as "confrontational."

Hannity asked Zimmerman about the moment when he told the dispatcher that Martin was running. "Is there any chance as you look back in retrospect as you look back on that night and what happened," Hannity asked, "that maybe he was afraid of you and didn't know who you were?"

"No," Zimmerman said firmly, shaking his head.

"Why do you think he was running then?"

"Um, maybe I said running but he was more—"

"You said running."

"Yes, it was like skipping, going away quickly, but he wasn't running out of fear."

"You could tell the difference?"

"He wasn't running."

"He wasn't actually running?"

"No, sir."

"OK, because that's what you said to the dispatcher. You thought he was running."

Hannity asked Zimmerman about following Martin.

"I meant that I was going in the same direction as him," Zimmerman explained, "so that I could keep an eye on him so that I could tell the police where he was going. I didn't mean that I was actually pursuing him."

◈

"A man assailed on his own grounds, without provocation, by a person armed with a deadly weapon and apparently seeking his life," wrote United States Supreme Court Justice John Marshall Harlan, "is not obligated to retreat, but may stand his ground and defend himself with such means as are within his control." Harlan was delivering the Court's opinion in *Beard v. United States*, an 1895 case in which Beard, "a white man, and not an Indian, was indicted in the Circuit Court of the United States for the Western District of Arkansas for the crime of having killed and murdered, in the Indian country, and within that district, one Will Jones, also a white person, and not an Indian." Beard was convicted of manslaughter. He was sentenced to eight years in prison and fined five hundred dollars.

"An angry dispute arose between Beard and the three brothers by the name of Jones—Will Jones, John Jones, and Edward Jones—in reference to a cow," Justice Harlan wrote in the Court's opinion. "The Jones brother, one of them taking a shotgun with him, went upon the premises of the accused for the purpose of taking the cow away whether Beard consented or not." But Beard stopped the brothers "and warned them not to come to his place again for such a purpose".

Later that day, the brothers returned to Beard's farm. One of the brothers, the one who was eventually killed by Beard, was "armed with a concealed deadly weapon". Beard's wife stopped the men from taking the cow, but before they left, Beard returned to his farm armed "with a shotgun that he was in the habit of carrying when absent from home". The men, the cow, and his wife were fifty or sixty yards from the farmhouse, and Beard "went at once" from the house to the "orchard lot" where the dispute was taking place.

"Beard ordered the Jones brothers to leave his premises,"

Justice Harlan wrote.

> They refused to leave. Thereupon Will Jones, who was on the opposite side of the orchard fence, ten or fifteen yards only from Beard, moved towards the latter with an angry manner and in a brisk walk, having his left hand (he being, as Beard knew, left-handed) in the left pocket of his trousers. When he got within five or six steps of Beard, the latter warned him to stop, but he did not do so. As he approached nearer the accused asked him what he intended to do, and he replied, "Damn you. I will show you," at the same time making a movement with his left hand as if to draw a pistol from his pocket, whereupon the accused struck him over the head with his gun, and knocked him down.

Dr. Howard Hunt testified that Will Jones died from a head injury delivered by Beard. The wound, according to Hunt, "was across the head, rather on the right side, the skull being crushed by the blow."

In ruling to reverse Beard's conviction, the Court wrote:

> In our opinion, the court below erred in holding that the accused, while on his premises, outside of his dwelling house, was under a legal duty to get out of the way, if he could, of his assailant, who, according to one view of the evidence, had threatened to kill the defendant, in execution of that purpose had armed himself with a deadly weapon, with that weapon concealed upon his person went to the defendant's premises, despite the warning of the latter to keep away, and by word and act indicated his purpose to attack the accused. The defendant was where he had the right to be, when the deceased advanced upon him in a threatening manner and with a deadly weapon, and if the accused did not provoke the assault, and had at the time reasonable grounds to believe, and in good faith believed, that the deceased intended to take his life, or do him great bodily harm, he was not obliged to retreat nor to consider whether he could safely retreat, but was entitled to stand his ground and meet any attack made upon him with a deadly weapon in such way and with such force as, under all the circumstances, he at the moment, honestly believed, and had reasonable grounds to believe, were necessary to save his own life or to protect himself from great bod-

ily injury.

Beard's conviction was overturned. The Court ordered a new trial.

The right of self-defense has a longstanding record in American jurisprudence, but for many years, Floridians were justified in the use of deadly force when faced with an imminent threat of death or great bodily harm only if they had no way to retreat from the impending danger, unless, of course, they were in their homes. But in 2005, the Florida legislature saw fit to enact what came to be known as the state's "Stand Your Ground" law, a statute that allows citizens to use deadly force without any duty to retreat if they reasonably believe "that such force is necessary to prevent imminent death or great bodily harm" or to "prevent the commission of a forcible felony" if the person using force is in a place where he or she is lawfully allowed to be and is not "engaged in an unlawful activity". Florida was the first state to enact a Stand Your Ground law. Twenty-four other states have since passed similar legislation.

In the wake of the shooting, Florida's Stand Your Ground law was cited as the reason Seminole County prosecutor Norm Wolfinger decided against charging Zimmerman with the killing. Negative publicity prompted Florida's governor, Rick Scott, to empanel a task force to review the legislation. Martin's mother, Sybrina Fulton, addressed the Task Force on Citizen Safety and Protection, urging the group to abolish the controversial law. "There is something seriously wrong when there is a minor child who was unarmed and he's dead right now and there is a law that the person is using to try to defend himself against killing a kid," Fulton said. "Please, I beg you, review the law again."

In August, Zimmerman's attorney, Mark O'Mara, said that he intended to file a motion to have Zimmerman's case dismissed based on the law. On August 9, O'Mara's staff posted a press release on the website for the attorney established for the case, gzlegalcase.com. "Since the beginning, there has been a rush to judgment in the case against George Zimmerman," the website explained. "Since the first day of his involvement, Mr.

O'Mara has emphasized that people should be patient and wait for the evidence to be released before forming opinions about the case." O'Mara described the Stand Your Ground hearing as a "mini-trial", one with no jury. The judge is the finder of fact. The defense has the burden of proof, but only to the preponderance of evidence: if it is more likely than not that Zimmerman was acting in self-defense, the judge must let him go. Under the law, if Zimmerman was acting in self-defense, he is immune from both criminal and civil prosecution. In other words, not only can he not be prosecuted, but he can't even be sued by Martin's family. But this protection applies not just to Stand Your Ground, but to self-defense in general.

Martin family attorney, Benjamin Crump, fired off a written statement in which he decried the use of Stand Your Ground and urged that "the unjustified killing of Trayvon Benjamin Martin should and will be decided by a jury."

"A grown man cannot profile and pursue an unarmed child, shoot him in the heart, and then claim stand your ground," Crump wrote. "We believe that the killer's motion will be denied during the Stand Your Ground Hearing, and as justice requires a jury will ultimately decide the fate of a man that killed an innocent child."

On June 10, journalist Jeff Weiner with the Orlando Sentinel wrote a piece on Stand Your Ground. Weiner quoted Jacksonville criminal defense attorney Keith Cobbin who explained the "mini-trial" aspect of a self-defense hearing. "You basically have a trial before the trial," Cobbin said. "Some of these things can actually be very much like trials, just without the jury."

If the judge grants Zimmerman's motion, the case will be dismissed. "If the judge dismisses the case, it's game over," Fort Lauderdale criminal defense lawyer Eric Schwartzreich told Weiner. Schwartzreich explained that there are other benefits for a defendant to request such a hearing. "You get to actually see in a courtroom how a witness will testify on the witness stand," he said.

Whether the judge will be willing to be the sole decider of both fact and law in a racially-charged, high-profile case is a question not easily answered by Zimmerman's defense team.

"There are some judges that don't want to stick their foot out there and say the buck stops here," Cobbin told Weiner.

Critics of Stand Your Ground argue that it allows criminals to get away with violence. In a July 22 article in the Tampa Bay Times, writers Kameel Stanley and Connie Humburg gave detailed accounts of several violent killers who had benefited from Florida's Stand Your Ground law, what they described as "the broadest self-defense law in the nation". "Killers have invoked stand your ground even after repeated run-ins with the law," the writers reported. "Forty percent had three arrests or more. Dozens had at least four arrests." But the writers did not make clear the distinction between those who had invoked the self-defense law and those who had been granted immunity.

Supporters of Stand Your Ground say the law makes Florida a safer state. In fact, they may be right. An April 15 article in the Miami Herald explained that violent crime in Florida dropped nineteen percent after the law was enacted in 2005, and the number of firearms crimes fell nine percent. But the number of murders increased twelve percent. Justifiable homicides have tripled.

On August 13, Associated Press journalist Kyle Hightower reported that Zimmerman's attorney, Mark O'Mara, would not pursue a Stand Your Ground argument but would instead move for a dismissal of the charges as a matter of "traditional self-defense". In O'Mara's view, Zimmerman couldn't retreat from Martin's attack. "The facts don't seem to support a 'stand your ground' defense," O'Mara said.

"People look at 'stand your ground' and immediately think somebody's standing there with deadly force—be it a gun or a weapon—and having the opportunity to back up but not having the need to under the statute," O'Mara explained. "I think the evidence in this case suggests that my client was reacting to having his nose broken and reacted to that by screaming out for help. He wasn't in position where I think there was any suggestion where he could retreat, which he is allowed to do under the statute."

"I think the facts seem to support that though we have a stand-your-ground immunity hearing, what this really is, is a simple, self-defense immunity hearing," Zimmerman's attorney said.

Harvard law professor Alan Dershowitz, writing for the Huffington Post, explained that Zimmerman's actions in following Martin do not deprive him of the right to defend himself. "A defendant, under Florida law, loses his 'stand your ground' defense if he provoked the encounter—but he retains traditional self-defense if he reasonably believed his life was in danger and his only recourse was to employ deadly force."

All of the nation's fuss about Stand Your Ground, it turns out, was for nothing. Stand Your Ground will not even be part of Zimmerman's defense.

# Prove It

*"Whether a judge or jury ultimately becomes the trier of fact in this case, I can assure you they will only get relevant, admissible evidence on which they can base their decision."*

—ANGELA COREY, SPECIAL PROSECUTOR

ANGELA COREY IS NO STRANGER to a courtroom. A prosecutor for over three decades, the bright-smiled lawyer has prosecuted over sixty-five homicides in her career. As the elected state attorney for the Fourth Circuit of Florida, she oversees the prosecution of hundreds of others. Born and raised in Jacksonville along with her brother and three sisters, the fifty-seven-year-old oversees all criminal prosecutions in three counties in coastal Northeast Florida.

For years, Duval, Nassau, and Clay counties rested on the bottom-end of the Old South, a place where the pace and purpose of life was just a little slower and a little more friendly than in other parts of the nation. Jacksonville used to be thought of as the biggest city in South Georgia until the real estate market boomed and Northerners looking for warmer weather and more sunshine couldn't find anyplace to live in South Florida, and even if they could find it, they couldn't afford it, so they steadily crept northward until suddenly Jacksonville's population grew by nearly six figures in just a decade and nearly a quarter million people since 1990. People from other parts of the country that couldn't find a place in Miami Beach or Boca Raton were more than happy to settle for a house in Atlantic Beach or Ponte Vedra or Amelia Island.

A military town, Jacksonville once boasted three major naval bases until Clinton-era cutbacks saw the closing of Cecil Field, a naval air station with a runway so long that it used to serve as one of the emergency landing sites for the space shuttle program. Two decades ago, almost everyone in Jacksonville was from the place or had moved there because of the military, but today things are different. It's busier. It's less friendly. It's not the biggest city in South Georgia anymore.

For eleven years running, Duval County had the highest murder rate among Florida's most-populated counties despite ranking sixth in population. But with over 821,000 residents, Jacksonville is both the largest and most populous city in Florida, but with a metropolitan population of 1.3 million, the five-county region falls behind the Miami, Fort Lauderdale, West Palm Beach, Tampa-St. Petersburg, and Orlando metro areas. Despite being farther north than any of those cities, Jacksonville is much more of a true Southern city. In Florida, the further north you go, the further south you get.

The St. Johns River runs through the middle of the city, a huge north-flowing waterway that in some places reaches three miles wide, in others ninety feet deep. Crossed by seven bridges, the river provides a view from Corey's office atop the fifteen-story City Hall Annex building. A photograph of Corey hangs on the wall next to photos of her predecessors, but this picture of an olive-complected, Middle Eastern woman is remarkably different than the portraits of all the older white men who held the job before her. A devout Episcopalian, Corey doesn't hide her faith, often wearing a cross around her neck.

Corey was hired as a prosecutor in 1981 by then-State-Attorney Ed Austin who went on to become mayor of Jacksonville. He was succeeded as state attorney by Harry Shorstein, a former Marine who served in combat as a captain in Vietnam and who was appointed by then-Governor Lawton Chiles after Austin resigned for his mayoral run. Shorstein was elected to the office in 1992 and again in 1996, and, unopposed in 2002 and 2004, he held the office until Corey took over in 2008.

During her time as an assistant state attorney, Corey earned a reputation as a tough prosecutor who was very friendly toward the police. Corey knew many of the 1,600 police officers at the Jacksonville Sheriff's Office, and her ties with officers often drew her into disputes between prosecutors and disgruntled policeman upset that their cases were being dropped. Corey's intervention on behalf of the police brought criticism from some of her colleagues who called Jacksonville's Finest Corey's "little babies". Corey spent many hours teaching officers about criminal law at the local police academy, and at one time rumors spread that she was contemplating running for sheriff of Duval County, a move that would have been highly popular with the rank-and-file officers.

While Corey was popular with police, Shorstein wasn't. His visits to the police academy were often a platform for war stories and explanations for why his office dropped so many cases. There has to be a reasonable probability of conviction, Shorstein would say, or we can't go forward. Corey, on the other hand, believed that cases should be heard by juries, not decided by prosecutors, and as the years passed, the relationship between Corey and Shorstein grew increasingly strained. Then, in November 2006, just days after Corey celebrated twenty-five years as an assistant state attorney, Shorstein fired her after having demoted her from being one of his top felony prosecutors to overseeing the office's misdemeanor division. The debacle came after Corey announced her intention to run against Shorstein in the upcoming election.

Corey had earned a reputation among lawyers, and an article in the Florida Times Union quoted Jacksonville attorney Bob Link who described Corey's dual personalities. "The standard comment about Angela was out of the courtroom she was a really nice person," Link said. "Inside the courtroom she was Attila the Hun."

Corey went to work in neighboring St. John's County for State Attorney John Tanner, one of Shorstein's many bitter foes. Then in February 2007, Shorstein announced that he would not seek reelection but would instead endorse the candidacy of his chief prosecutor, Jay Plotkin. In 2008, Corey handily defeated Plotkin with 64% of the votes.

When Corey took over the office, she made no bones about reorganizing. She fired ten attorneys and a slew of investigators and support staff. Corey implemented her policy of taking cases to trial to let the jury decide the accused's fate rather than dropping charges just because the case didn't appear to be a slam-dunk conviction. Corey re-opened a large number of cases that had been dropped by prosecutors while Shorstein was in office.

Corey's tough-on-crime approach did not come without cost. Defense attorneys complained that her approach allowed little room to negotiate plea bargains for clients whose guilt may have been mitigated by circumstances that weren't being considered by prosecutors. Judges complained that her policies were straining an already-overburdened justice system.

University of North Florida criminology professors Michael Halllett and Daniel Pontzer issued a report that questioned Corey's prosecution style. "While state attorney Angela Corey certainly lives up to every prosecutor's mantra to be 'tough on crime,'" they wrote, "is there a point where this becomes counter-productive?" The professors found that Corey's office was "a highly focused and hard-working office, driven by a sense of mission." They also found that, under Corey's leadership, the State Attorney's Office "had documented increases in filing rates, conviction rates and cases taken all the way to trial."

But the professors also complained that Corey's policies placed "great strain on the system" and had led to higher rates of incarceration, particularly of non-violent black offenders. "Is the political pressure to get tough on crime so powerful in Jacksonville that it has become the only viable 'brand' of Jacksonville criminal justice?" Hallett and Pontzer asked. "Even worse, is it possible that a political machine has emerged around the system with the power to sustain itself indefinitely, regardless of the costs to the community? These are serious questions, particularly given the well-documented economic and racial disparities that characterize Jacksonville crime and victimization rates."

In a March 6, 2012, article in the Folio Weekly, a Jacksonville-based periodical, Corey refused to back down from her prosecutorial record. "We don't apologize for prosecuting violent or repeat offenders," Corey explained. "We are filing more cases because we have a better relationship with the Jacksonville Sheriff's Office and are making better cases."

◈

Seminole County State Attorney Norm Wolfinger declined to charge Zimmerman citing Stand Your Ground. On March 22, Wolfinger announced that he was withdrawing from the case. "In the interest of the public safety of the citizens of Seminole County and to avoid even the appearance of a conflict of interest, I would respectfully request the executive assignment of another state attorney for the investigation and any prosecution arising from the circumstances surrounding the death of Trayvon B. Martin," the prosecutor wrote in a statement. "This request is being made in light of the public good with the intent of toning down the rhetoric and preserving the integrity of this investigation." Sanford police Chief Bill Lee stepped down the same day.

Jacksonville's News4Jax reported that Corey had been appointed to take over the investigation. "The governor called me late this afternoon and I accepted his request and we will begin tomorrow to look into the facts and circumstances in the shooting death of Trayvon Martin," Corey told WJXT. "It requires a thorough investigation, extensive interviews of every witness and extensive review of all evidence, and then a determination of how we apply Florida's law to the facts of any case."

"I believe Gov. Scott is very comfortable with the level of homicide prosecution that I have done myself," Corey was quoted in her hometown newspaper, the Florida Times-Union, "and he knows that we handle a lot of homicides and a lot of issues with justifiable use of deadly force."

Soon after Corey was appointed to take over the case, criticism was leveled at the decision. The New Black Panther Party and the Southern Christian Leadership Conference organized protests outside Corey's office because of their displeasure with her decisions to charge young black juveniles as adults, particularly a 12-year-old boy name Christian Fernandez who beat his two-year-old brother to death and sexually molested his five-year-old half-brother. The case has drawn critics from around the world who have urged Corey to charge the boy as a child, but Corey has steadfastly stood by her decision because, as she has explained, the juvenile justice system only has jurisdiction over the accused killer until the age of twenty-one. If he's still a threat to society then, the system can't do anything about it but wait for him to offend again.

On April 11, Corey announced that she had charged Zimmerman with second-degree murder. After introducing her two top homicide prosecutors, Bernie de la Rionda and John Guy, Corey told the nation what had taken place during the three weeks since her office took over the investigation. "I can tell you we did not come to this decision lightly," Corey said. "In fact, this case is much like the many difficult homicides in our circuit and we have made numerous decisions in the same manner. Let me emphasize that we do not prosecute by pressure or petition. We prosecute cases based on the relevant facts of each case and on the laws of the state of Florida."

"We launched an intensive investigation," Corey explained, "building on all of the work that Sanford police and the Eighteenth  Circuit [State Attorney's Office] had already done. . . . We've tried to leave no stone unturned."

Corey explained her duty as a prosecutor and told the nationwide audience that the courtroom was the place for the case to be tried. "We are held to a strict standard about what we can and cannot discuss about a criminal case," Corey said. "Details come out in front of the trier of fact, bit by bit, in painstaking detail, relevant fact by relevant fact, and it is done that way for a reason: to protect the rights of all involved."

"Whether a judge or jury ultimately becomes the trier of fact in this case," Corey said, "I can assure you they will only get relevant, admissible evidence on which they can then base their decision."

Corey had one last request for the news media: "[W]e implore you to allow this case to be tried in the proper arena, a court of jurisdiction in Seminole County."

The allegations against Zimmerman were detailed in what some have described as a "thin" probable cause affidavit signed by Corey's investigators, Dale Gilbreath and T. C. O'Steen, who between them have been investigating homicides for forty-four years. According to the affidavit, the investigators "along with other law enforcement officials have taken sworn statements from witnesses, spoken with law enforcement officers who have provided sworn testimony in reports, reviewed other reports, recorded statements, phone records, recorded calls to police, photographs, videos, and other documents" in order to develop their conclusions:

> On Sunday 2/26/12, Trayvon Martin was temporarily living at the Retreat at Twin Lakes, a gated community in Sanford, Seminole County, Florida. That evening Martin walked to a nearby 7-11 store where he purchased a can of iced tea and a bag of skittles [sic]. Martin then walked back to and entered the gated community and was on his way back to the townhouse where he was living when he was profiled by George Zimmerman. Martin was unarmed and was not committing a crime.
>
> Zimmerman who also lived in the gated community, and was driving his vehicle observed Martin and assumed Martin was a criminal. Zimmerman felt Martin did not belong in the gated community and called the police. Zimmerman spoke to the dispatcher and asked for an officer to respond because Zimmerman perceived that Martin was acting suspicious. The police dispatcher informed Zimmerman that an officer was on the way and to wait for the officer.[†]
>
> During the recorded call Zimmerman made reference to people he felt had committed and gotten away with break-ins in his neighborhood. Later while talking about Martin, Zimmerman stated "these assholes, they always get away" and also said "these fucking punks".
>
> During this time, Martin was on the phone with a friend and described to her what was happening. The witness advised that Martin was scared because he was being followed through the complex by an unknown male and didn't know why. Martin attempted to run home but was followed by Zimmerman who didn't want the person he falsely assumed was

---

†   The dispatcher never told Zimmerman to "wait for the officer". Zimmerman asked, "How long until you get an officer over here?" The dispatcher replied, "Yeah, we've got someone on the way. Just let me know if this guy does anything else."

going to commit a crime to get away before the police arrived. Zimmerman got out of his vehicle and followed Martin. When the police dispatcher realized Zimmerman was pursuing Martin, he instructed Zimmerman not to do that and that the responding officer would meet him. Zimmerman disregarded the police dispatcher and continued to follow Martin who was trying to return to his home.

Zimmerman confronted Martin and a struggle ensued. Witnesses heard people arguing and what sounded like a struggle. During this time period witnesses heard numerous calls for help and some of these were recorded in 911 calls to police. Trayvon Martin's mother has reviewed the 911 calls and identified the voice crying for help as Trayvon Martin's voice.

Zimmerman shot Martin in the chest. When police arrived Zimmerman admitted shooting Martin. Officers recovered a gun from a holster inside Zimmerman's waistband. A fired casing that was recovered at the scene was determined to have been fired from the firearm.

Assistant Medical Examiner Dr. Bao performed an autopsy and determined that Martin died from the gunshot wound.

The facts mentioned in this Affidavit are not a complete recitation of all the pertinent facts and evidence in this case but only are presented for a determination of Probable Cause for Second Degree Murder.

Critics were quick to lambaste Corey for presenting such a lacking affidavit of probable cause. On April 13, John Lott wrote an editorial for the National Review Online entitled, "Where's the 'Probable Cause'?" "The charges brought against George Zimmerman sure look like prosecutorial misconduct," Lott wrote, calling the affidavit "startlingly weak".

"As a former chief economist at the U.S. Sentencing Commission, I have read a number of such affidavits, and cannot recall one lacking so much relevant information," Lott explained. "The prosecutor has most likely deliberately overcharged, hoping to intimidate Zimmerman into agreeing to a plea bargain. If this case goes to trial, Zimmerman will almost definitely be found 'not guilty' on the charge of second-degree murder."

Lott criticized Corey for not taking the case before a grand jury. "A grand-jury indictment would have provided political cover; that charges were brought without one means that the prosecutor was worried that a grand jury would not give her the indictment."

Andrew McCarthy, who, in his words, has "nearly 20 years of writing and supervising the writing of complaint affidavits", blogged on April 13 saying the affidavit is "not law, it is agit-prop". "If I were a cynic," McCarthy wrote, "I'd say that an ambitious special prosecutor—exploiting the rabble-rousing of the U.S. attorney general and the racial grievance industry—filed an exceedingly serious charge for which she lacks evidence, second degree murder, in order to bask in the mob's adulation while pressuring Zimmerman to plead guilty to a lesser charge, manslaughter, on which the special prosecutor runs a high risk of losing if Zimmerman forces a trial. So I'm sure glad I'm not a cynic."

Harvard law professor Alan Dershowitz called the affidavit "irresponsible and unethical." "[Corey] was aware when she submitted an affidavit that it did not contain the truth, the whole truth and nothing but the truth," Dershowitz wrote in the Huffington Post on May 21. "She deliberately withheld evidence that supported Zimmerman's claim of self-defense."

One Internet commentator wrote that the affidavit "appears to say something while not really saying anything at all" and proposed how history would look if written the same way: "The United States profiled Japan. The United States confronted Japan and a struggle ensued."

Despite her critics, Corey also had her supporters. Writing for the National Review Online, David French commented that anytime "an armed man shoots an unarmed man, unless there are compelling facts to the contrary, charges are expected and routine." "While the affidavit is quite brief and lacks detail," French wrote, "it does contain three key factual assertions, that —if proven—will vindicate those who called for Zimmerman's arrest." French said that "the affidavit indicates that Zimmerman 'confronted' Martin, but it's agnostic on who initiated the 'struggle.'"

Orlando criminal lawyer and CNN legal analyst Mark Nejame commented on Dershowitz's criticism of the affidavit on June 22. "Dershowitz claims that Corey was required to include in her probable cause affidavit any information that would tend to exculpate Zimmerman of the charges against him," Nejame wrote. "He's incorrect, unfortunately." Nejame explained that "offering a bare-bones affidavit is relatively common and so long as the language is truthful, done in good faith and doesn't intentionally mislead the court, then the prosecutor is not obligated to provide evidence that might be exculpatory to a defendant in an affidavit."

Still, Nejame explained that, although not required by Florida law, he believes "such information should be included so that a judge can make a fully informed decision." "If the facts disclose that the court was intentionally misled by the way information was presented to it," Nejame wrote, "that is a cause for grave concern and reconsideration."

"[T]he affidavit Corey filed in the Zimmerman case," Nejame explained, "is about as minimal as I've seen in more than 30 years of practice as a criminal defense attorney."

But questions of whether or not the affidavit contained sufficient probable cause were answered the day after Zimmerman's arrest when Judge Mark Herr determined that there was. The case would move forward. The defense has not challenged the legal sufficiency of the affidavit.

Prosecuting Zimmerman will not be easy. On March 26, ABC News reported that Corey acknowledged the difficulty in proving the case against Zimmerman. "The stand-your-ground law is one portion of justifiable use of deadly force," Corey told ABC News. "And what that means is that the state must go forward and be able to prove its case beyond a reasonable doubt. . . . So it makes the case in general more difficult than a normal criminal case."

◈

Much has been said in this case about the fact that Zimmerman followed and even chased Martin. Many in the public and the news media have claimed that Zimmerman failed to stop when the dispatcher told him not to continue following Martin. Many, including the special prosecutor, even claim that Zimmerman was told not to follow Martin before he got out his car. But that simply isn't true.

In the probable cause affidavit filed by the Corey in the case, Zimmerman's failure to stop following Martin was cited as part of the reason for believing that he should be charged with second-degree murder. "When the police dispatcher realized Zimmerman was pursuing Martin," the affidavit reads, "he instructed Zimmerman not to do that and that the responding officer would meet him. Zimmerman disregarded the police dispatcher and continued to follow Martin who was trying to return to his home."

But did Zimmerman really "continue to follow Martin" as the affidavit alleges? The background wind that started when Zimmerman got out of his car ended within ten seconds of the dispatcher's chiding. As the background noise subsided, Zimmerman, clearly slowing his pace, told the dispatcher, "He ran." Zimmerman used the past tense. Just over half a minute earlier, Zimmerman used the present tense when he exclaimed, "Shit, he's running." He's running. He ran. Background noise. No background noise. The beginning and the end. Zimmerman stopped following Martin a minute and a half before his call to police ended.

Zimmerman's call to police lasted four minutes and thirteen seconds. Two minutes and fourteen seconds into the call, Zimmerman's car door closed as he began following Martin. Twenty-eight seconds later, the wind noise subsided indicating that Zimmerman had likely slowed his pace. Over the next minute-and-a-half, he told the dispatcher twice that Martin was gone. But where did he go?

The probable cause affidavit alleges that Martin was "trying to return to his home", although he was actually heading to Brandy Green's home where he was temporarily staying. Zimmerman told police that he parked his car near a cut-through, a sidewalk that connects two roads and intersects the sidewalk where the physical altercation eventually took place. The walking distance from where that cut-through begins to the front door of Brandy Green's townhouse—the residence where Martin was staying—is about six hundred fifty feet. The average normal walking speed for a young adult is about five feet per second, a brisk walk about seven feet per second. At that pace, seventeen-year-old Trayvon Martin would have been inside Green's residence in about a minute and a half to two minutes. Zimmerman was on the phone with police for two minutes and six seconds after telling the dispatcher that Martin was running. If Martin "was trying to return to his home", even walking at a leisurely pace, he would have been safely inside by the time Zimmerman's call to police ended.

Zimmerman was on the phone with Sanford police for a total of four minutes and thirteen seconds. The distance from where Zimmerman says he first saw Martin—which is near a cut-through in the gated community's fence—to Green's residence is about one-quarter mile. During the time that Zimmerman was on the phone with police, Martin could have walked all the way to Green's home at the comfortable pace of five-and-a-half feet per second—less than four miles per hour.

Martin's girlfriend, DeeDee, claimed that Martin, after running some distance from the "creepy" Zimmerman, was too tired to run anymore. But this claim simply doesn't make sense. The distance from where Martin likely entered the complex through an opening in the fence to the area where the shooting occurred was only one-sixth of a mile.[‡] Martin, a seventeen-year-old high school athlete, would have been able to walk that distance at the leisurely pace of five feet per second in only three minutes, and he should have been able to run the entire quarter-mile to his father's fiancée's house comfortably in a minute-and-a-half. In fact, for the sequence of events to have unfolded as DeeDee claims, Martin would have to have walked the distance from the fence opening to where he was killed at the incredibly slow pace of only three-and-a-half feet per second—less than two-and-a-half miles per hour. That's the average walking speed for adult pedestrians over the age of sixty-five.

---

[‡]    If Martin entered through the front gate, the distance would have been even less.

Zimmerman's defense team does not need a forensic expert to prove this point. They can simply demonstrate by walking Martin's route to prove that the teen had more than enough time to make it home. Start playing the recording of Zimmerman's call to police and then walk from where Zimmerman first saw Martin to Brandy Green's townhouse as the recording plays. Unless you walk really slowly, you'll make it to Green's house before the call ends. Do this with the judge and jury and they will be convinced beyond doubt that Martin could have made it home.

One interesting observation that has not been mentioned in this case is the location where Zimmerman said he first saw Martin relative to where the shooting took place. During his videotaped walk-through interview, Zimmerman pointed out a place in front of 1460 Retreat View Circle as the spot where he first saw Martin standing in the rain. From the cut-through in the fence where Martin likely entered the complex, that spot is in the opposite direction from where the shooting happened. The distance from the cut-through to Brandy Green's apartment is about the same whether one goes around the front of the complex or the back. If Martin walked from the cut-through to 1460, he was walking toward the back, away from where the shooting took place. That means he had to have changed course and gone toward the front of the complex past the clubhouse, the direction Zimmerman went after passing Martin. Did Martin see Zimmerman staring at him and decide to follow the "creepy" man to see where he was going? Nobody will ever know.

DeeDee also claimed when the confrontation began, Martin's cell phone fell to the ground. "Trayvon said, 'What are you following me for?' and the man said, 'What are you doing here?' Next thing I hear is somebody pushing, and somebody pushed Trayvon because the headset just fell. She told de la Rionda that she could "hear the grass". But Martin's cell phone was found near his body, about thirty-five feet from where the altercation began. Either he kept it in his hand during the struggle or it was in his pocket. Did he hang up on DeeDee and put the phone in his pocket in order to fight Zimmerman? Zim-

merman said that he thought Martin had something in his
hands when he was punching the neighborhood watchman.
Could it have been the cell phone? We'll probably never know.

Zimmerman claims he was never running. In his interview
with Sean Hannity, Zimmerman said that the background noise
and his stressed voice were due to wind on that rainy night.
However, records show that a weather station at Orlando-San-
ford International Airport, just five miles from the Twin Lakes
community, recorded a sustained wind speed of only seven
miles per hour at 6:53 p.m., twenty-three minutes before Zimmerman fired the fatal shot. No wind gusts were recorded.[†]

But just how fast was Zimmerman going? The distance
from where he parked his truck to the "T" in the sidewalk was
about 150 feet. Zimmerman told police that he was near the
"T" when the dispatcher asked him if he was following Martin.
If Zimmerman went from his vehicle to the "T" during the
twenty-three seconds of background noise, he was traveling at
about six-and-a-half feet per second—about four-and-a-half
miles per hour, a thirteen-and-a-half minute mile. He wasn't
running very fast. A scared seventeen-year-old high school athlete could have easily run that distance in half the time.[‡]

As much as Zimmerman tried to dance around the fact that
he followed Martin, his story of "going in the same direction"
as Martin and trying to find a street sign or an address he could
give police simply doesn't fit with what took place during his

---

[†]   Zimmerman led Sanford police through a videotaped walk-through of
      the events less than twenty-four hours after the shooting. There is very
      little wind noise present in the audio of that recording even though the
      recorded wind speeds at that time were over thirteen miles per hour,
      nearly double what they were during the actual incident. Zimmerman's
      voice also sounds normal, not stressed. On April 2, Martin's girlfriend,
      DeeDee, told Bernie de la Rionda that, at one point during her call to
      Martin, he was running and she "could hear that the wind [was] blow-
      ing." She did not report hearing wind blowing at any other point during
      the call.

[‡]   In 1994, at the age of twenty-two, while finishing the police academy
      and testing for a job with the Jacksonville Sheriff's Office, I ran a mile in
      five minutes and fifty-four seconds and a quarter mile in sixty-eight sec-
      onds. I was five feet six inches tall and weighed one hundred forty-seven
      pounds. (Unfortunately for me, those days are long gone.)

call to Sanford police. He claimed that he couldn't recall the name of Twin Trees Lane, so he was trying to get an address on Retreat View Circle. But if that was his intent, he never followed through. Zimmerman didn't give the dispatcher any address other than the Twin Lakes clubhouse, which he provided early in the call.

The distance from where Zimmerman parked his truck to Retreat View Circle is about 240 feet; the distance back from there to where the altercation began is another 100 feet—340 feet in total. At the leisurely walking pace of five feet per second, Zimmerman would have covered that distance in only sixty-eight seconds. Zimmerman, then, spent at least an additional minute and two seconds somewhere between Retreat View Circle and the "T" in the sidewalk, not including the thirty seconds Zimmerman said elapsed between the time the call ended and when the confrontation with Martin began.

If Zimmerman had walked the 240 feet from his truck to Retreat View Circle and then walked all the way back to his truck, at a pace of between five and six-and-a-half feet per second, it would have taken him between one minute and fourteen seconds and one minute and thirty-six seconds. In other words, he had plenty of time to walk, get the address, and walk back while he was still on the phone with police. But he didn't do that. He didn't walk back to his truck, and he didn't give the dispatcher an address.

We're left, then, with two apparent facts: Zimmerman's timeline doesn't square with the evidence, and Martin wasn't trying to get home. Exactly what either of them did during the extra time nobody really knows. What we do know is that Zimmerman, concerned that the "real suspicious" black teenager dressed in a dark-colored hoodie would be another one of "these assholes" that "always get away" ended up in a physical confrontation with Martin, who saw Zimmerman as a "creepy" white man who was following him.

Zimmerman said that as he walked past the "T" on the way back to his truck, Martin approached from between the buildings. Where did Martin come from? There are any number of places where he could have hidden from Zimmerman's view

and waited. Witnesses described the fifty-foot-wide stretch between the two rows of buildings as being very dark, so much so
that most of the witnesses really couldn't see anything. Zimmerman had a flashlight, but he told Serino that it wasn't
working, and Serino showed him that he had to bang on it to
make it work. Serino had a light just like it.[†]

The altercation clearly began where Zimmerman said it did,
near the "T" in the sidewalk. His flashlight and a key were
found right there. A brown plastic 7-11 bag was on the sidewalk just a few feet closer to where Martin's body was found.[‡]
Witnesses testified that they could hear the altercation getting
closer.

Exactly what happened at the "T" has yet to be fully explained, except by Zimmerman, who claims that Martin approached him, some words were exchanged, and then Martin
punched him in the nose. While some argue that Zimmerman
can't prove that is what happened, the fact is that the prosecutors can't prove that it didn't. As with any person accused of a
crime, Zimmerman is under no obligation to prove anything;
the State of Florida has the burden of proof. The jury does not
have the luxury of simply disbelieving Zimmerman; in court,
testimony under oath is assumed to be truthful unless proven
otherwise. If the prosecutors cannot put on a witness who saw
Zimmerman attack Martin, the jury will have to assume that
Zimmerman's testimony is true.

If Martin did punch Zimmerman in the nose, why did he do
it? Was he angered that this "creepy" man was following him?
That this "creepy" *white* man was following him? Many have
speculated that Zimmerman was motivated to his suspicions by

---

[†]  The Florida Department of Law Enforcement used a Total Station—a
laser surveying instrument—to diagram the scene. Their diagram notes
that a small flashlight was "illuminated". The flashlight was found next
to a Honda key. Zimmerman was a driving a silver Honda Ridgeline. Another larger black flashlight was on the ground closer to Martin's body,
but it is unclear who's flashlight that was. Witness 13 carried a flashlight
with him when he went to the scene after Zimmerman shot Martin.

[‡]  A white plastic WalMart bag was on the grass several feet away. However,
there has been no evidence released that explains where the WalMart
bag came from or if it is even connected to this case.

the fact that Martin was a black teenager dressed in a hoodie, but could Martin have likewise felt threatened that a white man was following him? Again, we'll probably never know.

Zimmerman told investigators that Martin confronted him, and DeeDee's testimony confirms that Martin was the first to say something when the two first came face-to-face. Although the language differs between DeeDee's account and Zimmerman's, it is clear that some verbal exchange took place. Zimmerman told investigators that he reached into his pocket to grab his cell phone to dial 911. Is it possible that Martin doubled back to confront Zimmerman to find out why he was following him? (DeeDee said that Martin asked, "What are you following me for?") If so, did Martin perceive that Zimmerman was reaching for a weapon and react by punching Zimmerman in the nose? Again, we'll probably never know for sure, but it is clear that Martin did not go home. Based on the testimony of both Zimmerman and DeeDee, it is most likely that Martin either waited somewhere out of Zimmerman's view or returned to the "T" after seeing Zimmerman walking back to his truck.

We do know that Zimmerman's nose was broken. We know that he had cuts on the back of his head that were photographed by police. We know that both Witness 13 and the first arriving police officer saw blood on Zimmerman's face and head. We know that the Sanford Fire Department reported that Zimmerman had "abrasions to his forehead" and "bleeding/tenderness to his nose", along with a "small laceration to the back of his head". We know that Zimmerman went to his doctor's office the following day and was diagnosed with "scalp lacerations", a broken nose, and black eyes.

Zimmerman was seen by Lindzee Folgate, a physician's assistant at Altamonte Family Practice. Folgate noted that Zimmerman complained of "nasal pain" and was "involved in an altercation" during which "he was assaulted, punched in the face, and shoved to the ground where his head was hit into the pavement multiple times." "During the altercation," Folgate noted, "he had a weapon as he is authorized to carry a firearm and he fired at the attacker, killing him. . . . He denies [headaches], change in [visual acuity], slurred speech, dizziness, or gait abnormality." Folgate also noted that Zimmerman admitted to "occasional nausea when thinking about the violence last night".

"No sutures needed given well-approximated skin margins," Folgate noted regarding the cuts on Zimmerman's head. "Continue to clean with soap and water daily. We discussed the red flag symptoms that would warrant imaging given the type of assault he sustained. Given the type of trauma, we discussed that it is imperative he be seen with his Psychologist [*sic*] for evaluation."

"We discussed that [his nose] is likely broken," Folgate reported, "but does not appear to have septal deviation. The swelling and black eyes are typical of this injury. I recommended that he be evaluated by ENT but he refused."[†]

How the altercation began may never be known, but the fact is that it did. The evidence shows that Zimmerman, at least during the time leading up to the shooting, was on his back while Martin had control of him. Zimmerman's back was wet and covered with grass. He had injuries to the back of his head. Witness 6 clearly saw Martin on top of Zimmerman "throwing down blows". Witness 12 is the only person who claims to have seen Zimmerman on top of the melee, but she didn't make that claim until a month after the shooting. Originally she told investigators that she couldn't tell, but on March 26 said that after seeing Martin and Zimmerman on television she believed it was Zimmerman that was on top "because of his size". But that testimony is tenuous at best, and if the prosecution elects to put her on the stand to testify to that claim, Mark O'Mara will have plenty of ammunition for cross-examination. None of the other witnesses could say who was on top except for Witness 3 who saw someone in a white shirt on top. Problem is, neither

† Some, especially bloggers, have claimed that these medical records cannot be believed because they are from Zimmerman's own doctor's office. However, making such accusations without any evidence to support it is irresponsible; in so doing, one is accusing a medical professional of ethics violations that could lead to loss of licensure. Furthermore, unless the prosecutors can disprove this evidence (and it is highly doubtful that they can), it is likely the only medical evidence that will be presented in court regarding Zimmerman's injuries.

Zimmerman nor Martin was wearing a white shirt, and the hysterical woman was so confused that she thought the guy in the
hoodie was the one who got handcuffed, but he was actually
the one who was lying on the ground dead from a gunshot
wound.

But there's more. The discrepancy between the autopsy
showing that the shot was fired from intermediate range and
the crime lab examination showing that the muzzle was in contact with the hoodie is a key piece of information. The discrepancy between the two means that the muzzle was touching the
sweatshirt but the sweatshirt wasn't touching the skin. There
were several inches of space in between them, several inches
that were likely caused by the loose-fitting sweatshirts (both
the hoodie and the light grey Nike sweatshirt Martin was wearing beneath the hoodie) were hanging down from Martin's
body as he leaned over Zimmerman.

Some have argued that Martin was just a "scrawny" kid and
Zimmerman was "twice his size". Martin stood five feet eleven
inches tall and weighed 158 pounds; Zimmerman stood five
feet seven-and-a-half inches tall and weighed 204 pounds.‡
Though Zimmerman had forty-six pounds on Martin, it didn't
matter much if he was on his back. Martial artists who ground
fight win competitions by getting their opponents off their feet
and pinning them to the ground. Once in that position, it takes
great strength or well-honed skill to regain control. Martin has
been described as an athlete, Zimmerman as obese. To assert
that Martin was at some great disadvantage is simply ignorant
of what it takes to win a ground fight. They weren't boxing.
They weren't sumo wrestling. They weren't competing to see
who would score the most points. They were fighting a real
fight, and as virtually every police officer knows, the person on
top is probably going to win—especially when being subjected
to a "ground and pound"—unless the person on the bottom is
armed.

Zimmerman claims he was getting his head pounded on the

---

‡    At the age of twenty-two, I was a police officer who stood five feet six
     inches tall and weighed 147 pounds, eleven pounds less than Trayvon
     Martin.

pavement. Prosecutors are likely to argue that his injuries weren't serious enough for him to have been getting hit hard on the concrete. But Zimmerman said it felt like his head was "going to explode." The defense argument will likely focus on what Zimmerman would perceive having his head repeatedly hitting the concrete. Mark O'Mara might argue to the jury that if getting your head banged against concrete has to be done so hard that it makes a sound that could be heard by Witness 6— as de la Rionda asked the man during a sworn statement—then who in the jury is willing to go outside and have his or her head banged against the concrete to test the theory? Serino indicated to Zimmerman during an interview that getting your head slammed against concrete results in "skull fractures", but did the investigator ever test the theory? Did he have his head banged against concrete to figure out how hard it would have to be struck to cause skull fractures? Virtually no rational person would, and that's the point.

But the State could test the theory if they are willing to go to that expense. Biomechanical engineers can employ biofidelic anthropomorphic mannequins—"crash test dummies"—to determine the force needed to cause skull fractures and to provide some idea of what effect such head strikes would have on a person experiencing them. That testing could cut either way: the results may favor the defense, and the prosecution, if it undertakes such testing, would be obligated to share the results with Mark O'Mara.

◈

Anyone who believes that the case against George Michael Zimmerman is a slam dunk win for prosecutors has no idea what it takes to prosecute a person for murder. Juries are finicky, even with the best of evidence. And in this case, the prosecution hasn't been handed the best of evidence.

Forensic evidence is, unfortunately, not like it looks on television. The police don't really have some super-high-tech computer that will access every database in the world instantly to provide the name, address, telephone number, height, weight, hair color, eye color, next-of-kin, and place of employment of a person and then bring up a live, real-time view of the person walking down the street. Those popular forensic-geek shows even use computers that don't look like normal computers but instead have magic holographic touch screens and flash all sorts of scrolling text and busy-looking windows on the computer screen so the the viewer thinks, Man, I wish my computer could do that.

Well, maybe the CIA has some of those make-believe television show toys, but the Sanford police certainly do not. The Florida Department of Law Enforcement doesn't, either, and, for that matter, neither does the special prosecutor's office. The FBI might have some super-secret, state-of-the-art technology, but probably not anything like what they have on *Criminal Minds*. There's no special technology out there that will tell the jury who was screaming for help, who was on top of the fracas, who chased whom, who ran, who walked, who hid, who lied, or who hit whom first.

We do know this: On the rainy evening of February 26, 2012, at the Retreat at Twin Lakes in Sanford, Seminole County, Florida, George Michael Zimmerman, the captain of the community's neighborhood watch program, saw Trayvon Benjamin Martin, an unarmed seventeen-year-old wearing a dark-colored hoodie, walking in the complex, apparently near 1460 Retreat View Circle. Zimmerman thought Martin looked suspicious, so he called the police non-emergency number. He told the dispatcher that Martin looked like he was up to no good, on drugs or something. These assholes, they always get away.

We know that Martin started running and that Zimmerman followed after him but quickly lost sight of the hoodie-wearing teen. We know that Zimmerman stayed on the phone with police long enough that Martin could have made it home, but he didn't. We know that Zimmerman said he walked across to get an address to give to the dispatcher, but he never gave it and he stayed out of his car much longer than it would have taken to simply walk across, get the nearest address on Retreat View Circle, and then walk back to the parked Honda Ridgeline.

We know that sometime after Zimmerman got off the

phone with police, he and Martin encountered one another near the "T" in the sidewalk. We know that words were exchanged. We know that one of them put his hands on the other, and they struggled, moving a distance of about forty feet from where they first started fighting to where George Zimmerman shot Trayvon Martin one time in the chest with his Kel-Tec 9mm pistol.

We know that Trayvon Benjamin Martin died. We know that his body was taken to the morgue tagged as John Doe and that it wasn't until the next day when his father called to report him missing that the police knew who he was or that his family knew he was dead.

But the physical evidence taken in context of the testimonial evidence tells us more. It tells us that the two were involved in a close-quarters struggle. It tells us that Zimmerman was on his back during much of the fight, including when he fired the fatal shot.

This is not a case in which the facts lead unambiguously to a conclusion that the killing falls on one side of the law or the other. It is also not a case in which Zimmerman did nothing right and Martin did nothing wrong.

The truth is that most of what we know about what happened that night we learned from George Zimmerman, and nothing in the physical evidence provides unequivocal proof that the killing happened in a way that was substantially different from what George Zimmerman claimed. Was Zimmerman's use of deadly force reasonable under the circumstances? That's an issue to be decided in court. Will he be convicted of second-degree murder or at least manslaughter? That remains to be seen, but the prospects aren't great. And despite Benjamin Crump's lamentations to the contrary, if the State has only George Zimmerman's account of what happened that evening, then they will have to convict him based on his words by proving to a jury that even what he says he did constitutes second-degree murder or some lesser included offense under Florida law.

If the State of Florida can't do that, then George Zimmerman will walk out of the courtroom a free man. Trayvon Martin, however, will still be dead.

# Time-Line of the Shooting

| | |
|---|---|
| 19:09:34 | Zimmerman calls Sanford police. |
| 19:10:02 | Begins giving a description of suspicious person |
| 19:10:12 | Jeans or sweat pants and white tennis shoes |
| 19:10:17 | Staring at the houses |
| 19:10:22 | Now he is staring at me |
| 19:10:32 | At clubhouse, coming towards me |
| 19:10:34 | Got his hand in his waistband |
| 19:10:57 | "He's coming to check me out." |
| 19:11:12 | "These assholes, they always get away." |
| 19:11:42 | "Shit, he's running." |
| 19:11:47 | Zimmerman exits his vehicle. |
| 19:11:50 | Wind noise can be heard in background of call. |
| 19:11:55 | Zimmerman stated, "These fucking punks!" |
| 19:11:57 | "Are you following him?" |
| 19:12:00 | "We don't need you to do that." |
| 19:12:01 | Zimmerman replied, "Okay." |
| 19:12:13 | Zimmerman stated, "He ran!" |
| 19:12:15 | Wind noise in background stops. |
| 19:12:30 | Will meet with the officer, gives directions. |
| 19:13:09 | Zimmerman begins to give his address. |
| 19:13:10 | "I don't know where this kid is." |
| 19:13:14 | "Do you just want to meet . . . near the mail-boxes?" |
| 19:13:22 | "Could you have the officer call me . . . ?" |
| 19:13:39 | Call Ends |

3:04 elapse from the end of Zimmerman's call to Witness #11's 911 call

| | |
|---|---|
| 19:16:43 | 911 call from witness #11 |
| 19:17:20 | Shot fired |

2:23 elapse from the time the shot is recorded until Officer Smith takes Zimmerman in custody.

19:17:40        Officer T. Smith arrives on scene
19:19:43        Officer T. Smith takes Zimmerman into custody

# List of People

Trayvon Martin      Victim of the Shooting

George Zimmerman    Charged with killing Trayvon Martin

## Sanford Police Department

| | |
|---|---|
| Bill Lee | Chief of Police |
| Trekell Perkins | Investigator |
| Timothy Smith | Patrol Officer |
| Ricardo Ayala | Patrol Officer |
| Jonathan Mead | Patrol Officer |
| William Ervin | Investigator |
| Mike Bernosky | Traffic Officer |
| Anthony Raimondo | Sergeant |
| Joseph Santiago | Sergeant |
| Stacie McCoy | Sergeant |
| Diana Smith | Crime Scene Technician |
| Michael Wagner | Patrol Officer |
| A. Johnson | Patrol Officer |
| Carlos Davila | Patrol Officer |
| Leon Ciesla | Sergeant |
| Kristen Bentsen | |
| Doris Singleton | Investigator |
| James McAuliffe | |
| Arthur Barns | Sergeant |
| Christopher Serino | Detective Major Crimes Unit |
| Rebecca Villalona | Major Crimes Investigator |
| Wendy Dorival | Community Volunteer Coordinator |
| Adam Johnson | Patrol Officer |
| Josh Memminger | Gang Suppression Intelligence Unit |
| Steve Lynch | Patrol Officer |
| Neil Robertson | Reserve Police Officer |
| Lonnie Taylor | Detective General Investigation |
| Mike Taylor | Lieutenant in Patrol |

David Morgenstern    Public Information Officer
**Seminole County Sheriff's Office**

Jordan Broderick    Deputy, Patrol Division

**Governor**

Rick Scott    Governor of Florida

**State Attorney's Office, 18th Circuit (Seminole County)**

Norm Wolfinger    State Attorney
Kelly Jo Hines    Assistant State Attorney
Bob Veaudry    Investigator
Jim Rick    Investigator
James Post    Investigator

**Special Prosecutor's Office**

Angela Corey    Special Prosecutor & State Attorney
Bernie de la Rionda    Assistant State Attorney
John Guy    Assistant State Attorney
Dale Gilbreath    Investigator
T. C. O'Steen    Investigator
Dave Bisplinghoff    Investigator
John Zipperer    Investigator

**Private Attorneys**

Benjamin Crump    Attorney for the Martin Family
Natalie Jackson    Attorney for Martin Family
Mark O'Mara    Attorney for George Zimmerman
Craig Sonner    George Zimmerman's First Attorney
M. Scott    Peeler  Attorney for Witness

## Family Members

| | |
|---|---|
| Tracy Martin | Trayvon Martin's Father |
| Brandy Green | Tracy Martin's Fiancee |
| Chad Green | Brandy Green's Son |
| Sybrina Fulton | Trayvon Martin's Mother |

## Volusia County Medical Examiner's Office

| | |
|---|---|
| Shiping Boa | Associate Medical Examiner |
| Tara Malphurs | Forensic Investigator |

## Sanford Fire Department

| | |
|---|---|
| Kevin O'Rourke | E.M.T., Station 38 |
| Michael Turner | Lieutenant, Station 38 |
| Stacy Livingston | Firefighter, Station 38 |
| Tyler Rochefort | Firefighter, Station 38 |
| Mike Brandy | Paramedic, Station 38 |

## Florida Department of Law Enforcement (FDLE)

| | |
|---|---|
| Anthony Gorgone | Laboratory Analyst |
| Alvin Guzman | Forensic Technologist |
| Stephen Krejci | Crime Lab Analyst |
| Megan Myburgh | Crime Lab Analyst |
| Amy Siewert | Crime Lab Analyst |
| John Batchelor | Special Agent |
| Steve Brenton | Special Agent |
| David Lee | Special Agent Supervisor |
| Dale Crosby | Special Agent |
| Jeffrey Duncan | Special Agent Supervisor |
| Rusty Rogers | Special Agent |
| Greg Holycross | Special Agent |

| | |
|---|---|
| James  Mullins | Special Agent |
| Luis Negrete | |
| Tony Rodriguez | Special Agent Supervisor |
| Mark Brutnell | Special Agent Supervisor |
| Gary Nehrbass | Special Agent Supervisor |

## Federal Bureau of Investigation

| | |
|---|---|
| Andrew Nadeau | Special Agent |
| James Majeski | Special Agent |
| Matthew Oliver | Special Agent |
| Elizabeth Alexander | Special Agent |
| Johnny Lavender | Special Agent |
| Patrick Walter | Special Agent |
| Samantha Medico | Special Agent |
| Andrew Culbertson | Special Agent |
| Alexis Brignoni | Special Agent |
| John Geeslin | Special Agent |
| James Roth | Special Agent |
| Mathew Pagliarini | Special Agent |

# Sources & References

**Official Documents & Recordings**

911 & Non-emergency Call Recordings
911 Call History of George Zimmerman
Affidavit of Probable Cause
Audio, SPD interview of Witness 1 on March 1, 2012
Audio, FDLE interview of Witness 1 on March 20 , 2012
Audio, SPD interview of Witness 2 on March 1 , 2012
Audio, SPD interview of Witness 2 on March 9, 2012
Audio, FDLE interview of Witness 2 on March 20, 2012
Audio, FDLE interview of Witness 3 on March 19, 2012
Audio, FDLE interview of Witness 6 on March 20 , 2012
Audio, FDLE interview of Witness 12 on March 20, 2012
Audio, SAO interview of Witness 12 on March 26 , 2012
Audio, SPD interview of Witness 13 on February 26 , 2012
Audio, FDLE interview of Witness 13 on March 20, 2012
Audio, SAO interview of Witness 13 on March 26 , 2012
Audio, SPD interview of Witness 14 on March 5, 2012
Audio, FDLE interview of Witness 17 on March 20 , 2012
Audio, SPD interview of Witness 18 on February 26 , 2012
Audio, SPD interview of Witness 20 on March 2 , 2012
Audio, FDLE interview of Witness 20 on March 19 , 2012
Audio, SPD interviews of George Zimmerman, February 26, 2012
Audio, SPD interview of George Zimmerman, February 27, 2012
Audio, SPD phone call to George Zimmerman, March 25, 2012
Audio, SPD phone call to George Zimmerman, March 26, 2012
Autopsy Report, March 15, 2012
Bank Statements of George Zimmerman
Capias Request, Sanford Police, March 13, 2012
Concealed Weapons Permit Issued to George Zimmerman
Crime Scene Contamination Logs
Crime Scene Sketch and Evidence Legend
FBI FAVIU Report of Examination, April 2, 2012

FBI Interview Reports
FDLE Crime Lab Report, Biology Section, March 26, 2012
FDLE Crime Lab Report, Biology Section, May 9, 2012
FDLE Crime Lab Report, Trace Evidence Section, March 21, 2012
FDLE Crime Lab Report, Gunshot Residue Section, March 28, 2012
FDLE Crime Lab Report, Latent Print Section, March 20, 2012
FDLE Crime Lab Report, Firearms Section, March 8, 2012
FDLE Crime Lab Report, Firearms Section, March 22, 2012
FDLE Crime Lab Report, Firearms Section, March 28, 2012
FDLE Investigative Reports
FDLE Total Station Drawing
Incident Reports for Twin Lakes
Medical Records for George Zimmerman, February 27, 2012
Sanford Fire Department Dispatch Records
Sanford Fire Department Report
Sanford Police Emails
Sanford Police Latent Print Report, March 12, 2012
Sanford Police Major Crimes Report, February 26, 2012
Sanford Police Major Crimes Report, March 6, 2012
Sanford Police Major Crimes Report, March 2, 2012
Sanford Police Major Crimes Report, March 13, 2012
Sanford Police Major Crimes Report, March 18, 2012
Sanford Police Major Crimes Report, March 19, 2012
Sanford Police Major Crimes Report, March 22, 2012
Sanford Police Offense Report
Sanford Police Press Releases
Sanford Police Property and Evidence Chain of Custody
State Attorney's Office Investigative Memoranda
Photographs of George Zimmerman in Sanford Police Car
Twin Lakes Newsletters
Twin Lakes Resident Flyer
Video, CVSA interview of Zimmerman, February 27, 2012
Video, walk-through interview of Zimmerman, February 27, 2012
Written Statement of George Zimmerman, February 26, 2012
Written Statements of Witnesses

## News Articles & Editorials

Abad-Santos, A. "George Zimmerman's defenders come out." *Associated Press*. Accessed from *The Atlantic Wire*. March 26, 2012.

Alcindor, Y. "Test identify only Zimmerman's DNA on handgun." *USA Today*. September 20, 2012.

Alcindor, Y. "Witnesses in Trayvon Martin case offer differing accounts." *USA Today*. June 3, 2012.

Alcindor, Y., and Bello, M. "Zimmerman passed lie detector test." *USA Today*. June 27, 2012.

Alvarez, L. "City criticizes police chief after shooting." *The New York Times*. March 22, 2012.

Barry, D., Kovaleski, S., Robertson, C., and Alavarez, L. "Race, tragedy and outrage collide after a shot in Florida." *The New York Times*. April 1, 2012.

Boedeker, H. "George Zimmerman: Angela Corey needs her head examined." *Orlando Sentinel*. May 19, 2012.

Broward, C. "Angela Corey takes on well-known legal commentator, Harvard professor Alan Dershowitz." *The Florida Times-Union*. June 7, 2012.

Broward, C. "Angela Corey threatened to sue Harvard Law over professor's criticism, educator says." *The Florida Times-Union*. June 6, 2012.

Buiso, G. "'Witness' supports self-defense story." *New York Post*. March 25, 2012.

Burch, A., and Isensee, L. "Trayvon Martin: A typical teen who loved video games, looked forward to prom." *The Miami Herald*. March 22, 2012.

Butler, P. "Paul Butler on Trayvon Martin and racial profiling." *The Daily Beast*. March 26, 2012.

Cadet, D. "Trayvon Martin's parents: Sybrina Fulton, Tracy Martin say they're prepared for any outcome in trial." *The Huffington Post*. July 25, 2012.

Canada, D. "George Zimmerman's friend: He called Trayvon Martin a goon, not a coon." *Rollingout.com*. March 26,

2012.

Caputo, M. "Stand Your Ground may yet survive." *The Miami Herald.* April 15, 2012.

Caulfield, P. "Angela Corey, prosecutor in Trayvon case, is tough on crime." *The New York Daily News.* April 10, 2012.

Causey, A. "Angela Corey charges George Zimmerman with second-degree murder." *The Florida Times-Union.* April 11, 2012.

Cohen, J. "Trayvon: Justice or just us?" *The Huffington Post.* May 2, 2012.

Cooper, A. "New developments in Trayvon Martin case." *CNN, Anderson Cooper 360.* Transcript. May 17, 2012.

Coursey, L. "Calls for Angela Corey to quit Trayvon Martin investigation." *ActionNewsJax.* March 26, 2012.

Corley, C. "Trayvon Martin case: Attorney choice sparks division." *National Public Radio.* March 31, 2012.

Cristopher, T. "Debunking right-wing 'media conspiracy' theory of Trayvon Martin story." *Mediaite.* March 27, 2012.

Dade, C. "Trayvon Martin case 2.0: Digital trial before jury." *National Public Radio.* May 3, 2012.

Dahl, J. "Trayvon Martin special prosecutor Angela Corey is tenacious, dedicated and set in her ways, says former colleague." *CBS Crimesider.* April 11, 2012.

Dahl, J. "Trayvon Martin shooting: A timeline of events." *CBS News.* April 11, 2012.

Davenport, L. "Our black boys are not trash: From Emmett Till to Trayvon Martin." *NewsOne.* March 21, 2012.

DeGregory, L. "Trayvon Martin's killing shatters safety within Retreat at Twin Lakes." *Tampa Bay Times.* March 25, 2012.

Delinski, R. "Chief Myers says PIO lacked skills to handle Trayvon Martin case." *The Sanford Herald.* September 10, 2010.

DeLuca, M. "Did Trayvon shooter abuse 911?" *The Daily Beast.* March 22, 2012.

Dershowitz, A. "Dershowitz: Zimmerman prosecutor threatening to sue Harvard for my criticism." *Newsmax.* June 5, 2012.

Dershowitz, A. "New forensic evidence is consistent with George Zimmerman's self defense claim." *The Huffington*

*Post*. May 21, 2012.

Dorell, O. "Florida state attorney known to 'vigorously' prosecute cases." *USA Today*. April 11, 2012.

Erbentraut, J. "Heaven Sutton, Chicago 7-year-old girl, fatally shot while selling snow cones with her mother." *The Huffington Post*. June 28, 2012.

Franescani, C. "George Zimmerman: Prelude to a shooting." *Reuters*. April 25, 2012.

French, D. "The three legal keys of the Trayvon Martin affidavit." *National Review Online*. April 13, 2012.

Fung, K. "Geraldo River apologizes for Trayvon Martin hoodie comments." *The Huffington Post*. March 27, 2012.

Fung, K. "Geraldo Rivera: Trayvon Martin's 'hoodie is as much responsible for [his] death as George Zimmerman'." *The Huffington Post*. March 25, 2012.

Gershman, B. "Were Trayvon Martin witnesses coached to change their stories?" *The Huffington Post*. May 30, 2012.

Gershman, B. "Whose voice is screaming for help? Zimmerman's or Martin's?" *The Huffington Post*. May 4, 2012.

Gianatasio, D. "Skittles, Arizona iced tea caught in no man's land in Trayvon Martin case." *AdWeek*. March 28, 2012.

Goldberg, J. "Playing the race card again." *National Review Online*. March 28, 2012.

Gray, M. "George Zimmerman's gun: A popular choice for concealed carry." *Time*. March 28, 2012.

Gray, M. "New evidence: No trace of Trayvon Martin's DNA on George Zimmerman's gun." *Time*. September 19, 2012.

Gray, M. "Zimmerman's brother comes to his defense: 'He stopped someone from disarming him." *Time*. March 30, 2012.

"Ground and pound." *Urban Dictionary*. Accessed August 9, 2012.

Gutman, M. "Trayvon Martin case: Timeline of events." *ABC News*. May 8, 2012.

Gutman, M., and Tienabeso, S. "George Zimmerman tells Trayvon Martin's parents 'I am sorry'." *ABC News*. April 20, 2012.

Gutman, M., and Tienabeso, S. "Trayvon Martin exlusive:

Friend on phone with teen before death recalls final moments." *Good Morning America*, March 20, 2012.

Gutman, M., and Tienabeso, S. "Trayvon Martin's last phone call triggers demand for arrest 'right now'." *ABC News.* March 20, 2012.

Hallett, M., and Pontzer, D. "No peace dividend for Duval? Posing questions about Jacksonville's punitive civic infrastructure." *University of North Florida.* February 15, 2012.

Hamacher, B., and Emmanuel, L. "George Zimmerman makes first appearance before judge." *NBC Miami.* April 13, 2012.

Hannity, S. "Exclusive: George Zimmerman breaks silence on 'Hannity'." *Fox News, Hannity.* Transcript. July 18, 2012.

Hart, B. "Trayvon Martin autopsy report: Killed by a bullet fired at intermediate range." *The Huffington Post.* May 17, 2012.

Hernandez, R. "George Zimmerman answers lie detector questions." *Orlando Sentinel.* June 21, 2012.

Hightower, K. "Zimmerman lawyer pursuing traditional self-defense." *The Associated Press.* August 13, 2012.

Hinkel, D., Rhodes, D., and Sobol, R. "Judge to man charged with killing girl: 'You're dangerous'." *Chicago Tribune.* July 1, 2012.

Horwitz, S., and McCrumman, S. "Trayvon Martin documents reveal new details in shooting." *The Washington Post.* May 17, 2012.

Jim H. "Critiques of Zimmerman affidavit." *AMNation.com.* Comment. April 17, 2012.

Johnston, I. "Trayvon Martin case: How courts in other countries might deal with a similar killing." *NBC News.* August 22, 2012.

Jonsson, P. "Geraldo Rivera (again) says Trayvon Martin's 'thug wear' got him profiled." *The Christian Science Monitor.* May 19, 2012.

Jonsson, P. "Trayvon Martin case's mystery man: George Zimmerman's cop connection." *The Christian Science Monitor.* July 14, 2012.

Kassab, B. "What Angela Corey may be thinking about 'stand your ground'." *Orlando Sentinel.* April 12, 2012.

Kovaleski, S. "Trayvon Martin case shadowed by series of police missteps." *The New York Times*. May 16, 2012.

Kuo, V. "Fatal shooting of Florida teen turned over to state attorney." *CNN*. March 15, 2012.

Lavin, S. "Lawyer: Angela Corey missed deadline to release evidence." *The Free Republic*. April 28, 2012.

Layton, J. "People of East St. Louis rally behind Trayvon's parents." *AlestleLive.com*. May 30, 2012.

Lee, T. "Trayvon Martin case salts old wounds and racial tension." *The Huffington Post*. March 14, 2012.

Levs, J. "Trayvon Martin case's tough, controversial prosecutor." *CNN*. April 10, 2012.

Lewis, S. "Mother of slain girl speaks out." *WGN*. March 19, 2012.

Liverman, M. "Rev. Al Sharpton and the families of Trayvon Martin and Robert Champion commemorate social justice in Tallahassee." *WTXL*. August 26, 2012.

Littlepage, R. "Ron Littlepage: Angela Corey's hissy fits, threats unprofessional." *The Florida Times-Union*. June 8, 2012.

Lott, J. "Where's the 'probable cause'?" *National Review Online*. April 13, 2012.

Lynch, R. "Trayvon Martin case: 'Blacks are under attack,' says Jesse Jackson." *The Los Angeles Times*. March 23, 2012.

Lysiak, M., and Siemaszko, C. "Trayvon Martin corpse photo accidentally released by Florida prosecutors as part of botched evidence dump." *New York Daily News*. August 10, 2012.

Lysiak, M., and Siemaszko, C. "Trayvon Martin's accused killer was a lousy criminal justice student." *The New York Daily News*. August 9, 2012.

MacDonald, H. "The media and black homicide victims." *National Review Online*. March 29, 2012.

MaCrae, K., and Vann, M. "Martin family responds to firing of police chief." *Huffington Post*. June 22, 2012.

Malveaux, S. "Experts: Cries on 911 tape probably not Zimmerman's." *CNN Newsroom*. Transcript. April 2, 2012.

Martel, F. "Anonymous witness police used tells Orlando station Trayvon Martin attacked George Zimmerman." *Mediaite*. March 24, 2012.

Martin, T., and Fulton, S. "Charges brought against killer of Trayvon Martin." *Change.org*. Petition website. Accessed July 7, 2012.

Martosko, D. "Public opinion shifts on Trayvon Martin case." *The Daily Caller*. March 31, 2012.

McAdam, D. "History of Jigsaw Puzzles." *American Jigsaw Puzzle Society*. Accessed on July 8, 2012.

McCarthy, A. "Martin case affidavit." *National Review Online*. April 13, 2012.

Mirkinson, J. "Geraldo Rivera sharply criticized by Trayvon Martin lawyer Benjamin Crump: 'You're embarrassing your son again'." *The Huffington Post*. May 29, 2012.

Mungin, L. "Investigator: Zimmerman missed opportunities to defuse situation." *CNN*. June 27, 2012.

Murphy, B. "Shorstein dismisses longtime assistant." *The Florida Times-Union*. November 17, 2006.

Muskal, M. "George Zimmerman's DNA, not Trayvon Martin's, found on gun." *Los Angeles Times*. September 19, 2012.

Nejame, M. "Did politics drive prosecution in Trayvon Martin case?" *CNN*. June 22, 2012.

Nejame, M. "The facts must decide Trayvon Martin case." *CNN*. April 24, 2012.

Nejame, M. "Trayvon Martin shooting wasn't a case of racial profiling." *CNN*. May 30, 2012.

Newman, A. "Experts weigh in after four witnesses in Trayvon Martin case change story." *The New American*. May 28, 2012.

Nittle, N. "The real Trayvon Martin: Facts about the slain youth's life." *About.com*. Accessed July 7, 2012.

Oldenburg, A. "Geraldo Rivera blames hoodie for Trayvon Martin's death." *USA Today*. March 25, 2012.

Olorunnipa, T. "Tough-mided prosecutor in spotlight on Trayvon Martin case." *The Miami Herald*. March 28, 2012.

Peralta, E. "Poll: Opinion on Trayvon Martin case divided along racial lines." *National Public Radio*. April 6, 2012.

Pinkham, P. "Shorstein says he won't seek '08 re-election; The state attorney intends to practice law with his sons." *The Florida Times-Union*. February 7, 2007.

Prieto, B., and Nolin, R. "Tensions still simmer in Trayvon Martin shooting case." *Orlando Sentinel*. March 17, 2012.

RhettMiller, J. "Dershowitz: Zimmerman prosecutor threatened to sue Harvard." *Fox News*. June 7, 2012.

Robles, F. "Medical records: George Zimmerman had black eyes, painful broken nose but no head trauma." *The Miami Herald*. July 4, 2012.

Robles, F. "Multiple suspensions paint complicated portrait of Trayvon Martin." *The Miami Herald*. March 26, 2012.

Robles, F. "Sanford detective wanted manslaughter charge for George Zimmerman." *The Christian Science Monitor*. June 27, 2012.

Robles, F. "Shooter of Trayvon Martin a habitual caller to cops." *The Miami Herald*. March 21, 2012.

Robles, F. "Trayvon Martin's social media posts may come up at trial." *The Miami Herald*. May 3, 2012.

Robles, F. "Witnesses in Trayvon Martin case contradict, change their stories." *The Miami Herald*. May 26, 2012.

Roig-Franzia, M., Jackman, T., and Fears, D. "Florida shooter George Zimmerman not easily pigeonholed." *The Seattle Times*. March 22, 2012.

Roig-Franzia, M., Jackman, T., and Fears, D. "Who is George Zimmerman?" *The Washington Post*. March 22, 2012.

Rutland, M. "Sanford police chief Bill Lee in wake of Trayvon Martin case." *The Miami Herald*. June 20, 2012.

Savage, B. "George Zimmerman prosecutor: Wait for all the evidence." *Central Florida News 13*. May 19, 2012.

Savali, K. "Bill Maher: 'Obama couldn't be less threatening if he was walking home with iced tea and Skittles'." *NewsOne*. May 28, 2012.

Schindler, A. "Prison break." *Folio Weekly*. March 20, 2012.

Schneider, M. "Emails show vitriol toward Sanford police chief." *The Seattle Times*. August 2, 2012.

Schneider, M. "Experts see inconsistencies in Zimmerman's account of his encounter with Martin." *The Florida Times-Union*. June 22, 2012.

Schneider, M. "Trayvon Martin's DNA not found on George Zimmerman's gun." *The Huffington Post*. September 19,

2012.

Schneider, M. "Zimmerman asks for delay, information on Martin." *ABC News*. October 9, 2012.

Sharpton, A. "Interview with Cheryl Brown." *PoliticsNation*. Transcript. March 28, 2012.

Smith, M. "Mourners say goodbye to Heaven Sutton." *Chicago Tribune*. July 6, 2012.

Staff. "Accused Trayvon Martin killer George Zimmerman leaves jail on $1M bond." *CBS News Crimesider*. July 6, 2012.

Staff. "Affidavit alleges George Zimmerman 'confronted' Trayvon Martin." *Fox News*. April 12, 2012.

Staff. "Angela Corey to take over investigation into Sanford shooting death of Trayvon Martin." *The Florida Times-Union*. March 22, 2012.

Staff. "Autopsy: Trayvon Martin killed by single gunshot fired at 'intermediate range'." *The Grio*. May 16, 2012.

Staff. "Behind the handgun George Zimmerman used to kill Trayvon Martin." *The Orlando Sentinel*, reprinted in *The Florida Times-Union*. May 15, 2012.

Staff. "Cop's son accused of beating man walks out of jail." *WFTV*. January 3, 2011.

Staff. "Experts argue appropriateness of murder charge in Martin case." *CNN*. April 12, 2012.

Staff. "Five questions for Angela Corey." *News Service of Florida,* published in *Orlando Sentinel*. June 13, 2012.

Staff. "George Zimmerman evidence shows extent to which police doubted self-defense claim." *The Huffington Post*. June 26, 2012.

Staff. "George Zimmerman leaves Fla. Jail on $1M bond." *First Coast News*. July 6, 2012.

Staff. "George Zimmerman running out of money for defense." *First Coast News*. August 15, 2012.

Staff. "George Zimmerman, Trayvon Martin case: Next court hearing set, Zimmerman asking for Martin's Twitter." *Associated Press*. October 9, 2012.

Staff. "George Zimmerman, Trayvon Martin case: Zimmerman asking for info from Martin's social media accounts." *The*

*Associated Press*. October 8, 2012.

Staff. "New accusations in Trayvon Martin shooting." *CBS Miami*. April 3, 2012.

Staff. "New video shows George Zimmerman telling police about struggle with Trayvon Martin." *Associated Press*. Posted on *The Florida Times-Union*. June 21, 2012.

Staff. "Outrage escalates following Trayvon Martin death." *WESH*. March 19, 2012.

Staff. "Rev. Jesse Jackson talks Obama, Zimmerman at DNC." *Central Florida News 13*. September 4, 2012.

Staff. "Sybrina Fulton: 'I can wait a year' for justice." *National Public Radio*. April 26, 2012.

Staff. "Tape showed Zimmerman's anger over black man's beating." *CNN*. May 24, 2012.

Staff. "The events leading to the shooting of Trayvon Martin." *The New York Times*. June 21, 2012.

Staff. "Trayvon Martin attorney responds to Zimmerman's 'stand your ground' hearing." *Global Grind*. August 9, 2012.

Staff. "Trayvon Martin case: Skittles, Arizona iced tea speak about 'commercial gain' in death of Florida teen." *International Business Times*. March 27, 2012.

Staff. "Trayvon Martin case: State attorney quites investigation as state studies 'stand your ground' law." *The Huffington Post*. March 22, 2012.

Staff. "Trayvon Martin killed by single gunshot fired from 'intermediate range,' autopsy shows." *NBC News*. August 18, 2012.

Staff. "Trayvon Martin's DNA not found on Zimmerman's gun." *CBS Miami*. September 19, 2012.

Staff. "Trayvon Martin's parents react to defense's request for access to social media accounts." *WFTV*. October 8, 2012.

Staff. "Witness, Zimmerman attorneys address key questions in Trayvon Shooting." *CNN*. April 7, 2012.

Staff. "Who is special prosecutor Angela Corey?" *CBS Miami*. April 11, 2012.

Staff. "Zimmerman atty: Family 'made a mistake' with defense funds." *CBS News*. June 4, 2012.

Stanley, K., and Humburg, C. "Many killers who go free with

Florida 'stand your ground' law have history of violence."
*Tamba Bay Times*. July 22, 2012.

Steele, S. "Shelby Steele: The exploitation of Trayvon Martin."
*Wall Street Journal*. April 6, 2012.

Stein, S. "Obama on Trayvon Martin case: 'If I had a son, he'd
look like Trayvon." *The Huffington Post*. March 23, 2012.

Strassmann, M. "What happened right after Trayvon Martin's
shooting?" *CBS News*. March 27, 2012.

Stuart, D. "Newly elected state attorney Angela Corey." *About.-
com*. Accessed August 26, 2012.

Stutzman, R. "George Zimmerman's father: My son is not a
racist, did not confront Trayvon Martin." *Orlando Sentinel*.
March 15, 2012.

Stutzman, R. "O'Mara to depose eight Sanford cops next week."
*Orlando Sentinel*. October 12, 2012.

Stutzman, R. "Trayvon Martin facts vs. rumor." *Orlando Sentinel*. April 2, 2012.

Stutzman, R. "Experts: Trayvon Martin's heart kept pumping after shooting." *Orlando Sentinel*. August 17, 2012.

Stutzman, R., and Prieto, B. "Trayvon Martin shooting: Gun
that killed teen was fired once." *Orlando Sentinel*. March
20, 2012.

Stutzman, R., and Weiner, J. "New George Zimmerman evidence: Details on Trayvon's DNA on Zimmerman and vice
versa." *Orlando Sentinel*. September 19, 2012.

Stutzman, R., and Weiner, J. "Several George Zimmerman witnesses change their accounts." *Orlando Sentinel*. May 22,
2012.

Thomas, P., and Tienabesco, S. "George Zimmerman's reenact-
ment of Trayvon Martin shooting released." *ABC News*. Accessed from *First Coast News*. June 21, 2012.

Tumulty, K. "Obama says this hope stuff only goes so far." *Time*.
July 8, 2008.

Velez-Mitchell, J. "New info released in Trayvon Martin case."
*HLN, Jane Velez-Mitchell*. Transcript. May 17, 2012.

Weigel, D. "Witnesses Mary Cutcher and Selma Mora offer their
account of what happened the night Trayvon Martin died."
*Slate.com*. April 6, 2012.

Weiner, J. "Will jury, or judge, decide George Zimmerman's fate?" *Orlando Sentinel*. June 10, 2012.

Weiner, J. "Trayvon Martin: New photo, details of George Zimmerman's employment." *Orlando Sentinel*. March 23, 2012.

Wemple, E. "Why did New York Times call George Zimmerman 'white Hispanic'?" *The Washington Post*. March 28, 2012.

*Wikipedia*. "Emmett Till." Accessed August 16, 2012.

*Wikipedia*. "The shooting of Trayvon Martin." Accessed October 15, 2012.

Williams, W. "Should black people tolerate this?" *CNSNews.com* May 22, 2012.

Winch, G. "Cops: Zimmerman wasn't afraid of Trayvon." *HLN*. June 27, 2012.

Winter, M. "Report: Shot fired from 'intermediate range' killed Trayvon." *USA Today*. May 17, 2012.

Word, R. "The punisher." *Folio Weekly*. March 6, 2012.

Zehnder, I. "Autopsy report reveals Trayvon Martin was shot at 'intermediate range'." *Examiner.com*. May 18, 2012.

## Books

Adams, R., McTernan, T., & Remsberg, C. *Street survival: Tactics for armed encounters*. Northbrook, IL: Calibre Press, 1980.

Artwohl, A., and Christensen, L. *Deadly force encounters*. Boulder, CO: Paladin Press, 1997.

Bevel, T., & Gardner, R. *Bloodstain pattern analysis with an introduction to crime scene reconstruction* (3rd ed.). Boca Raton, FL: CRC Press, 2008.

Carlucci, D., & Jacobson, S. *Ballistics: Theory and design of guns and ammunition*. Boca Raton, FL: CRC Press, 2008.

Chapman, A. *Biomechanical analysis of fundamental human movements*. Champaign, IL: Human Kinetics, 2008.

Chisum, W., & Turvey, B. *Crime reconstruction*. Burlington, MA: Academic Press, 2007.

Di Maio, V. *Gunshot wounds: Practical aspects of firearms, ballis-*

*tics, and forensic techniques* (2nd ed.). Boca Raton, FL: CRC Press, 1999.

Gardner, R., & Bevel, T. *Practical crime scene analysis and reconstruction*. Boca Raton, FL: CRC Press, 2009.

Geberth, V. *Practical homicide investigation: Tactics, procedures, and forensic techniques* (3rd ed.). Boca Raton, FL: CRC Press, 1996.

Grossman, D. *On killing: The psychological cost of learning to kill in war and society*. Boston, MA: Little, Brown and Company, 1995.

Grossman, D., & Christensen, L. *On combat: The psychology and physiology of deadly conflict in war and peace*. Millstadt, IL: Warrior Science Publications, 2008.

Haag, M., & Haag, L. *Shooting incident reconstruction* (2nd ed.). Burlington, MA: Academic Press, 2011.

Heard, B. *Handbook of firearms and ballistics: Examining and interpreting forensic evidence*. West Sussex, UK: John Wiley & Sons, 2008.

Houck, M. A philosophy of forensic science. FDIAI/GDIAI Joint Educational Conference, Panama City Beach, FL, October 2011.

Hueske, E. *Practical analysis and reconstruction of shooting incidents*. Boca Raton, FL: CRC Press, 2006.

James, S., & Eckert, W. (Eds.). Interpretation of bloodstain evidence at crime scenes (2nd ed.). Boca Raton, FL: CRC Press, 1998.

James, S., & Nordby, J. (Eds.). *Forensic science: An introduction to scientific and investigative techniques* (3rd ed.). Boca Raton, FL: CRC Press, 2009.

Kirk, P. *Crime investigation* (2nd ed.). Malabar, FL: Robert E. Kreiger Publishing Company, 1974.

Landenheim, J., & Landenheim, E. *Firearms and ballistics for physician and attorney* (2nd ed.). Jacksonville, FL: Institute of Police Technology and Management, 2002.

Moran, B. Shooting incident reconstruction. In W. J. Chisum & B. E. Turvey (Eds.) *Crime reconstruction* (pp. 215-312). Burlington, MA: Academic Press, 2007.

O'Hara, C., & O'Hara, G. *Fundamentals of criminal investigation*

(Rev. 5th ed.). Springfield, IL: Charles C. Thomas, 1988.

Osterburg, J., & Ward, R. *Criminal investigation: A method for reconstructing the past*. Cincinnati, OH: Anderson Publishing Co., 1992.

Spitz, W., & Spitz, D. (Eds.). *Spitz and Fisher's medicolegal investigation of death: Guidelines for the application of pathology to crime investigation* (4th ed.). Springfield, IL: Charles C. Thomas, 2006.

Tilley, A. *The measure of man and woman: Human factors in design* (Rev. ed.). New York: John Wiley & Sons, 2002.

Wallace, J. *Chemical analysis of firearms, ammunition, and gunshot residue*. Boca Raton, FL: CRC Press, 2008.

Warlow, T. *Firearms, the law, and forensic ballistics* (3rd ed.). Boca Raton, FL: CRC Press, 2012.

Wonder, A. *Blood dynamics*. San Diego, CA: Academic Press, 2001.


**Other Research**

Bureau of Justice Statistics, Homicide Trends in the United States, 1980-2008.

Florida Department of Agriculture and Consumer Services, Division of Licensing, Concealed Weapon/Firearm Holder Profiles as of July 31, 2012

Florida Department of Agriculture and Consumer Services, Division of Licensing, Concealed Weapon or Firearm License Summary Report, October 1, 1987 through June 30, 2013

Kel-Tec PF9 Manual

Weather History, Sanford Airport, February 26, 2012

Weather History, Sanford Airport, February 27, 2012

# About the Author

Michael A. Knox is a forensic consultant who specializes in reconstructing crime scenes and traffic accidents for clients from all over the United States. For over fifteen years, Mr. Knox was a police officer and detective with the Jacksonville (FL) Sheriff's Office where he served in patrol, DUI enforcement, crime scene investigations, and traffic homicide investigations. Mr. Knox has investigated hundreds of homicides by gunfire and other means.

In his consulting practice, Mr. Knox has reconstructed shootings of all types for both criminal and civil cases including police-involved shootings, homicides, self-defense claims, and accidental shootings. Mr. Knox has reconstructed shootings in Florida, Georgia, Alabama, Mississippi, Texas, Ohio, Illinois, New Jersey, and Pennsylvania.

Mr. Knox has a Bachelor of Science degree in mechanical engineering from the University of North Florida and a Master of Science degree in forensic science from the University of Florida. He is currently a doctoral student in criminal justice at Nova Southeastern University. Mr. Knox has attended hundreds of hours of advanced training in forensic technology.

Mr. Knox has taught courses on crime scenes and forensic technology to law enforcement officials in Peru, the United Arab Emirates, the Republic of Georgia, and throughout the United States. He has taught for the Northeast Florida Criminal Justice Training Center, the Institute of Police Technology and Management, the U.S. State Department, Sirchie Fingerprint Laboratories, and Keiser University.

Mr. Knox has testified as an expert in crime scene reconstruction in state and federal courts in Florida, Alabama, Texas, and Illinois.

www.ingramcontent.com/pod-product-compliance
Lightning Source LLC
LaVergne TN
LVHW011220080426
835509LV00005B/231